CW01511924

POVERTY AND THE WORLD O...

Sustainability Matters

This series provides accessible introductions to the many facets of sustainability and sustainable development. Each book explores a specific topic – for example, poverty, gender equality, water security, peace and justice – to consider the possibilities and challenges to achieving a sustainable future for all. The authors bring incisive analysis and theoretically robust thinking to the complex and interrelated issues.

Published

Poverty and the World Order: The Mirage of SDG1
Robert Walker

POVERTY AND THE WORLD ORDER

The Mirage of SDG1

ROBERT WALKER

agenda
publishing

For my colleagues, kin, friends and everyone else.

First published in 2023 by Agenda Publishing
Agenda Publishing Limited
The Core
Bath Lane
Newcastle Helix
Newcastle upon Tyne
NE4 5TF
www.agendapub.com

ISBN 978-1-78821-554-1 (hardcover)
ISBN 978-1-78821-555-8 (paperback)

British Library Cataloguing-in-Publication Data
A catalogue record for this book is available from the British Library

Typeset by Newgen Publishing UK
Printed and bound in the UK by TJ Books

CONTENTS

LIST OF FIGURES, TABLES AND CASE STUDIES

Figures

Tables

Case studies

1

SDG1 AND THE NATURE OF POVERTY

Only a special kind of person would pick up and start reading a book on the Sustainable Development Goals (SDGs). Few people have ever heard of the goals and even fewer know much about them (Hudson *et al.* 2020; Tedeneke 2019).

This immediately points to a major challenge. The SDGs were launched as part of the United Nations' 2030 Agenda for Sustainable Development in 2015, accompanied by an official video entitled "*We the People*". There are 17 goals of which the first, No Poverty, is the focus of this volume (Figure 1.1).

The agenda and video offered "a globally shared development program, involving the whole population in a common mission aimed to put an end to any form of poverty, to fight against inequalities and to face climate change" (Smaniotto *et al.* 2020: 2). The 2030 Agenda is approaching its halfway stage but, seemingly, without many of us – "we the people" – being aware of the need for our involvement.

Figure 1.1 The Sustainable Development Goals

The goals and 169 targets to be achieved by 2030 truly do present a "supremely ambitious and transformational vision", one that is relevant and should be important to everyone. They aim:

> to end poverty and hunger everywhere; to combat inequalities within and among countries; to build peaceful, just and inclusive societies; to protect human rights and promote gender equality and the empowerment of women and girls; and to ensure the lasting protection of the planet and its natural resources; ... to create conditions for sustainable, inclusive and sustained economic growth, shared prosperity and decent work for all, taking into account different levels of national development and capacities.   (UN 2015a: para. 3)

Unlike the Millennium Development Goals (MDGs) that the SDGs replaced, they are "universal goals and targets which involve the entire world, developed and developing countries alike. They are integrated and indivisible and balance the three dimensions of sustainable development [economic, social, and environmental]" (UN 2015a: para. 4). Even so, each country is required to assume "primary responsibility for its own economic and social development" and each government must set "its own national targets guided by the global level of ambition but taking into account national circumstances" (UN 2015a: para. 55).

However, the scale of ambition requires:

> a revitalized Global Partnership to ensure its implementation ... This Partnership will work in a spirit of global solidarity, in particular solidarity with the poorest and with people in vulnerable situations. It will facilitate an intensive global engagement in support of implementation of all the Goals and targets, bringing together Governments, the private sector, civil society, the United Nations system and other actors and mobilizing all available resources. [...] Public finance, both domestic and international, will play a vital role in providing essential services and public goods and in catalysing other sources of finance.
> (UN 2015a: paras 39, 41)

There is also a role foreseen for "the diverse private sector, ranging from micro-enterprises to cooperatives to multinationals, and that of civil society organizations and philanthropic organizations in the implementation of the new Agenda" (UN 2015a: para. 41).

The 2030 Agenda, therefore, envisages a global partnership involving governments, business and the world's people both as individuals and as civil society. Members of the public surveyed in 2021 in 28 countries placed either zero hunger or no poverty as their top priority goal (Broom 2021). This is quite congruent with rank ordering of the SDGs with poverty first and hunger second. However, even before the onslaught of the Covid-19 pandemic in 2020, the world was "off-track" to eradicate extreme poverty by 2030 and food insecurity was increasing (UN 2020a). Moreover, there was already a shortfall of US$2.5 trillion in the finance needed to achieve the SDGs (WEF 2019).

While not necessarily informed of this situation, people in most countries surveyed in 2021 felt that their government was taking "less than its share of responsibility for achieving the SDGs", although this was not true in Germany or in Asia – China, India, Japan, Malaysia and South Korea. In marked contrast, respondents typically considered that "most ordinary people" and even businesses were satisfactorily sharing responsibility for achieving the SDGs. Insofar as the global public perceive the need to strengthen the global partnership to address the SDGs, it would seem to be one limited to governments.

As will become increasingly apparent, many governments, especially those of developing countries, will have great difficulty in achieving the SDGs if acting alone. Therefore, the global partnership cannot be purely rhetorical but must involve the transfer of resources and expertise from more to less developed countries. This represents a radical and transformative change in the way that nation states usually interact. Companies and countries typically compete in the global economy for resources, markets and wealth. Diplomatically, governments jockey to advance national interests with the most powerful countries seeking dominance. The institutions of global governance, such as the United Nations, are generally weak and, indeed, are often controlled or stymied by their most powerful members. As a result, states rarely enter partnerships promoting a global good that conflicts with their immediate national interests. Even when they do, and public opinion is supportive as in the case of climate change, collective progress may be very slow. For the 2030 Agenda to be completed and SDG1 to be attained, governments, as the lead actors, will need the active support of "we the people" in helping them to make the moral but politically brave choices that will be required.

While acknowledging the challenges that lie ahead, it is important to recognize that there have been successes since the world came together in 2000 to address poverty and the plethora of related issues. These are considered in Chapters 2 and 3 that respectively focus on MDG1 (to end poverty and hunger), and SDG1 (to end poverty in all its forms everywhere). Overall, poverty has fallen, education coverage has risen, and health has improved. Some forms of inequality have been reduced, although others have been attenuated as the living standards of the rich and super-rich have sped ahead of the global average. The fact that the world agreed in 2015 to continue working to address poverty and to expand the agenda for action must equally be seen as a success. Furthermore, the architects of the SDGs are clearly not short of the necessary ambition.

However, as evidenced in Chapters 4 and 5, progress since 2015 has been lethargic while the Covid-19 pandemic has added to the challenge of accomplishing SDG1 by 2030. In these new circumstances, added to by the global fallout from Russia's invasion of Ukraine, the support of "we the people" will not be enough and may not even be forthcoming. The structures of international governance must change. These currently support the workings of a global economy that favours developed countries over developing ones and daily reproduces inequality and poverty. The nature of the reforms necessary if poverty is to be eradicated are explained in the second section of this volume.

Before leaping ahead to conclusions, however, it is important to explain SDG1 and what "ending poverty in all its forms everywhere" means. It certainly does not mean ending poverty as "we the people" might understand it.

1.1 Poverty and the SDGs

The 2030 Agenda is premised on the assumption that "eradicating poverty in all its forms and dimensions, including extreme poverty, is the greatest global challenge and an indispensable requirement for sustainable development" (UN 2015a: preamble). It is important to note that eradicating poverty is viewed as a prerequisite for development, not an outcome of it. Hence, the 2030 Agenda would appear to exclude developmentalist strategies previously adopted by many countries especially in East Asia. As an example, China's President Deng Xiaoping encouraged some individuals and areas to get rich first when opening the economy to foreign investment in the 1980s. The intention was to generate wealth quickly that could subsequently be used to achieve a shared prosperity earlier than would otherwise have been possible (Gong 2018).

There is no definition of poverty included in the 2030 Agenda, instead there are targets and indices. As will be explained next, the lack of a definition is judicious both for practical and political reasons. However, this means that indicators, which are inevitably partial and often defined with respect to readily available data, substitute for goals. Policies may then be designed to have maximum impact on the indicators irrespective of their effect on poverty per se. This is a variant of the distortion often observed when targets are used to drive policy design and implementation that has come to be called Goodhart's Law after Charles Goodhart, the British economist who first discussed the problem (Mattson *et al.* 2021). In this case, however, the distortion may not be malign – a product of governmental actors seeking to appear to perform well – but result from a lack of strategic direction.

Like many concepts grounded in social science, the meaning of poverty is contested. Moreover, poverty and poverty alleviation are inherently political; no politician wishes to be associated with an increase in poverty, merely to be able to announce a reduction. Poverty alleviation is therefore a strong campaign ticket and a major stimulus to policy development. It correspondingly carries major political risks because the lack of consensus as to what it is, or how it should be tackled, makes it difficult to secure positive results that go uncontested.

Concepts of poverty are also culturally bound, varying in meaning in different parts of the world. This is because of the association of poverty with a lack of economic development, but also because poverty plays different roles in the national psyche. In Anglo-Saxon countries, poverty provides the justification for, and limit on, the legitimacy of the welfare state. In much of continental Europe, poverty, as social exclusion, marks a failure of social solidarity. In the developing world, poverty often way-marks the direction of history describing the world as it used to be; its absence being a measure of progress, its presence signifying political or national failure.

As symbols of cultural reproduction, paupers in folk tales are to be pitied, celebrated, despised or loved and, while their motives may be good or bad, they usually represent a division in society between "us" and "them" (Chase & Bantebya-Kyomuhendo 2015). In Britain, in the 1940s, "want" – poverty – was a giant standing in the way of progress. In 1960s China, poor peasants were the heroes of the continuing revolution; today they are castigated for not wanting to get rich quickly enough. Even in Norway, arguably the world's richest country, domestic poverty "grabbed the political spotlight" as recently as 2018 (Berglund 2018). Given the need to accommodate such diversity and political sensitivity across the 193 countries participating in the SDGs, it is understandable that the definition of poverty was left open.

The seven targets associated with SDG1 are reproduced in Table 1.1. The first two are substantive, targets relating to the eradication and reduction of poverty. The next three targets focus on policy responses, while the last two targets deal with resources and strategies including international cooperation in development. All seven targets will be discussed in detail in Chapter 3 but first, it is important to understand the often heated debates about the nature of poverty.

Almost all commentators agree that poverty refers to the lack of something. Those writing within the income-poverty tradition consider poverty to be the lack of income and its consequences while those adopting the capability approach, with Amartya Sen as the most eminent proponent, view poverty as the denial of freedom or the inability to realize one's potential. Within both traditions there is debate about whether poverty is an absolute or relative concept, about the degree to which poverty is multidimensional and about the relationship between poverty and human rights. Beyond these conceptual distinctions, there are debates

Table 1.1 Targets associated with Sustainable Development Goal 1

Target number	Target
1.1	By 2030, eradicate extreme poverty for all people everywhere, currently measured as people living on less than US$1.25 a day.
1.2	By 2030, reduce at least by half the proportion of men, women and children of all ages living in poverty in all its dimensions according to national definitions.
1.3	Implement nationally appropriate social protection systems and measures for all, including floors, and by 2030 achieve substantial coverage of the poor and the vulnerable.
1.4	By 2030, ensure that all men and women, in particular the poor and the vulnerable, have equal rights to economic resources, as well as access to basic services, ownership and control over land and other forms of property, inheritance, natural resources, appropriate new technology and financial services, including microfinance.
1.5	By 2030, build the resilience of the poor and those in vulnerable situations and reduce their exposure and vulnerability to climate-related extreme events and other economic, social and environmental shocks and disasters.
1.a	Ensure significant mobilization of resources from a variety of sources, including through enhanced development cooperation, in order to provide adequate and predictable means for developing countries, in particular least developed countries, to implement programmes and policies to end poverty in all its dimensions.
1.b	Create sound policy frameworks at the national, regional and international levels, based on pro-poor and gender-sensitive development strategies, to support accelerated investment in poverty eradication actions.

about measurement, about indicators, and about the causes and consequences of poverty. Not everyone considers that measurement is possible or desirable (Palacio 2013).

1.2 Poverty as low income

Conceptualizing poverty as a lack of income has a long history. It can be traced back until at least the provision of subsidized grain in Imperial Rome and may even date to the origins of coinage. Throughout this long history, the concept and its measurement have been so intimately connected as to sow confusion. Income is relatively simple to measure and so it is easy to think of poverty as being the lack of an adequate income. Nowadays, however, it is generally accepted within the Anglo-Saxon tradition that lack of money income, or a deficit in money-like resources, is the proximate cause of poverty rather than being poverty itself. Poverty, therefore, comprises the direct manifestations of this lack of income (Ringen 1988).

The apparent ease with which income can be measured helps to explain why the first target associated with SDG1 is expressed in terms of income using the international poverty line (IPL): 1.1 By 2030, eradicate extreme poverty for all people everywhere, currently measured as people living on less than US$1.25 a day.

While estimates of income are relatively straightforward to obtain, accuracy is more difficult to assure. Relying on recall is problematic but insisting on documentation is intrusive. In many rural economies the value of home production, voluntary exchange and bartering all need to be estimated, otherwise income will be understated. Similarly, it is notoriously difficult to assess the incomes of either people working in informal economies which, when reliant on recall, are often underestimated, or those of residents in institutions since most surveys restrict coverage to domestic addresses.

Expenditure may be a better gauge of consumption and a more direct measure of poverty than income, but it is more difficult to assess (Falkingham & Namazie 2002). Whereas income is usually a continuous flow, albeit sometimes intermittent, expenditure is inherently lumpy with the need to factor in the durations between expenditures and to consider item-specific rates of depreciation. Estimates of expenditure are also much influenced by the layout and content of the research instruments: they tend to increase with the number of items included in the interview schedule but to fall inversely with the duration of recall. When making comparisons between jurisdictions, it is important to recognize that some forms of consumption, health care for example, may be subsidized or available free of charge and so not be recorded in money terms.

1.2.1 Needs and relative poverty

Understanding poverty as relating to low income or expenditure draws attention to the fact that poverty is an inherently relative concept, necessitating an answer to the question, "Low in relation to what?" Intuitively, the simplest answer is low in relation to needs, which then demands an answer to the further question, "Which needs?" At this point it is helpful to refer to Maslow's much cited hierarchy of needs while not necessarily accepting its validity as an accurate portrayal of universal human needs (Maslow 1954; Cianci & Gambrel 2003). Maslow argued that physiological needs, including food, water, clothing and housing, needed to be met first and the pioneers on poverty research, such as William Booth (1892) and Seebohm Rowntree (1901) in the UK, and W. E. B. Du Bois (1996 [1899]) and Robert Hunter (1904) in the US, took a similar view.

In 1857, the German statistician Ernst Engel noted that as family income falls, the proportion spent on food increases, that on housing and clothing remains constant, and that assigned to recreation, education and health declines (Zimmerman 1932). These observations remained relevant into the twenty-first century although different ratios applied in rural and urban settings given that food is typically more expensive in cities (Anker 2011). It should be noted that Engel assumed that income was equitably shared within families. This assumption has been retained in much current research and policy, although its validity has been vigorously contested (Fialová & Mysíková 2021; Howard & Bennett 2021).

Criticisms apart, until recently many countries have followed Engel and defined poverty by establishing the cost of purchasing a suitable diet (the UN Food and Agriculture Organization recommends a daily nutritional allowance of 2,100 calories/per day) and adding an amount for non-food expenditure – often 40 per cent as proposed by Houthakker in 1957 (UN 2005a). In 1978, when China's Bureau of Statistics first started measuring poverty, it added 15 per cent for non-food costs, increasing this to 40 per cent in 2008 (based on 2000 prices), and to 53.5 per cent in 2011 (Freije et al. 2020). The United States' principal poverty index, originally developed by Mollie Orshansky in 1963, adds 66 per cent to the cost of food (Fisher 1992).

Children, and possibly elders, may have different physiological and other needs while larger households are thought likely to benefit from economies of scale. Engel's observations again have proved useful in taking account of the needs of households of different composition. Comparing the incomes of households that differ in membership but spend the same percentage of their income on food provides a means of calculating the expenditures and savings associated with variations in household composition. Orshansky (1969) employed this technique when devising the weights, termed equivalence scales or relativities, used to adjust for differences in household composition in the US poverty index.

However, the application of Engel's Law for determining equivalence scales can, on occasion, generate implausible results and many other scales have been developed, the most used being the OECD Modified Scale and square root scale (Dudel et al. 2021). The former assigns a value of 1 for the household head, 0.5 for each additional adult member and 0.3 for each child; the latter divides household income by the square root of household size with the result that the needs of a household of four are assumed to be twice those of a person living alone.

Although it is usual practice to adjust for family or household composition in developing poverty indicators, this was not done when creating the World Bank's international poverty line (IPI), which is used for monitoring progress towards SDG1. Set at per capita income of less than US$1.25/day, but increased to US$1.90 in 2017 and to US$2.15 in 2022, it is based on the needs of an adult from a household of unspecified composition. This significantly reduces the reliability of poverty estimates and international comparisons based on the IPI (Batana & Cockburn 2018).

The measures discussed so far focus on physiological needs, notably minimal food requirements. It is, however, pertinent to ask what is, or should be, included among the "other expenditures". This amounts to asking which other needs from Maslow's hierarchy do persons forgo due to poverty that can be assigned a monetary value: safety, belongingness and esteem, and cognitive, aesthetic and spiritual well-being (Koltko-Rivera 2006). The question is complicated by the fact that the proportion of spending on other than physiological needs is observed to rise in richer societies. Therefore, it becomes necessary when fixing a poverty threshold to determine which needs, normally met in a particular society, must be denied a person if they are to count as poor.

The British sociologist, Peter Townsend (1979), initiated a body of scholarship to determine empirically the things and activities that people forgo because they cannot afford them. This work has now been replicated in countries as diverse as Benin, Britain, Japan and Tonga (Nandy & Pomati 2015; Bramley & Bailey 2018; Abe 2010; Catalán *et al.* 2020). In parallel, experts have costed minimum "baskets of goods", normatively defined in terms of both quantity and quality (WFP 2020; Deeming 2017, 2020). Yet other scholars have consulted members of the public to ascertain the incomes and/or expenditures that are generally believed to be necessary to avoid experiencing poverty or being labelled as poor (Davis *et al.* 2021; Thornton & Boylan 2021). Each of these approaches is therefore defining poverty, not in absolute terms concerned solely with physiological needs, but relative to the incomes or consumption of the society as a whole. Adopting the spirit of these approaches, while avoiding the high fieldwork costs associated with detailed measurement, many national governments, especially in Europe, have adopted simpler but more arbitrary indices of relative poverty. Most of these set poverty thresholds as a proportion of national median household disposable income, typically 40, 50 or 60 per cent.

1.2.2 Poverty, relative or absolute

There is much debate about the merits of relative versus absolute poverty that sometimes degenerates into a normative demarcation between the political right and left, the Global South and North, or between the USA and Europe (Norrie 2018; Dunn 2017; Besharov & Call 2009). Some consider that relative measures conflate poverty with inequality and prevent poverty from ever being eradicated since some inequality, and therefore poverty, is inevitable. Certainly, relative poverty when defined as a proportion of median income cannot, unlike absolute poverty, be eradicated by economic growth alone. This is because a rise in median income lifts the poverty threshold thereby increasing the poverty rate (Foster 1998). Furthermore, relative poverty can appear to fall, counterintuitively, during an economic recession (because falling median income lowers the poverty threshold) and rise in the ensuing recovery in line with increased median income.

Others argue that the relative concept does not match the public's understanding of poverty. There is some merit in this. Adults, like children, in advanced economies typically imagine poverty to be associated with famine, filth and failure until informed of the nature of deprivation within their own communities (Chase & Bantebya-Kyomuhendo 2015; Chase & Walker 2013; Yang *et al.* 2021b).

Finally, certain scholars contend that measures of relative poverty simultaneously understate the effectiveness of poverty alleviation while obscuring abject poverty in rich countries (Gilbert 2017). Abject poverty can, however, be effectively measured in relative terms simply by lowering the poverty threshold to focus attention on those in deep poverty. Alternatively, the poverty gap can be measured, that is shortfall in people's resources relative to the poverty threshold (Muñoz *et al.* 2018). Moreover, while the relative poverty rate does not fall if national income increases and is equally shared, this is consistent with the fact that social expectations tend to rise with median income leaving low-income families no better able to participate in society than before.

Whatever criticisms are levelled against relative poverty and for whatever reason, few would deny that real poverty is experienced in every advanced post-industrial society, albeit poverty that reduces life expectancy rather than imminently kills (Chase & Walker 2013; Ali *et al.* 2018).

An unfortunate consequence of the distinction between absolute and relative poverty has been to separate debates about poverty in the Global South, reliant on measures of absolute poverty, from those in the North, with governments there, the US being the notable exception, choosing to focus on relative poverty. The World Bank did not include estimates of relative poverty among its world development indicators until 2014, and then only for countries in the east of Europe. With respect to the Global South, it is still developing a measure of what it terms "societal poverty", a hybrid concept that counts someone as poor if they have an income of less than the sum of one US dollar a day and 50 per cent of the national median (Feng & Nguyen 2014; Jolliffe & Prydz 2021).

The Millennium Development Goals were only concerned with absolute poverty. The two principal measures – income is less than US\$1/day (increased to US\$1.25 in 2008) and the proportion undernourished – were therefore largely immaterial for rich countries. Even in the era of the SDGs, the division created by absolute and relative definitions is merely sidestepped with the introduction of a second target: "1.2 By 2030, reduce at least by half the proportion of men, women and children of all ages living in poverty in all its dimensions according to national definitions."

This second target, being based on national definitions of poverty, serves to confound multiple concepts of poverty since countries variously use relative, absolute, composite and, occasionally, multidimensional indices of poverty.

The distinction between absolute and relative poverty has proved to be counterproductive and is unnecessary. All poverty is relative in that resources are related to what is necessary for life. At a given point in time, poverty thresholds, absolute or relative, can all be compared in terms of the extent to which they exceed or fall short of a given index of needs. One might term this a measure of the adequacy, generosity or, indeed, the meanness of a particular poverty threshold. The use of relative poverty is largely restricted to more affluent countries where poverty thresholds tend to be more generous than in poorer countries. The latter more often define poverty in absolute terms.

Incomes rise over time as economies grow richer and governments often respond by increasing the poverty line or threshold. The degree to which the threshold is increased as national income rises is termed the income elasticity of the poverty threshold. Absolute and relative measures of poverty are characterized by different income elasticities, implying also varying degrees of generosity (Fisher 1995; Foster 1998). An elasticity of 1, meaning that the poverty threshold rises in line with national income, corresponds to a purely relative definition of poverty and to a society in which the benefits of economic growth are fully reflected in the poverty threshold. If there is perfect targeting of welfare benefits, the benefits of growth will also be fully shared by people living in poverty. An elasticity of 0, indicative of an absolute definition of poverty, implies that none of the benefits of growth are shared with the poor. The political reality is that absolute poverty thresholds tend gradually to rise, if only because it becomes increasingly expensive to satisfy basic needs as affluence increases (Fisher 1995).

1.2.3 Poverty as the absence of rights

Often seeming to stand in opposition to an income-based approach, proponents of capability theory construct poverty as the denial of people's freedom to achieve well-being. As with the distinction between relative and absolute poverty, the difference between income and capability poverty is more illusionary than real. As is traditional in academic discourse, with the new presented as better than the old, Amartya Sen offered the capability approach as a corrective to traditional economics with its focus on utility and resources. While introducing terminology that even Sen has subsequently admitted was "not awfully attractive", he simply sought to shift the focus from means, that is resources, to ends, how people are able to use resources to do or become things. His distinction, therefore, is much the same as that made by Ringen (1988) from within the income-based tradition: namely, that lack of income is not poverty but its cause.

Sen introduced the term "functionings" to describe the "doings and beings" that people might be expected or aspire to undertake or become; "capabilities" refers to the "real, or substantive, opportunity" to achieve or to be these things (Robeyns & Fibieger Byskov 2021). Capabilities are described by Sen as real freedoms, meaning that the opportunity can truly be accessed, and that the person has the wherewithal to achieve chosen functionings. A person's ability to "convert" a set of resources, the means, into ends depends on their endowments and the socio-political and environmental conditions.

Sen himself has repeatedly refused to offer a definitive list of capabilities, although many others have done so. His reasoning is that there must be a place for public discussion and that such a list "will be very contingent on the kind of society we live in" (Tasioulas & Sen 2018). He has, however, discussed the concept of basic capabilities when "deciding on a cut-off point for the purpose of assessing poverty and deprivation" (Sen 1987: 19). Basic capabilities embrace "the freedom to do some basic things considered necessary for survival and to avoid or escape poverty or other serious deprivation" and poverty is thus defined as "the failure of basic capabilities to reach certain minimally acceptable levels" (Sen 1992: 45, 109).

Advocates of the capabilities approach, the Office of the High Commissioner for Human Rights among them, believe that it has many virtues. One is that "once poverty is seen to consist in the failure of a range of basic capabilities, it immediately becomes a multidimensional concept. Poverty can no longer be defined uni-dimensionally as lack of adequate income, as has traditionally been done" (OHCHR 2004: 7).

Few people now, almost two decades after this statement was published, would consider poverty to be uni-dimensional. But even at the time, it was to confuse concepts and indicators; in the nineteenth century, Charles Booth (1892) and W. E. B. Du Bois (1996 [1899]) were both aware of the multifaceted nature of poverty, as were most scholars, if not all economists, in subsequent years.

Confusion or not, Sen's influence in shifting attention away from income as an indicator of poverty has been profound. The Human Development Index (HDI) is considered to embody Sen's capabilities approach to understanding human well-being (Stanton 2007). Devised in 1990, it adds schooling and life expectancy at birth to gross national income to create a country level score, while the Multidimensional Poverty Index (MPI), introduced by United Nations Development Programme in 2010, aggregates micro-level data for the same three dimensions to permit nation by nation comparison of poverty rates. Furthermore, the SDGs themselves are considered by some to be the policy expression of capability thinking: they provide a multidimensional, multisectoral approach that stresses interconnections and multidisciplinary engagement, and ends the old division between developed and developing countries (Crabtree & Gasper 2020). That said, SDG Target 1.1 – income poverty – and SDG Target 1.2 – poverty "in all its dimensions" – might be thought to continue the old divisions, the former being predominantly for the developing world and the latter for the developed one. Moreover, while SDG Target 1.1 is prescriptive, ending US$1.25/day poverty, SDG Target 1.2 leaves the definition open to nation states. Perhaps such division could have been avoided had Sen chosen to define a canonical list of capabilities.

Sen sought further to reconcile absolute and relative conceptions of poverty arguing that "poverty is an absolute notion in the space of capabilities but very often it will take a relative form in the space of commodities or characteristics" (Sen 1983: 161). Sen considers absolute poverty to take one of two forms. First, there is poverty that is indisputably absolute: starvation, for example, in which poverty demarcates life from death. Second, citing Adam Smith's observation that, to avoid shame in eighteenth-century Britain, it was necessary to be able to wear leather shoes, he sees the unavoidable experience of shame as being indicative of absolute poverty: "on the space of the capabilities themselves – the direct constituent of the standard of living – escape from poverty has an absolute requirement, to wit, avoidance of this type of shame. Not so much having equal shame as others, but just not being ashamed, absolutely" (Sen 1983: 161).

The commodities that a person needs to acquire to avoid shame will be context-specific and therefore relative but, in their absence, poverty and the concomitant shame is absolute. Although Macdonald (2018) claims that Adam Smith has been misread, in that he attached shame to behaviour, choosing not to wear leather shoes rather than not being able to afford them, Chase and Bantebya-Kyomuhendo (2015) have found shame to be inextricably associated with poverty in many cultural and economic settings.

It is not altogether clear whether, in explaining two different meanings of the word absolute as applied to poverty, Sen was considering two levels of poverty, extreme and less extreme, or merely viewing poverty through two different lenses. The aforementioned "societal poverty", currently being considered by the World Bank, corresponds with the first possibility, albeit limited to income alone; it adds an index of relative poverty on top of an absolute one, an approach that Li and Yue (2020) have developed conceptually in the context of China. However, Chase and Bantebya-Kyomuhendo's (2015) work points to the reality of the second possibility with shame and deprivation both being integral to the experience of poverty. They found that shame is ubiquitous within the space of capabilities irrespective of the commodities needed to release people from poverty-related shame. Moreover, recent work by Bray *et al.* (2020) and Yang *et al.* (2021a, 2021b) has found shame attaching to a much wider set of poverty dimensions than currently accounted for in the HDI or MPI.

A further contribution of the capability approach relevant to the development of the SDGs is to provide "a conceptual bridge between the discourses on poverty and human rights" (OHCHR 2004: 3). The 2030 Agenda, itself, is "grounded in the Universal Declaration of Human Rights, international human rights treaties, the

Millennium Declaration and the 2005 World Summit Outcome. It is informed by other instruments such as the Declaration on the Right to Development" (UN 2015a: para. 10).

Capability theory links poverty to human rights through the former's denial of freedom and dignity. These links are established in the conceptual framework on *Human Rights and Poverty Reduction* released by the UN Office of the High Commissioner for Human Rights in 2004. Poverty defined as the deprivation of capability represents the "inadequate realization of certain basic freedoms" both negative and positive:

> Thus, a person's freedom to live a healthy life is contingent both on the requirement that no one obstructs her legitimate pursuit of good health – negative freedom, and also on the society's success in creating an enabling environment in which she can actually achieve good health – positive freedom.
>
> The reason why the conception of poverty is concerned with basic freedoms is that these are recognized as being fundamentally valuable for minimal human dignity. But the concern for human dignity also motivates the human rights approach, which postulates that people have inalienable rights to these freedoms.   (OHCHR 2004: 9)

Of course, poverty is only one cause of the denial of human rights, and the different causes must be distinguished from each other. Therefore, the OHCHR stipulates that "Inadequate command over economic resources must play a role in the causal chain leading to the non-fulfilment of human rights". And, also, that "The human rights involved must be those that correspond to the capabilities that are considered basic by a given society".

With income broadly defined as economic resources these stipulations serve both to reconnect the income-deficit and capability approaches and to support a minimal conception of a poverty threshold. While the conceptual framework speaks of the gradual realization of rights, those specifically mentioned include only: adequate nourishment, clothing and shelter; avoiding preventable morbidity; participation in community life; and being able to appear in public with dignity. A legacy of this minimalist conception is also to be found in the OHCHR's *Guiding Principles on Human Rights and Extreme Poverty*, adopted in 2012, which refer only to extreme poverty.

Nevertheless, the linkage of poverty with human rights has advantages beyond its constitutive relevance. It offers the potential to ensure that governments take preventive action and to make certain that the kinds of anti-poverty programmes that are implemented are effective and dignity enhancing. Human rights also seek to empower people through stipulating entitlements, encouraging participation, specifying principles of accountability, and insisting on non-discrimination and equality of treatment. These principles inform the targets associated with SDG1 that have to do with policy responses and provide a mechanism through which governments can be held responsible for the quality of policy implementation.

1.3 Conclusion

The 2030 Agenda provides the glimpse of a much better world that is fairer, cleaner, peaceful and without poverty and hunger. The Sustainable Development Goals provide ambitious targets to aid the realization of this vision; a vision for the world's people to be achieved with the world's people.

That is the plan, the viability of which is to be considered in subsequent chapters in relation to just one of the 17 goals, ending poverty. This chapter has considered what is meant by poverty, drawing attention to the two main interpretations, low-income and capability theory. In the past, each approach has been so rigorously defended by its proponents that their similitudes have been overlooked such that conceptual progress and policy advance have arguably both been impeded. On close inspection the two interpretations reduce to one.

Poverty is an undesirable state of life being restricted by the multiple consequences of a shortage of resources in relation to needs. It denies people the opportunity actively to engage as full members of society and adequately to play the roles expected of them, causing them to feel shame. Moreover, they are habitually subjected to stigma and social exclusion by others. Persons experiencing poverty often feel powerless, and frequently are so. Hence, they are denied, to borrow Sen's terminology, the freedom to achieve capabilities equating to an acceptable life and a satisfactory level of well-being. Insofar as they are not accorded dignity on account of their poverty, their human rights are infringed.

While poverty probably exists in every society, it is difficult empirically to determine a threshold that is not, in large measure, subjective and normative. The poverty rate, the proportion of people who count as poor, depends on the level of resources in relation to needs that is chosen as a poverty threshold. The extent to which the poverty rate will appear to fall in the context of economic growth depends on the sensitivity of the poverty threshold to increases in median incomes and social expectations.

Turning to the measures of poverty presented as SDG Targets 1.1 and 1.2, the threshold for Target 1.1 is based solely on income and set very low in global terms, it is the average of the poverty threshold of the world's poorest 15 countries. Moreover, the threshold is fixed, that is absolute, meaning that numbers should fall with even minimal rates of economic growth unless offset by increasing inequality. It is only this kind of poverty that is be eradicated by 2030.

Target 1.2 requires poverty to be reduced by a minimum of half by 2030 but poverty is ill-defined. The metric offered is "poverty in all its dimensions according to national definitions" but there is no list of dimensions since this is left for individual states to determine. Comparatively few countries embrace an official multidimensional poverty index, while the UNDP's Multidimensional Poverty Index (MPI) for most countries only includes deficiencies in income, schooling and health. National poverty measures are usually uni-dimensional, relating either to income or expenditure, and may be relative or absolute and, therefore, more or less sensitive to the rate of economic growth. In sum, Target 1.2 speaks to individual countries but offers no basis for international comparison or any degree of precision as to what is expected.

There is, then, an enormous gap between the rhetoric of "ending poverty in all its forms everywhere" and Targets 1.1 and 1.2 which, although demanding when compared to past achievements, fall far short of the rhetorical aspiration. But "we the people" may not care or may not care sufficiently.

CASE STUDY 1 ON THE NATURE OF POVERTY

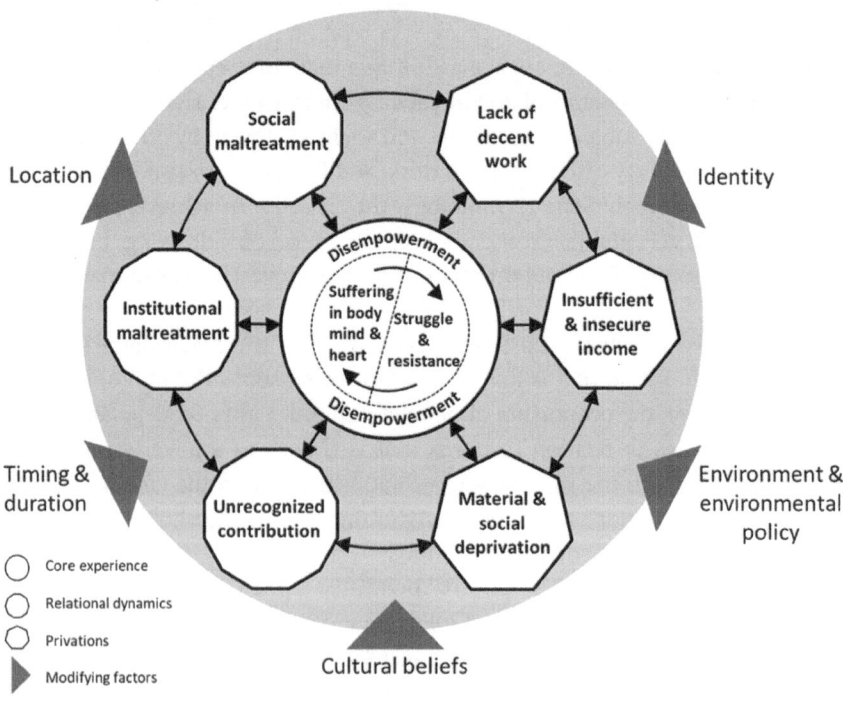

Figure CS1 Dimensions of poverty

The above portrayal of poverty was described by Angel Gurria, when director general of the OECD, as the first which "places a bridge across the gulf in the measurement approaches to poverty in rich and poor countries … allowing us to see poverty through a single perspective". It was prepared in 2019 by research teams in Bangladesh, Bolivia, Britain, France, Tanzania and the United States that all included people who, according to local standards, were living in poverty. Each of the nine dimensions of poverty was salient in every country although its precise manifestation was influenced by timing, location, the natural environment, culture, and identity. The 2030 Agenda refers to two separate conceptions of poverty represented by SDG1.1 for poor countries and SDG2 for rich ones. Only one of the nine dimensions – insufficient income – is to be measured explicitly under the SDG rubrics. While the goal to end "poverty in all its forms everywhere", is ambitious, SDG1 represents a partial response to a partial understanding of poverty.

Further reading

Bray, R. *et al.* 2020. "Realising poverty in all its dimensions". *World Development* 13(4). https://doi.org/10.1016/j.worlddev.2020.105025.

Godinot, X. 2019. "Unveiling the hidden dimensions of poverty". *Spotlight on Sustainable Development*. Special Contribution 1. www.2030spotlight.org/en/book/1883/chapter/unveiling-hidden-dimensions-poverty.

2

PROGRESS TO 2015

The Sustainable Development Goals (SDGs) did not simply replace the Millennium Development Goals (MDGs), they were a reaction to them.

The eight Millennium Development Goals (Table 2.1), introduced with the signing of the Millennium Declaration at the United Nations headquarters in September 2000 were described by some as being "revolutionary" (SDGF 2022). Supported by the leaders of 189 countries, the goals seemed to offer "a common language to reach global agreement". Not only were the goals generally considered to be realistic, but they also came with an approved mechanism for measurement and monitoring. Moreover, by 2015, the world seemed to be inching towards attaining several of the goals; it was even possible to claim that the goal of halving extreme poverty had been achieved five years ahead of schedule. For 15 years, therefore, the MDGs helped keep poverty and world development, if not in the public eye, at least as a focus for potential global collaboration.

Table 2.1 The Millennium Development Goals

Goal	Targets (in italics added in 2006/8)
1. Eradicate extreme poverty and hunger	A: Halve, between 1990 and 2015, the proportion of people whose income is less than US$1/day (US$1.25/day) *B: Achieve full and productive employment and decent work for all, including women and young people* C: Halve, between 1990 and 2015, the proportion of people who suffer from hunger
2. Achieve universal primary education	A: Ensure that, by 2015, children everywhere, boys and girls alike, will be able to complete a full course of primary schooling
3. Promote gender equality and empower women	A: Eliminate gender disparity in primary and secondary education, preferably by 2005, and in all levels of education no later than 2015
4. Reduce child mortality	A. Reduce by two-thirds, between 1990 and 2015, the under-five mortality rate
5. Improve maternal health	A. Reduce by three quarters, between 1990 and 2015, the maternal mortality ratio *B. Achieve, by 2015, universal access to reproductive health*

(continued)

Table 2.1 *(Cont.)*

Goal	Targets (in italics *added in 2006/8*)
6. Combat HIV/AIDS, malaria and other diseases	A: Have halted by 2015 and begun to reverse the spread of HIV/ AIDS *B: Achieve, by 2010, universal access to treatment for HIV/AIDS for all those who need it* C: Have halted by 2015 and begun to reverse the incidence of malaria and other major diseases
7. Ensure environmental sustainability	A: Integrate the principles of sustainable development into country policies and programmes and reverse the loss of environmental resources *B: Reduce biodiversity loss, achieving, by 2010, a significant reduction in the rate of loss* C: Halve, by 2015, the proportion of people without sustainable access to safe drinking water and basic sanitation D: By 2020, to have achieved a significant improvement in the lives of at least 100 million slum dwellers
8. Develop a global partnership for development	A: Develop further an open, rule-based, predictable, non-discriminatory trading and financial system B: Address the special needs of the least developed countries C: Address the special needs of landlocked developing countries and small island developing states D: Deal comprehensively with the debt problems of developing countries through national and international measures in order to make debt sustainable in the long term E: In cooperation with pharmaceutical companies, provide access to affordable essential drugs in developing countries F: In cooperation with the private sector, make available the benefits of new technologies, especially information and communications

However, by 2011, when the planning for the SDGs began in earnest, a large body of opinion considered that the MDGs were too narrowly focused and had therefore prevented poverty from being tackled in the round (UNEP 2012; Ivanova & Escobar-Pemberthy 2016). Some even suggested that the goals were fundamentally flawed ignoring the underlying causes of global poverty (Bello 2013; McCloskey 2015). The SDGs were therefore intended to take forward the collective energy inspired by the MDGs but to rectify at least some of their deficiencies. Hence, to understand the SDGs it is necessary to understand the MDGs.

The origins of the MDGs and the thinking behind them are considered before examining the extent to which they were truly successful. Viewed as an example of global international governance built around consensus, they stand as beacons of hope given previous failures. However, when the focus shifts to performance in relation to targets, and beyond to consider the impact on individual lives and the well-being of communities, the achievements begin to look more mundane, if not truly disappointing.

2.1 On the origins of the MDGs

Much is in the name. The Millennium Development Goals were products of their time and concerned development, not just poverty.

The development agenda in the modern era dates from the aftermath of the Second World War when it was hoped that providing for basic needs would foster peace, avoid conflict, and support the newly established world order. Key institutions established at this time were the United Nations and the Bretton Woods Institutions comprising the International Monetary Fund (IMF) and the International Bank for Reconstruction and Development (hereafter referred to as the World Bank). The focus of the World Bank, initially established to assist with the rebuilding of war-ravaged Europe, soon shifted, in the context of rivalries stemming from the Cold War, to development of the Global South. This first meant supporting investment by colonial powers but later became a system to provide financial assistance to newly emergent nations.

2.1.1 Once upon a time

The Declaration of Human Rights of 1948 should likewise be interpreted in the immediate postwar context. Inalienable rights were not justified in their own terms but as the foundation of freedom, justice and, significantly, world peace.

Article 25, which asserts that everyone has a right to an adequate standard of living, embraces the foundation needs of physiology and safety articulated by Maslow and discussed in the previous chapter. With mention of out-of-wedlock births, a particular Western concern at the time fuelled by the sexual freedoms that wartime dislocation had engendered, it also hints at the higher needs of respect, recognition and self-esteem. While such higher-order needs were not generalized, Article 25 does include a vision of the postwar social settlement in Western Europe and the needs that social protection systems were then being developed to meet. During the decolonization period of the 1950s and 1960s, varyingly successful attempts were made by emergent states to establish parallel systems of state welfare provision supported, on occasion, by the World Bank (Surender 2013). By the 1970s, however, the prevailing view was that economic growth needed to be established before welfare provision could be considered.

While the World Bank directed support to individual countries, the United Nations sought to take a global perspective with several summits around a range of topics. However, with the turn in the 1980s towards neoliberalism advocated by the Reagan administration in the United States and the Thatcher government in Britain, the balance of influence shifted firmly towards the World Bank and the IMF with the emergence of the so-called Washington Consensus. The "Consensus" was that state intervention should be curtailed and developing economies opened to the free movement of goods, services and capital (Wade 2002). To achieve this, the World Bank, and latterly the IMF, made a total of 958 loans between 1989 and 1998 that were conditional on structural adjustment designed to shift the balance of economic activity from the public to the private sector (Easterly 2001). Throughout this period, most international debate on poverty was silenced while the world waited for economic growth to lift people out of poverty and, additionally, to generate resources that might be directed towards welfare spending.

The two decades to 2000 were, in fact, characterized by economic stagnation rather than by growth, which permitted an alternative discourse on poverty to open (Archibong *et al.* 2021). Emblematic of this change was the release of the World Bank's *World Development Report 1990* (World Bank 1990); the thirteenth in the series, it was the first to be devoted to poverty. In the same year, the first *Human Development Report* was published by the United Nations Development Programme (UNDP 1990) and, significantly, the word "human" was used to qualify development rather than "economic", as had previously been common practice. The latter report, much influenced by Amartya Sen's capability approach, conceptualized human development as "a process of enlarging people's choices". It also expanded the coverage of Maslow hierarchy of human needs to "include political freedom, guaranteed human rights and self-respect" (UNDP 1990: 10).

While the report mentioned poverty 161 times, the concept was not defined. By implication, however, the UNDP had moved beyond income poverty noting that "income is a means, not an end" and that well-being "depends on the uses to which incomes are put". It also rejected the idea that "income is a good proxy for all other human choices". In contrast, the World Bank's *World Development Report 1990* defined poverty as "the inability to attain a minimal standard of living" and measured it with respect to two income/consumption thresholds. The lower threshold was set at US$275 per person a year (1985 purchasing power parity [PPP] prices), the poverty line in India, while the upper one, US$370 per person each year, was the average of the poverty lines in Bangladesh, Egypt, India, Indonesia, Kenya, Morocco and Tanzania. This distinction in the conceptualization and measurement between the United Nations and the Bretton Woods institutions persists until this day, albeit the World Bank has begun to entertain ideas of relative and multidimensional poverty (Jolliffe & Prydz 2021; World Bank 2021).

It is important to recall that 1989 witnessed the fall of the Berlin War and the collapse of East European communism. The ending of the Cold War fuelled Western confidence which infected both the UN and the Bretton Woods institutions. This euphoria and the UNDP's attachment of Western values is captured in the forward to the first *Human Development Report*:

> We live in stirring times. An irresistible wave of human freedom is sweeping across many lands. Not only political systems but economic structures are beginning to change in countries where democratic forces had been long suppressed. People are beginning to take charge of their own destiny in these countries. Unnecessary state interventions are on the wane. These are all reminders of the triumph of the human spirit.
>
> (UNDP 1990: 10)

It was in this context that the United Nations resumed its earlier strategy of topic-based summits with the World Summit for Children held in 1990 often being seen as the progenitor of the MDGs (Bradford 2002; Hulme 2009). Specific goals were established including: universal access to safe water; reduced malnutrition; decreased under-five and maternal mortality; and universal access to – and completion of – primary education.

2.1.2 Towards the Millennium Development Goals

It was by no means inevitable that the world would unite around a set of global goals. Somewhat inadvertently, officials in the OECD grouping of rich countries initiated a process when, in 1996, they synthesized outcomes from UN summits into a set of goals. These were subsequently championed by the four development ministers of Britain, Germany, the Netherlands and Norway, who all happened to be women.

The idea "to do something" to coincide with the millennium came from the United Nations. Goals were on the agenda, but, since politically these had to be taken from the UN's membership, predominantly drawn from the Global South, a second set of goals was developed. The two sets subsequently had to be merged through a process of intense negotiation, something that was not achieved until 12 months after the MDGs were formally ratified. Even so, the MDGs stand as testimony to the possibility of global governance.

The 1992 Rio Summit placed environmental issues before the world's public while the 1994 Cairo Summit made connections between reproductive health, gender and development. However, the World Summit on Social Development in Copenhagen in 1995 had a more direct impact on the formulation of MDG1. Promoted by the International Labour Organization (ILO), the summit merged poverty, defined as a multidimensional concept, with employment and social integration. Criticized at the time by some non-governmental organizations

(NGOs) for being insufficiently radical in not addressing economic globalization, delegates signed up "to the goal of eradicating poverty in the world, through decisive national actions and international cooperation, as an ethical, social, political and economic imperative of humankind" (UNDP 1997: 106). The UNDP subsequently refocused its mission on poverty reduction and, in 1999, the World Bank introduced Poverty Reduction Strategy Papers (PRSPs) as the basis for allocating aid.

But the success of the Copenhagen Summit needs to be set against the fiscal conservatism of the time. While neoliberalism had not delivered, it was far from dead. *The OECD Jobs Study*, which was published in 1994, brought workfare to European countries and suggested making last-resort benefits conditional on behaviour as well as need (Lødemel & Trickey 2001). US President Clinton, although a Democrat, was a fiscal conservative or needed to present himself as one. Likewise, the incoming Labour government in Britain in 1997 felt compelled to demonstrate its careful management of the economy. Domestic poverty rates were increasing across much of Europe leading to the refrain that "charity begins at home" at a time when the amount of overseas development assistance (ODA) provided by OECD countries was already in long-term decline (Sainsbury & Morissens 2002).

In this context, the OECD's Development Assistance Committee (DAC), meeting in Paris in May 1995, felt under considerable pressure. After the meeting, a conversation reputedly in the carpark between Colin Bradford, the US representative on the Committee, and Jan Pronk, the Dutch Minister for International Development, resulted in the establishment of a ministerial level *Groupe de Réflexion*. In May 1996, the *Groupe* proposed a set of targets that rapidly came to be called the International Development Targets (IDTs).

The IDTs embraced well-being, social development and environmental sustainability and regeneration. The British and Japanese representatives were not enamoured by the concept of multidimensional poverty and wanted, instead, to focus on lifting incomes through economic growth. The first compromise, therefore, was to place economic welfare first, with a focus on income poverty reduction, while embracing the other dimensions within a second goal relating to social development. The second compromise, at the insistence of the Japanese, was to limit the scope of gender equality included within the social development goal to equity within education. The third compromise was to omit any mention of the level of development aid to be provided by OECD countries.

While the IDTs briefly attracted positive coverage in the Western media, they were the initiative of rich Northern countries drafted without wide consultation and so might never have gained traction. The response of civil society was split on interest lines: those whose concerns could be found within the IDTs were broadly supportive; but those NGOs representing women's interests were loudly critical of the compromise on gender. The reaction of the international governmental organizations was also somewhat mixed with guarded approval by the World Bank, but a cool reception from the IMF.

The IDTs fell far short of the Copenhagen Commitment and the aspirations of the UNDP. Whereas the DAC proposed a goal of halving poverty, the UNDP wanted to eradicate it and tackle many more dimensions. While the UNDP justified their ambition on the basis that poverty was an infringement of human rights, the DAC's motivation was largely pragmatic and self-interested: eliminating poverty would reduce South–North migration, increase global solidity and, hence, enhance security. DAC set global goals and prioritized national economic growth as the principal mechanism for achieving them. The UNDP, however, preferred developing countries to establish their own targets and expected a financial commitment from OECD members.

This impasse took time to resolve with much credit being apportioned to the four aforementioned female ministers for international development who became known as the "Utstein Group" (after the venue of a joint World Bank/ IMF meeting where they first met). They made real the practical relevance of the goals in ways that appealed to technocrats in the UNDP and IMF. They also invested time in explaining and "selling" the IDTs to the leaders of recipient countries with varying degrees of success.

2.1.3 Making of the Millennium Development Goals

While the IDTs established a model of global targets, it was the United Nations that turned them into a global reality, although it is not clear that this was anyone's prior intention. Under the leadership of Secretary-General Kofi Annan, the UN recognized the promotional value of the millennium, a once-in-a-thousand-year event that could re-energize the global community, and re-establish the UN's relevance and credibility after a decade or more of increasing criticism.

The UN Assembly in 2000 was designated as "the Millennium Assembly" comprising a Millennium Summit and Declaration, the latter to be based on a report circulated earlier for comment. Much formal and informal lobbying followed as groups tried to get their special interest included in the pre-conference report and onto the millennium agenda. When the pre-conference report, *We the Peoples: The Role of the United Nations in the 21st Century*, was launched in April 2000 under the Secretary-General's name, poverty eradication had become the lead topic with a set of poverty reduction goals that were very different from the IDTs (Annan 2000). The difference was perhaps inevitable in that the UN's goals were both informed and constrained by its much broader constituency. Relevant for discussion in later chapters, *We the Peoples* included specific commitments for the Global North, noting that "At the international level, the more fortunate countries owe a duty of solidarity to the less fortunate" (UN 2000: 78).

The two sets of goals created political as well as policy difficulties. The UN needed to demonstrate that it was working in concert with the international agencies favoured by its principal sponsor, the USA, namely the IMF and World Bank. Intense and extensive lobbying and frantic negotiations took place right up to the eve of the Millennium Assembly and Summit. The resultant Millennium Declaration, that was unanimously approved on 8 September 2000, judiciously excluded any definitive list of global poverty goals (UN 2000). Moreover, "Development and poverty alleviation" had slipped to second place below "Peace, security and disarmament" and the declaration contained two lists of potential targets: the first prefaced by "We resolve further"; and the second by "We also resolve".

With the dilemma of different goals merely postponed and still strong institutional backing for the IDTs, it looked as if no reconciliation would be possible. Nevertheless, following agreement that there would be a clear division of responsibilities – with the World Bank and IMF having oversight of the PRSPs and the UN that of the Millennium Goals, the task of reconciling the goals was initiated. The process, presented as a purely technical exercise in the UN Secretary-General's first Millennium Summit follow-up report to General Assembly in September 2001, was profoundly political with participants in constant touch with their capitals and headquarters (UN 2001). While most countries immediately accepted the newly formulated goals as technical refinements, the USA refused to do so for four years on the valid grounds that they were "a Secretariat product, which member states never formally ratified" (quoted in Hulme 2009: 42).

2.1.4 The MDGs as lowest common denominator

The IDTs became the basis for MDGs because indicators were needed and the DAC was four years ahead in developing these (Hulme 2009). The only element of the IDTs that did not make the final list concerned birth control; this had faced concerted opposition from the Vatican and conservative Islamic states at the time of the *We the Peoples* report. Goal 8, "Develop a global partnership for development", had seven targets and 17 indicators attached to it, the largest number for any goals. This was perhaps intended to appease demands that the Global North had to be made accountable but, unlike the other targets, no dates were included. This enabled rich countries to choose to be semi-detached from the process since most of the other targets were inapplicable to them.

As a technocratic solution, the MDGs were certainly closer to the IDTs than the ambitious Copenhagen Declaration with its emphasis on human rights and multidimensionality. While the MDGs were framed within a human rights perspective, the logic was not much pursued in the targets, lost during nego-tiations. No goals, targets or indicators referred to unemployment or to decent work, health was not comprehensively covered despite being the focus of three goals and, while structural adjustment had already been replaced by system of PRSPs by the time that the MDGs were finalized, pressure on donors to reform and enhance the system of development aid under MDG8 was extremely limited.

The discrepancy between the Copenhagen and Millennium Declarations is perhaps most marked in terms of the goals, targets and indicators that were to be the precursors of SDG1. Copenhagen envisaged that poverty would be conceptualized in multidimensional terms and extend beyond physiological needs to include participation in social and cultural life, social integration, employment and livelihoods. MDG1, in contrast, adopted an exceedingly restrictive definition of poverty, limiting poverty to that which was "extreme" and coupling it with hunger by way of emphasizing the extremity. Moreover, whereas Copenhagen sought to eradicate absolute poverty, MDG1 targeted halving it by 2015. Three other basic needs were captured in indicators relating to Goal 7, Environmental Sustainability: access to an improved water source, improved sanitation and secure tenure.

The five indicators associated with MDG1 reflected the extremity of poverty. Poverty was measured as income of less than US$1/day while hunger was taken to be the prevalence of underweight children (when aged less than five) and the proportion of the population below the minimum level of dietary energy con-sumption. With respect to hunger, therefore, the indicators sought evidence of actual damage caused by poverty, not merely the risk of it.

When compared with today's Sustainable Development Goals, it is evident the MDGs were only about development, not about continuing progress. They reflected the distinction between rich and poor countries and between donors and recipients. While the product of negotiation, they were shaped by the interests and expertise of developed countries for the presumed benefit of developing ones. Although made possible by a once-in-a-thousand-year event, they were nevertheless inherently divisive with precise targets across seven goals for poorer countries to attain and one goal with imprecise targets for rich ones. Viewed from the Global North, the targets seemed reasonable, indeed basic, and not very challenging. Experience was to teach otherwise as is explained in the next section

2.2 Achievements of the MDGs

Some of the conceptual and technical limitations of the MDGs were soon recognized. Revisions were made in 2003 and four new targets were added in 2007 and implemented in 2008. These included an additional target appertaining to MDG1: namely, "to achieve full and productive employment and decent work for all, including for women and young people". The poverty threshold was also increased from US$1/day to US$1.25 in 2008.

There remains much debate as to achievements of the MDGs and the reasons for them. Viewed from the perspective of the United Nations' summary evaluation, the MDGs were a great success, albeit with "uneven achievements and shortfalls in many areas" (UN 2015b: 4):

> the world community has reason to celebrate. Thanks to concerted global, regional, national and local efforts, the MDGs have saved the lives of millions and improved conditions for many more. The data and analysis ... prove that, with targeted interventions, sound strategies, adequate resources and political will, even the poorest countries can make dramatic and unprecedented progress.

The *2015 MDG Progress Chart* (UN 2015c) which takes 16 of the 19 targets and uses a traffic light system to assess progress across nine geographic sub-regions presents an image that is predominantly green or light green, indicating sub-regions where the "target was met or excellent progress" made or where there was "good progress". Only 11 per cent of target/regions were recorded as experiencing "poor progress or deterioration" (subdued red in colour) with another 16 per cent in which progress was considered "fair" (amber).

This impression of success fits uneasily next to the judgement on Oxford University's *World in Data* website, which asserts that: "Overall, the world achieved three and a half out of the 14 Targets which can be assessed quantitatively" (Ritchie & Roser 2018). The Oxford study takes each of the indicators literally and determines whether the overall global target was met. The synthesis of the Oxford analysis, summarized in Figure 2.1, shows considerable variation across the different targets. The targets for reducing income poverty and improving the supply of clean water were both exceeded, while the employment rate fell rather than increasing (from 62 to 60 per cent of the working age population).

2.2.1 Success or maybe not

The difference between the positive official presentation and the Oxford's more pessimistic account reflects, of course, political considerations: the UN's need to prove its relevance and competence; to justify the resources and human effort involved in developing and managing the MDGs; the wish to demonstrate the worlds' agency in tackling social phenomena that kill and maim; and the desire

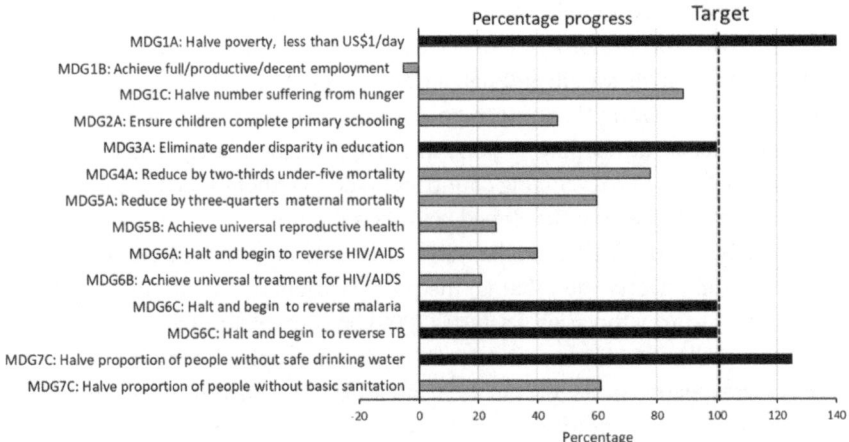

Figure 2.1 Progress towards MDG targets, 1990–2015
Source: Calculated from Ritchie and Roser (2018).

to build support for continuing with a similar strategy that would continue to keep the issues in the public's eye with the UN in the lead (Jolly 2004). But the difference also draws attention to the varying capacities of countries (and arguably of geographic regions that share similar characteristics) to respond to the problems that they confront.

Countries clearly differ in terms of wealth, infrastructure, state capacity and their point on the trajectory of development. There are generally decreasing returns to policy investment that make it, for example, theoretically easier for country A to reduce its poverty rate from 90 per cent to 80 per cent than for country B to cut poverty from 20 to 10 per cent; that said, country A is likely to have less economic and administrative capacity than country B. Likewise, the target of halving poverty is likely to be more challenging for a country with high levels of poverty than one with few people who are poor. The implication, therefore, is that ostensibly similar targets create different challenges for countries, stretching some governments more than others.

Aggregate measures of global success also turn out to be problematic. Success measured in terms of the number of countries hitting the target mean that a single laggard country would prevent the world from claiming full success. Aggregate measures, for example, adding up all the people lifted out of poverty mean that the success of large countries might conceal the failure of several smaller ones. The approach adopted in the *2015 MDG Progress Chart*, presenting results based on relatively homogeneous regions with laggard regions not being allowed to detract from the success of others, provides the most optimistic reckoning of the effectiveness of the MDGs.

There were three targets associated with MDG1: halving the proportion of people with income of less than US$1/day; achieving full, decent and productive employment for all; and halving the proportion suffering from hunger (Table 2.1). Comparing the performance of the group of least developed countries with that of developing regions in respect of these targets is instructive (Figure 2.2). Whereas developing countries taken together exceeded the poverty reduction target, the least developed countries did not.

The likely reason is that similar rates of economic growth have a different impact on the poverty rate; that is, the poverty reduction elasticity associated with economic growth varies. Easterly (2009) has demonstrated that Target 1.A disadvantaged low-income countries. Target 1.A required countries to halve poverty irrespective of its level in 1990, an ambition which it turns out can be achieved with less economic growth by richer countries than poorer ones. This is illustrated in Figure 2.3. Economic growth is generally presumed to lift all incomes, moving the income distribution curve portrayed in the figure to the right. The income curve for the poorer country needs to move further to the right – implying the need for greater income growth – before the poverty rate is halved. In effect, poorer countries must grow their economies faster than richer ones to achieve the same proportional decline in poverty.

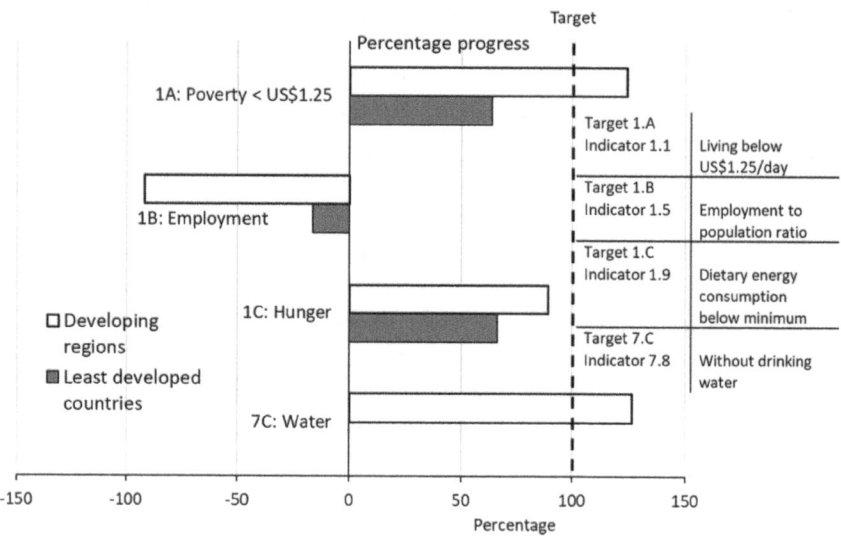

Figure 2.2 Progress towards MDG poverty and hunger targets, 1990–2015
Source: Calculated from UN (2015d). The employment values are multiplied by ten to make visible the differences.

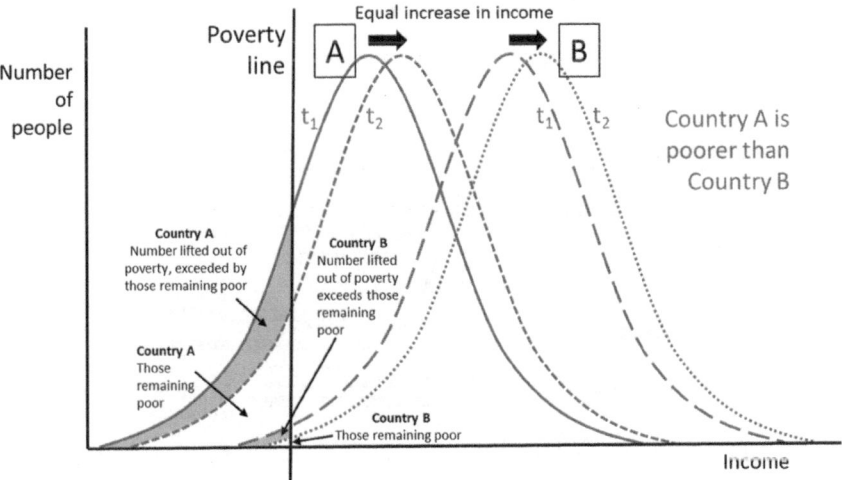

Figure 2.3 MDG Target 1.A disadvantages poorer countries
Source: Adapted from Easterly (2009).

The target of halving hunger was achieved by neither the least developed countries nor by the developing regions. Unlike income poverty measured in absolute terms, which can be reduced automatically through economic growth, tackling extensive hunger requires planning to secure and distribute food to families that are going short. The families may also feel that other priorities are more important than eating, for example, putting children through school. The discrepancy in outcomes with respect to income poverty and hunger might also raise concern about the adequacy of the income-based international poverty line which, at very least, should allow hunger to be avoided (Sundaram 2016).

The employment target, attaining full employment, was exceedingly ambitious and probably unattainable. The developing regions and the least developed countries both slipped backwards. (The employment values in Figure 2.4 are multiplied by ten to make visible the differences.) The least developed countries fared a little better with employment falling by 1.7 percentage points in relation to the target compared to 9.2 per cent across the developing world. This difference could be because the least developed countries were less integrated into the global economy and were, therefore, less affected by negative consequences of the international competitive forces that were then in play.

There was considerable regional variation in the number of goals that were successfully attained by 2015 (Figure 2.4). Countries everywhere largely succeeded in halving income poverty and often exceeded the target by a considerable margin; the only exception was the countries of Sub-Saharan Africa.

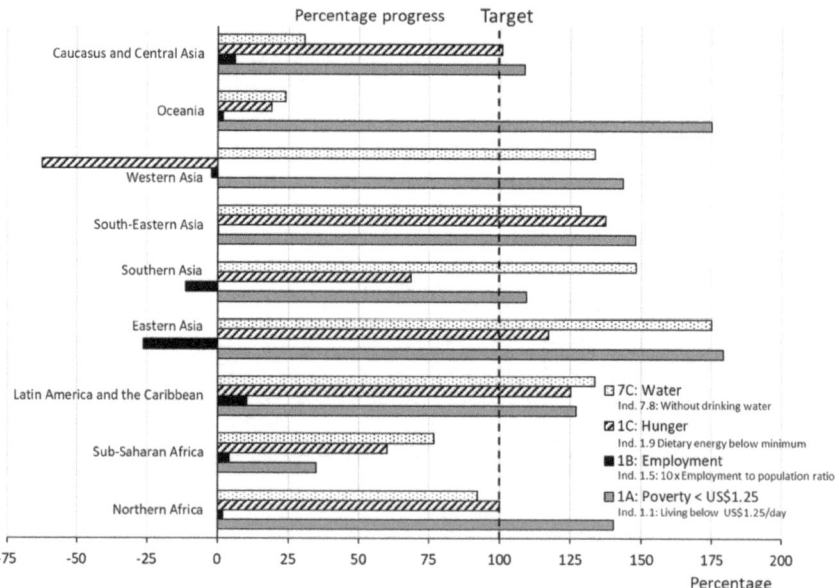

Figure 2.4 Regional progress towards MDG poverty targets, 1990–2015
Source: Calculated from UN (2015d).

Sub-Saharan African countries also generally failed to halve the number of people consuming insufficient calories or those without access to clean drinking water. This was also true of countries in the Oceania region. By way of contrast, countries in Latin America and the Caribbean, and those in East and Southeast Asia, were particularly successful in reducing all forms of poverty; that said, the goal was only to halve poverty not to eradicate it, leaving many millions without access to adequate diets and clean water. In West Asia, the proportion of people with inadequate diets actually rose, the result of war, civil unrest and a rapidly growing number of refugees (UN 2015a).

While poverty generally fell during the MDG era, this does not automatically mean that these advances had anything to do with the existence of the goals. Indeed, as is evident from Figure 2.5, absolute poverty fell noticeably in both developing regions and among the least developed counties during the decade before the introduction of the MDGs. Projecting this trend of declining poverty through to 2015 provides a simple counterfactual, an estimate of what might have happened had the MDGs not been instigated. On this basis, developing countries would have exceeded the target of halving poverty by 2015 even without the Millennium Declaration. This points to the limited ambitions of those setting the original target – or perhaps their keenness to ensure that the MDGs would ultimately be declared a success.

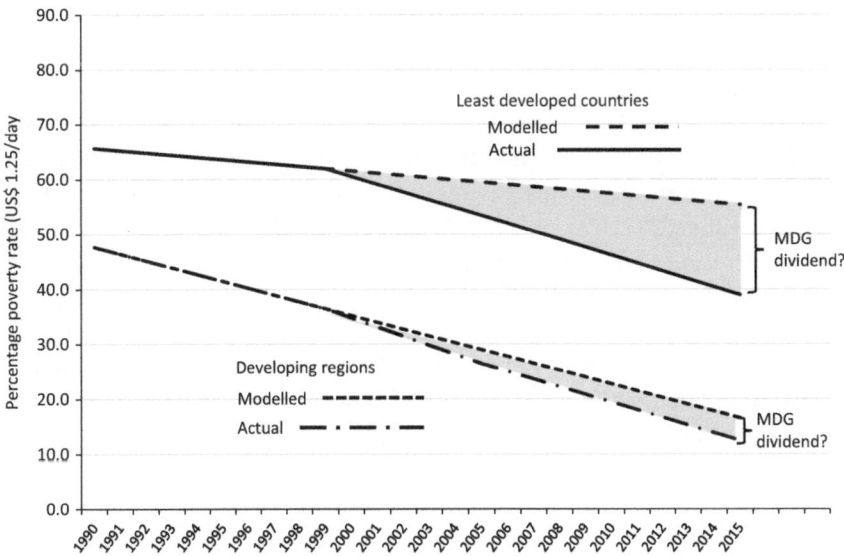

Figure 2.5 Modelling the impact of the MDGs: MDG1, Indicator 1.1
Source: Calculated from UN (2015d).

However, poverty fell faster during the MDG era than in the previous decade. This was particularly true of the least developed group of countries; the difference of 16 percentage points between the observed and predicted poverty rate was four times greater than that witnessed for developing regions taken as a group. It suggests that the MDGs – or something else occurring during the first 15 years of the millennium – brought unusual benefits to the least developed countries. However, the effect was not uniform. In almost half (46 per cent) of the least developed countries, poverty fell more slowly between 2000 and 2015 than during the previous decade.

2.2.2 Why poverty fell

Before considering the factors that might explain falling poverty rates in developing countries, it is important to draw attention to the poor quality of the statistics upon which any assessment of the effectiveness of the MDGs needs to be made. Gathering monitoring information requires states to have an institutional infrastructure with sufficient resources to facilitate regularly collecting micro data from reliable samples of the national population (Ferreira *et al.* 2016). There needs also to be competent statisticians available who are immune to political interference. With many states not having such an infrastructure, the comprehensive tables included in UN documents reporting on the MDGs are based on much statistical simulation by the World Bank, that is generating estimates in the absence of real data.

Since the upgrading of the World Bank's minimum income floor from US$1.25/day to US$1.90/day in 2015, it is no longer possible readily to evaluate the MDGs against the original targets of halving poverty defined as income of less than either US$1/day or US$1.25/day. Hence, the modelling reported in Figure 2.6 relates to the poverty line of US$1.90/day. It is based on World Bank simulations for 101 countries included in the PovcalNet database for which there are relevant information. Poverty averaged across these countries fell from 47 per cent in 1990 to 12 per cent in 2015 implying that around a billion people were lifted out of poverty. The global poverty rate stood at 34 per cent in 2001, the base year used in the modelling and the date when the MDGs were introduced.

If the modelling is to be believed, what most drove poverty down in the years before 2015 was economic growth. It did so through its impact on per capita GDP and, partially independently, on median income. These latter two factors were independent because increases in economic production do not always result

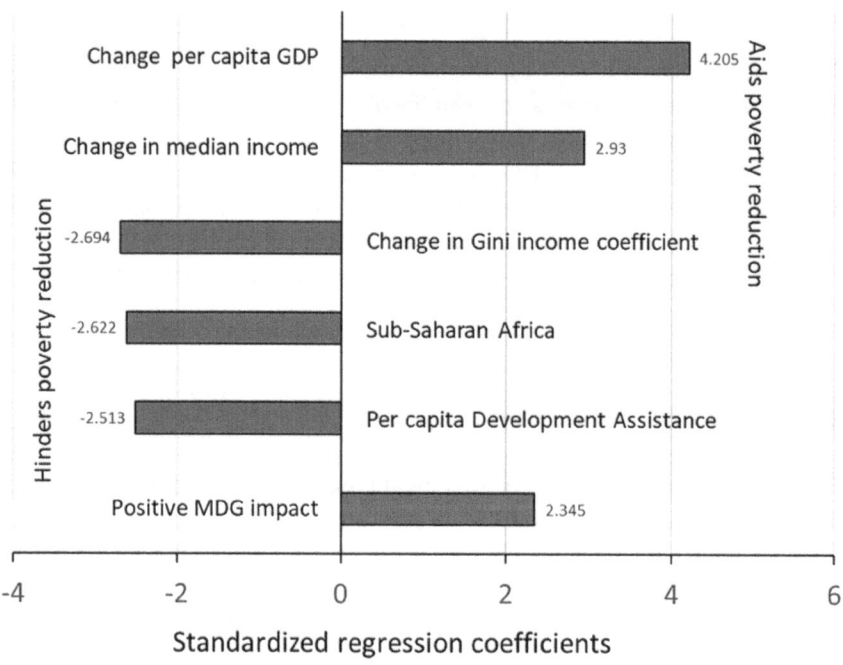

Figure 2.6 Factors associated with MDG1 poverty reduction, 2001–15
Source: Calculated from the World Bank's *PovcalNet* database and official sources.

in a rise in individual incomes. Indeed, increases in income inequality slowed down the rate of poverty reduction by almost as much as rising median incomes increased it. Interestingly, poverty in countries that received large amounts of foreign aid (including official development assistance as well as guaranteed export credits, private direct investment and portfolio investment) did not fall as quickly as elsewhere. It might be tempting to conclude, as others have done (Lyons 2014), that foreign aid inhibits economic growth but there was no evidence of this in the data analysed. It could be, of course, that development aid is directed to countries facing intractable difficulties that limit governments' ability to reduce poverty. Unfortunately, this hypothesis cannot be adequately tested with the data available. Countries with the highest poverty rates did not appear to be receiving a disproportional share of aid in 2000 but, then again, donors will have had far more information about national needs and circumstances than contained in the PovcalNet database.

The four factors mentioned explain 52 per cent of the variation in rate of poverty reduction among the 101 countries considered with development aid, the sole indicator of policy, not having the positive impact anticipated. A fifth variable, indicating those countries in which the poverty rate fell faster after 2000 than beforehand, is seen to have a positive and independent effect on poverty reduction. This variable might be considered tautological, in that it relates directly to poverty reduction, but it does point to a change in outcome coincident with the introduction of the MDGs in the 49 countries so affected. However, it only adds about 4 per cent to the explanatory power of the model.

Finally, it is important to acknowledge the importance of poverty reduction in China and its contribution to the global fall in poverty recorded during the era of the MDGs. Estimates suggest that around 57 per cent of worldwide decline in poverty was due to falls in China (*China Power* 2021). In modelling the factors associated with poverty reduction, China has the same weight as any other country despite its size and success in bringing down poverty. To counterbalance this, the analysis reported in Figure 2.7 weights countries according to the natural logarithm of population size which gives more influence (but not too much) to larger countries such as China and India. The principal determinants of poverty reduction remain altered: economic growth and rising median wages offset by increasing income inequality, with international aid continuing to seemingly dampen predicted falls in poverty. However, three other national characteristics emerge as important (a function of the weighting process that simulates an increased sample containing more larger countries). It seems that the least developed group of countries, including those in Sub-Saharan Africa and others with high baseline levels of poverty, confront additional difficulties in bringing down poverty rates. This remains the case even

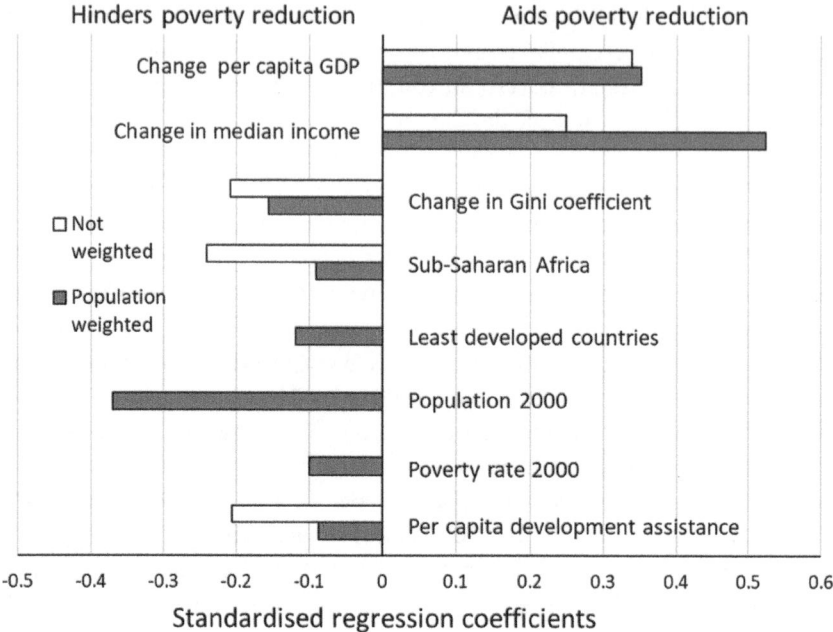

Figure 2.7 Taking account of population size in MDG1 poverty reduction, 2001–15
Source: Calculated from the World Bank's *PovcalNet* database and official sources.

though, as noted above, poverty in the least developed countries fell noticeably faster under the MDG period than previously. The weighted analysis
also reveals that poverty tended to fall faster in smaller countries than in large
ones. Although China lifted almost half a billion people out of poverty between
2000 and 2015, it ranked only twenty-first according to the rate of poverty
decline, with smaller countries, including Jordan, Jamaica and Fiji, heading
the list.

Judging the outcome of the MDGs as a strategy to promote poverty reduction
and human development is akin to determining whether a glass is half full or half
empty while having one's eyes almost closed. Closed eyes represent the lack of
reliable evidence and reliance on simulated data. Half full and half empty relate to
some apparent successes and some failures. A bookkeeping exercise would note
that 86 per cent of countries witnessed a fall in income poverty but be grateful
for the entry of China, very large, reasonably successful in reducing poverty, but
experiencing a marked increase in income inequality. The sceptic would note
that the world performed less well against the goals that required active intervention unlike the lead indicator, income poverty, which in most instances would
have fallen simply on account of economic growth.

2.3 Conclusion

The MDGs were not imposed on the world ready-formed but emerged through a sometimes tortuous process of negotiation, producing what might be described as a convenient compromise between the world's richest nations and its poorest. As a political exercise the Millennium Declaration and the subsequent follow-through should be considered successes, facilitating and legitimating a global discourse around development which helped to cultivate a constituency willing to promote further reform. Surprisingly large number numbers of states actively participated in the process with both donors and developing countries framing their policies, or at least their policy rhetoric, in relation to the goals (Joulaei *et al.* 2016; Moss 2010). By the time that preliminary thinking on the SDGs began in 2010–11, civil society was very vocal about wishing to be involved. This level of engagement and visibility surely stems from the vision of linking the goals to the millennium, the possibility of a new era with the world collectively addressing social injustice. Given that the goals were also seemingly consensual, the result of extensive consultations ahead of the Millennium Declaration, they were relatively immune to criticism (Fukuda-Parr 2013).

Furthermore, since the MDGs were not legally binding, governments could decide which goals to focus on, and which to ignore, while remaining within the spirit of a collective enterprise. This, however, enabled governments to select easy targets consistent with existing policy, ones that did not necessitate structural change. It also allowed countries in the Global North to condition their overseas development assistance on compliance with the MDGs, while largely ignoring MDG8. MDG8 sought their compliance with the need to reform the discriminatory global trading and financial system, and to respond to the special needs of the least developed countries (Bello 2013).

Between 1990 and 2015, the rate of absolute income poverty fell from 47 per cent to 12 per cent in the countries for which data were available and the number of people living in poverty fell by 1.1 billion. While it is difficult to know to what extent the MDG agenda contributed to these falls, since economic growth drove much of the decline in poverty, the rate of poverty reduction increased after the turn of the millennium. Many countries, however, failed to attain all or indeed any of the goals, some of which were simply too ambitious.

The simplicity of the MDGs was in some respects a weakness. While ideal for messaging, fuelling moral outrage and building popular support, the goals scarcely addressed the real-world complexities of policymaking and implementation. The targets and indicators tended to become goals in themselves, leading to "rigid national policy agendas, following international benchmarks, rather than local conditions" (UN 2012d: 47). Moreover, despite revisions in 2007/08, issues of inequality, gender, decent work, environmental sustainability and many dimensions of health were never adequately accommodated within the millennium agenda. Nor were the connections between the goals positively exploited.

The results-based management literature that may have indirectly spawned the MDGs proposes individualized targets that, while stretching organizations, are nevertheless attainable when accompanied by positive incentives. This contrasts markedly with one-size-fits-all nature of the MDGs goals that emphasized the risk of failure rather than the progress accomplished. Whether the objective was to shame national governments into taking further action, or to encourage donors to direct resources to nations that were not "on track", is unclear. Either way, the psychological and managerial evidence is that shaming does not stimulate positive behavioural change (Walker 2014). Rather, when the goals are beyond reach – as was the case for many of the least developed countries – it simply discourages commitment.

The United Nations' 2012 evaluation of the MDGs noted "the perception of a donor-centric agenda" (UN 2012d: 46) and, in many respects, the agenda was undoubtedly donor-centric. This is illustrated by the prominence of the OECD's IDT indicators and the willingness of the donor governments to impose targets on donees while refusing to countenance any quantitative targets applying to themselves. The proposition from the Copenhagen Summit that developing countries would be enabled to establish their own targets was rejected with international ones imposed instead. These took no account of local circumstances and disadvantaged countries in Sub-Saharan Africa (Easterly 2009).

Indeed, Easterly (2009) has scrutinized each of the MDGs and the associated indicators and concluded that they all disadvantaged countries in Sub-Saharan Africa. Because his reasoning is not regionally specific but relates to level of economic development, his analysis implies that the indicators penalized all the least developed countries. Whether this was an oversight or by design – Easterly leans to the second interpretation – cannot be determined but, in the context of a competition successfully to achieve the MDGs, the least developed countries needed to run either further or faster to come first.

Away from technicalities, the MDGs have been criticized for lacking a credible model of development or, alternatively, for fundamentally misrepresenting the reasons for global inequality, merely perpetuating the already discredited theorizing that underpinned the Washington Consensus (Bello 2013; McCloskey 2015; Sundaram 2016). The criticisms cohere around the view that the MDGs were premised on an individualistic model of poverty rather than a structural one. The critics reject the idea that poverty can be solved by giving a little more cash and micro loans to individuals in poverty, or that developing countries needed merely to be encouraged or instructed to replace existing policies with the "correct" ones. They point, instead, to the missed opportunity to address the negative effects of globalization, to revise the mechanisms of international trade and finance that favoured advanced economies, to amend trade rules that insisted on developing countries opening their economies prematurely, and to reform of the policies and practice of international development itself.

Building on the experience gained from the MDGs, the Sustainable Development Goals (SDGs) provided an opportunity to respond positively to these criticisms and many of those involved in the worldwide consultation and detailed negotiations believe this to have been the case. While this belief is questioned in later chapters (especially Chapters 6, 7 and 9), it is necessary first to understand the metamorphosis that created the SDGs from the MDGs.

CASE STUDY 2 ON CHINA'S ACHIEVEMENTS

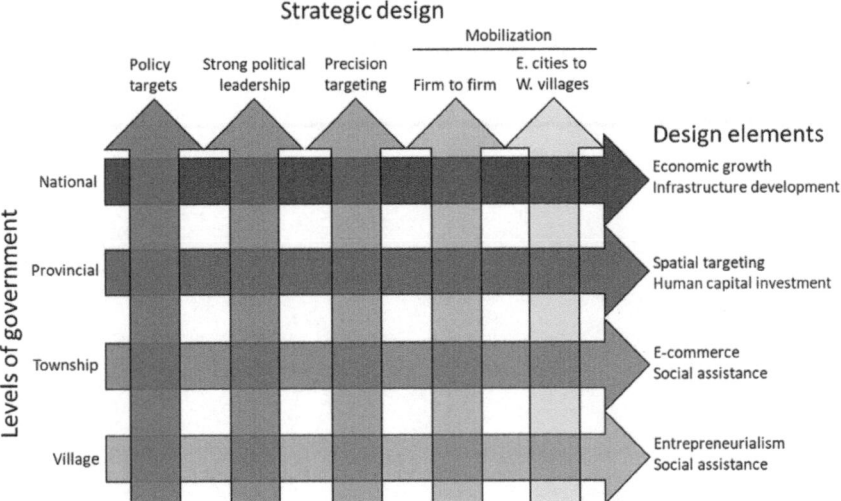

Figure CS2 China's poverty eradication strategy

China accounted for more than half of the global reduction in poverty achieved to 2015 and, having eradicated extreme poverty, the government reports meeting the 2030 Agenda poverty reduction "10 years ahead of schedule" (CIKD 2021: 11).

A nationally coordinated poverty alleviation strategy was first launched in China in 1986 and, from 2015, prioritized under the visible leadership of Chairman Xi Jinping. Complementary strategies were adopted by all tiers of government ranging from physical infrastructure – including 37,900 kilometres of high-speed rail – to the village delivery of social assistance within a national framework of targets and community mobilization involving firm-to-firm and city-to-village technical and financial support. In 2015, a comprehensive list of all families in poverty was compiled with government officials charged to assist named individuals out of poverty as an additional duty. In some provinces, Sunday was called "Xi-day", the day when officials worked with their allotted families.

While China's achievements are impressive, poverty was measured against an absolute poverty standard with most of the reduction resulting from economic growth. In 1990, when the international poverty rate (income below US$1.90/day) for China was estimated at 66 per cent, the official rural poverty rate was 74 per cent. The latter subsequently fell to 50 per cent in 2000, to 6 per cent in 2015 and, officially, to zero in 2021. Urban poverty is not recorded in China.

Further reading

CIKD 2021. *China's Progress Report on Implementation of the 2030 Agenda for Sustainable Development*. Beijing: Center for International Knowledge on Development.
Walker, R. & L. Yang 2023. "The politics of poverty alleviation in China". In S. Pellissery, S. Biswas & C. Sambo (eds), *Politics of Welfare in the Global South*. New York: Oxford University Press.

3

THE ORIGINS OF SDG1

> The new Agenda builds on the Millennium Development Goals and seeks to complete what they did not achieve, particularly in reaching the most vulnerable.

Reading this sentence from *Transforming our World*, the UN declaration announcing the Sustainable Development Goals in 2015, one could be forgiven for assuming that they are simply the MDGs Mark 2 (UN 2015a: para. 16). The reality, however, is very different. While homage is paid to the MDGs, it is only as relics belonging to an earlier civilization. Although SDG1, like MDG1, relates to poverty, the real action in negotiating the SDGs took place elsewhere, leaving SDG1 poorly specified.

This situation arose for several reasons to be elucidated in the first part of this chapter. In summary, the momentum behind the SDGs came, not from the poverty lobby, but from environmentalists schooled in ideas of sustainable development. In addition, state actors from the Global South, reacting to the MDGs drawn up by donor countries, aspired to do things differently. However, governments of many OECD countries resisted fundamental change, making it remarkable that agreement was achieved and that outright confrontation between North and South was avoided. It is generally recognized that this was made possible by skilled leadership operating in a new consultative way that weakened pre-existing alliances and power structures. It must be noted, however, that this recognition rests heavily on the writings of the main protagonists who shaped the negotiations and brokered the outcome (Kamau *et al.* 2018).

The influence of the sustainability lobby is evident in the expansion of the goals to embrace environmental, economic and social objectives and in the emphasis given to the interconnectedness of goals. The SDGs also differ from the MDGs in that they include targets relating to the "means of implementation". Given that these targets necessarily allude to resources, they emphasize the need for global partnership and transfers in cash and in kind to assist less developed nations.

The five substantive and two means of implementation targets associated with SDG1 are examined in the second section along with the most important of the 13 indicators. Taken together, the targets and indicators appear as casualties of the confusion between the different concepts of poverty discussed in Chapter 1. Incompatible definitions of poverty perpetuate distinctions between the Global North and South and lead to targets that impose the greatest demands on the least advantaged countries. There is also a failure to ensure an explicit commitment to the international cooperation or partnership necessary to attain the targets.

3.1 Shaping the SDGs

The political challenges facing the world in 2010–11 were very different than at the time of the millennium. The 9/11 attack on the World Trade Center in New York had created different global security fault lines. The 2007–09 Great Recession had temporarily reduced employment, increased hunger, and led some rich countries permanently to cut back on overseas development assistance (ODA). The economic rise of China and its informal but continuing alliance with the G77 voting bloc in the United Nations had altered the balance of power between the Global South and North. These developments affected both the content of the SDGs and their development.

3.1.1 Formal modus operandi

One set of facts makes it possible to present the development of the SDGs as a model of rationalistic policymaking with three stages involving different groups of policy actors.

First, following a High-level Plenary Meeting of the General Assembly on the Millennium Development Goals in September 2010, the so-called "MDG summit", the UN Secretary-General established a UN System Task Team in 2011 comprising experts from over 50 UN system entities and other international organizations. In parallel, the UN also commissioned a participatory evaluation of the MDGs from the perspective of 2,000 people living in extreme poverty in 22 countries; this was undertaken by ATD Fourth World, Social Watch and the International Trade Union Confederation (ITUC) (ATD4W 2014). In 2012, the Secretary-General appointed a High-Level Panel of Eminent Persons (HLP) which reported in 2013. In addition, the Task Team initiated a "global conversation" that included an open website and consultations within 84 countries led by UN resident coordinators that is thought to have reached seven million people (UNDP 2013; SDG Zone 2021). In June 2012, the UN System Task Team published *Realising the Future We Want*, which determined the terms of the ensuing debate (UN 2012d).

Second, an Open Working Group (OWG) was established in 2013 that was open to all UN member states with civil society in attendance. The group was charged with developing goals and targets, which it did by August 2014. The UN General Assembly then accepted the Group's recommendations as the "main basis for integrating sustainable development goals into the post-2015 development agenda" (Resolution 68/309).

Thereafter, as the third stage, indicators were developed by a specially constituted technical group – the Inter-Agency and Expert Group on SDGs (IAEG) – which involved representatives from 28 member states working under the authority of the UN Statistical Commission (UNSC). This group engaged in several waves of consultation with stakeholders with some meetings open to civil society groups, academia and business. It subsequently presented a framework of global indicators that was agreed, first by the UNSC in March 2017, and then adopted by the UN General Assembly on 6 July 2017.

3.1.2 Sustainable development

However, the dominant account of the evolution of the SDGs is much more expansive than the bureaucratic exercise presented above. It is one traceable back to the late 1960s and to the Club of Rome, a grouping of intellectuals from the Global South that challenged the dominant motif of the earth as a resource to be exploited (Fukuda-Parr & Muchhala 2020). Notable publications from the Club of Rome, *Limits to Growth* (Meadows *et al.* 1972) and *Mankind at the Turning Point* (Mesarovic 1974), emphasized limited resources and environmental degradation resulting from continued development and precipitated the subsequent emergence of sustainable development as a normative philosophy. The Northern response to this line of reasoning, that development in the South should be curtailed, prompted threats of a Southern boycott of the 1972 Stockholm Conference on Development and the Environment. In the event, the boycott was avoided primarily because of the work of an interdisciplinary preparatory group that was convened ahead of the conference with representation from the Global South.

The preparatory group formulated three key requirements that informed the resultant Stockholm Declaration: people-centred development that recognized pollution and environmental degradation as causes of poverty; reform of global economic governance to enable the restructuring of developing economies, breaking their dependency status as suppliers of unprocessed resources and cheap trinkets; and third, the transfer of finance and technology from the Global

North. The Stockholm Declaration also asserted that "in the developing countries most of the environmental problems are caused by under-development" (UN 1973: para. 4)

In 1987, the influential Brundtland Commission appointed by the UN Secretary-General, with a majority membership from the Global South, provided a lasting definition to the term "sustainable development": "development that meets the needs of the present without compromising the ability of future generations to meet their own needs" (Brundtland 1987: para. 1).

It argued that sustainable development should become "a goal not just for the 'developing' nations, but for industrial ones as well" (Brundtland 1987: para. 10) and that industrialized countries had a responsibility to reduce global inequality that added to the numbers hungry and in poverty.

These ideas were centre-stage at the time of the Rio "Earth Summit" in 1992. Sustainable development was explicitly referred to in 12 of the 27 principles included in the Rio Declaration, and was to be achieved by "establishing a new and equitable global partnership through the creation of new levels of cooperation among States, key sectors of societies and people" (UN 1992a: preamble). The partnership document, *Agenda 21*, called for the "progressive integration of economic, social and environmental issues in the pursuit of development", possibly the first policy recognition of the tripartite nature of sustainable development (UN 1992b; Mensah 2019; Harris 2000).

At informal consultations ahead of the opportunistically timed Rio+20 UN Conference on the Environment and Development (UNCED) in 2012, Colombia and Guatemala proposed that the Rio+20 Declaration should contain a set of Sustainable Development Goals (SDGs) and the procedure for agreeing them. The idea, which has been attributed to Paula Caballero Gómez, then Director of Economic, Social and Environmental Affairs for Colombia's Ministry of Foreign Affairs, was "to galvanize political will for an agenda for sustainability and equity" that was "deeply transformative" (Fukuda-Parr & Muchhala 2020: n.p.).

By the time of the Rio+20 UN Conference, the report of the aforementioned UN System Task Team had been published proposing goals covering inclusive social development, inclusive economic development, environmental sustainability and peace and security. Despite these topics coinciding with the dimensions of sustainable development, these proposals were pejoratively dubbed "the MDG-Plus" agenda by proponents of SDGs and seem only to have informed the conciliatory tone of the outcome document *The Future We Want*. This "underscored" the MDGs "as a useful tool in focusing achievement of specific development gains" and that the development of the SDGs "should not divert focus or effort from the achievement of the Millennium Development Goals" (UN 2012a: para. 246). The document was also very precise in determining how the SDGs should be developed:

An open working group shall be constituted no later than at the opening of the sixty-seventh session of the Assembly and shall comprise thirty representatives, nominated by Member States from the five United Nations regional groups, with the aim of achieving fair, equitable and balanced geographical representation. At the outset, this open working group will decide on its methods of work.   (UN 2012a: para. 248)

Fukuda-Parr and Muchhala (2020: n.p.) are clear that the proposal to create the SDGs was the initiative of individual delegates, not states, an epistemic community associated with UNCED that was "dominated by environmentalists" with persons from developing countries being well represented. They actively "persuaded their delegations and organizations to support the initiative" and were clearly successful; the proposal was not only included in the Rio+20 outcome document but was subsequently approved by the UN General Assembly, seemingly supplanting the procedures that had previously been established by the UN Secretary-General.

3.1.3 The Open Working Group

Much has been written about the Open Working Group (OWG) since it marked a major departure from the conventional rule-bound system of participation involving all member states (Chasek & Wagner 2016; Dodds *et al.* 2017; Kamau *et al.* 2018; Fukuda-Parr & Muchhala 2020). The system it supplanted often meant that small numbers of states could frustrate the view of the majority and that Northern governments frequently found themselves in opposition to those from the South. The limit of 30 representatives was extended first to 70, by allowing two or three countries to occupy each seat, and then to all member states but without increasing the number of seats. Regional groupings decided how the seats would be shared and the effect was that participants spoke on behalf a group of countries (termed "troikas") rather than representing solely national interests. While, formally, non-governmental organizations (NGOs) could only observe the proceedings, they, in practice, were allowed to engage actively with the process through informal out-of-hours meetings.

The OWG met on 13 occasions with the first eight sessions, each lasting between two and five days to "stocktake", that is to assemble evidence with respect to each the topics (Chasek & Wagner 2016: 406). The topics were ostensibly taken from the sections of the Rio+20 UN Conference outcome document with the "easier" ones (including poverty) being considered first. During this stage the OWG heard presentations from 80 experts. The final five sessions were devoted to identifying the goals and targets with the discussion seeded by a list of 19 "focus areas", "based on the exchange of views during the eight stock-taking sessions and other communications from OWG members and observers" (Kamau *et al.* 2018: 135–6). Seventeen of the 19 focus areas are recognizably the same as the final 17 SDGs. The working style adopted by the OWG was for a revised document, prepared by the co-chairs and the secretariat, to be tabled for discussion at each meeting as the single negotiating text. The "zero version" of the final list of goals and targets was first presented as late as the twelfth meeting.

There is some disagreement as to which goals were the most contentious but SDG1, ending poverty, was not one of them. It was agreed that the goal should apply to all countries – apparently a presentation by Nobel laureate Joseph Stiglitz was influential in raising awareness of poverty in developed countries. Nevertheless, the least developed countries "wanted to emphasize their particular challenges and insisted that they should not be left behind" and the reconciliation was to include two targets that, without comment, related to different definitions of poverty (Kamau *et al.* 2018: 162).

More contested was the inclusion of a separate goal relating to inequality. While after the Stiglitz presentation there was agreement that inequality within countries was a universal issue, the United States resisted its inclusion as a separate goal. This was resolved through "a philosophical and conceptual breakthrough – inspired by the World Bank – that focused on the relative position of the poorest 40 per cent of a country's population" (Kamau *et al.* 2018: 184–5).

However, this "resolution", which is discussed further below, did not address the second issue of contention, inequality between nations. "Impassioned" arguments for including a target of reducing global inequality were put forward by Brazil but successfully resisted by "the United States/Canada/Israel and a few others" that also objected, although in vain, to the compromise which was to seek "a greater voice for the developing world in global economic and financial institutions" which found a place in Target 10.6 (Kamau *et al.* 2018: 184–5).

3.1.4 The achievements of the OWG

The achievements of the OWG and the advocates of sustainable development that preceded it can be presented in different ways. Fukuda-Parr and Muchhala (2020: n.p.) believe that it demonstrates the "agency of Southern actors" in that "sustainable development originated with challenges from the South to a Northern led analysis of the world's environmental challenge". They consider that the "adoption of the SDGs is a game changer in thinking about development. Its redefinition transitions development from a post-colonial to a global project". A counter perspective is that the SDG agenda was highjacked by self-interested middle-class intellectuals and environmentalists with little knowledge of poverty or much understanding of the circumstances of people living in poverty. A third view is that the achievements of the OWG were more procedural and symbolic than substantive.

The differences between the SDGs and the MDG-Plus agenda seem overplayed (Table 3.1). As previously noted, the UN System Task Team argued that the Post-2015 Agenda needed to cover the three dimensions of sustainable development, economic, social and environmental, and that it "should be conceived as a truly global agenda with shared responsibilities for all countries" built on the three

Table 3.1 Evolution of the Sustainable Development Goals

High-Level Panel May 2013	Priorities on member states[1] December 2012	OWG Topic List February 2014	OWG Sustainable Development Goals August 2014
1. End poverty	4. Poverty eradication	1. Poverty eradication	Goal 1. End poverty in all its forms everywhere
2. Empower girls and women and achieve gender equality	10. Gender[2]	5. Gender equality and women's empowerment	Goal 5. Achieve gender equality and empower all women and girls
3. Provide quality education and lifelong learning		4. Education	Goal 4. Ensure inclusive and equitable quality education and promote lifelong learning opportunities for all
4. Ensure healthy lives	5. Health	3. Health and population dynamics	Goal 3. Ensure healthy lives and promote well-being for all at all ages
5. Ensure food security and good nutrition	1. Food security and sustainable agriculture	2. Food security and nutrition	Goal 2. End hunger, achieve food security and improved nutrition and promote sustainable agriculture
6. Achieve universal access to water and sanitation	2. Water and sanitation	6. Water and sanitation	Goal 6. Ensure availability and sustainable management of water and sanitation for all
7. Secure sustainable energy	3. Energy	7. Energy	Goal 7. Ensure access to affordable, reliable, sustainable and modern energy for all
8. Create jobs and sustainable livelihoods, and equitable growth	9. Employment	8. Economic growth 11. Employment and decent work for all	Goal 8. Promote sustained, inclusive and sustainable economic growth, full and productive employment and decent work for all

(continued)

Table 3.1 (*Cont.*)

High-Level Panel May 2013	Priorities on member states[1] December 2012	OWG Topic List February 2014	OWG Sustainable Development Goals August 2014
9. Manage natural resource assets sustainably	8. Environment/ management of natural resources		Goal 15. Protect, restore and promote sustainable use of terrestrial ecosystems, sustainably manage forests, combat desertification, and halt and reverse land degradation and halt biodiversity loss
10. Ensure good governance and effective institutions	6. Means of implementation		
11. Ensure stable and peaceful societies			Goal 16. Promote peaceful and inclusive societies for sustainable development, provide access to justice for all and build effective, accountable and inclusive institutions at all levels
12. Create a global enabling environment and catalyse long-term finance			Goal 17. Strengthen the means of implementation and revitalize the Global Partnership for Sustainable Development
		12. Promoting equality	Goal 10. Reduce inequality within and among countries
	12. Cities and housing[2]	13. Sustainable cities and human settlements	Goal 11. Make cities and human settlements inclusive, safe, resilient and sustainable
	11. Sustainable consumption and production[2]	14. Sustainable consumption and production	Goal 12. Ensure sustainable consumption and production patterns
	7. Climate change	15. Climate	Goal 13. Take urgent action to combat climate change and its impacts
		16. Marine resources, oceans and seas	Goal 14. Conserve and sustainably use the oceans, seas and marine resources for sustainable development

Table 3.1 *(Cont.)*

High-Level Panel May 2013	Priorities on member states[1] December 2012	OWG Topic List February 2014	OWG Sustainable Development Goals August 2014
		9. Industrialization 10. Infrastructure	Goal 9. Build resilient infrastructure, promote inclusive and sustainable industrialization and foster innovation
		17. Ecosystems and biodiversity	

Source: Kamau *et al.* (2018); UN (2012b); UN (2013).

[1]More than 50% of replies
[2]More than 40% of replies

principles of human rights, equality and sustainability. Eleven of the SDGs are direct images of those laid out by the High-Level Panel, which, although not including climate as a separate goal, also stated that "the biggest challenge of all" was "adaptation to climate change". Moreover, the High-Level Panel's report also supplied the unifying "no one should be left behind" motif that was conceived to reflect universality and the need to "tackle the causes of poverty, exclusion and inequality". This motif, not least because of its origins in the High-Level Panel, was immediately taken up by NGOs with consultation rights at the UN and became the basis of an international seminar held at the UN in June 2013 (ATD4W 2014). The additional goals, five more than the 12 proffered by the Panel, might be viewed as little more than an elaboration of the Panel's core concept of sustainable development. Indeed, unlike in the report of the UN's High-Level Panel that sought to ensure that "globalization brings maximum benefits to all", the 2030 Agenda contains no reference to the economic status quo. Instead, *Transforming Our World* simply argues that "sustained, inclusive and sustainable economic growth is essential for prosperity" (UN 2015a: para. 27).

Similarity is to be expected with intelligent people thinking about the same issues and needing to accommodate different experiences and perspectives. Moreover, the Secretariat for the Open Working Group on Sustainable Development Goals was staffed by the UN Department of Economic and Social Affairs' (DESA) Division for Sustainable Development (DSD). In addition, the initial input to the OWG from the UN Secretary-General was explicitly informed by the work of the High-Level Panel and the UN System Task Team, as well as by responses to a questionnaire returned by approximately a third of member states. The Secretary-General's input included the suggestion that goals and targets would be "made relevant through the formulation and application of national sustainable development strategies or their equivalents, and application through inter-ministerial management schemes and other cooperation mechanisms" (UN 2012b: para. 37). This suggestion became the "Means of Implementation" targets that accompany each of the SDGs that represent perhaps the most fundamental change from the MDGs.

The OWG process represented a marked departure in the classic negotiating procedures within the UN and, through the observers and qualified participation of NGOs and other groups, made public the cut and thrust of international political debate and compromise that is often hidden behind closed doors. Its success is illustrated by the fact that the recommendations of the OWG were taken forward as the basis of the subsequent negotiations to elaborate the 2030 Agenda for Sustainable Development and that the wording of the 17 SDGs was to remain intact. However, the OWG's deliberations were heavily circumscribed by the material and evidence provided to them by the UN secretariat and it seems unlikely that they resulted in outcomes that were radically different to what might otherwise have been achieved. It is, however, possible to argue that the OWG had a detrimental effect on the drafting of SDG1.

3.2 SDG1 targets and indicators

The OWG process was a product of the norm entrepreneurs committed to the tenets of sustainable development and "the rise of the South". However, the group was sorely lacking in expertise about the nature of poverty and especially its existence in the developed world (Fukuda-Parr & Hulme 2011; Gasper 2019). As noted already, representatives were surprised to learn from Stiglitz about the prevalence of poverty in the Global North. Moreover, the experts recruited to advise the OWG were specialists in development, mostly economists and all trained in the United States, a jurisdiction which has resisted the concept of relative poverty and that is notorious for high rates of poverty – even when assessed against a low absolute poverty threshold.

This configuration of circumstances might account for why the measurable targets are based on varying concepts of poverty; these apply differentially to developing and developed countries, thereby giving lie to the universality of the goals. It might also explain the continued use of the MDG definition of extreme poverty, one so low as to deny persons the dignity promised by the UN guidance on extreme poverty and human rights (UN 2012c). However, it is also important to acknowledge the politics that were in play.

Low-income countries did not want to be subject to targets that they considered to be over-ambitious and could leave them open to unfair criticism as they felt had happened – and indeed did happen (as shown in Chapter 2) – under the

MDGs. Furthermore, World Bank calculations that most persons experiencing extreme poverty were living in middle-income countries expanded the number of governments that were hesitant to accept what they considered to be external prescription (Kamau *et al.* 2018). The G-77 and China grouping correspondingly resisted review mechanisms that would place them under "unreasonable pressure" or mean that they would be able to be judged by high-income countries. Several high-income countries were reluctant to accept the universality of the goals that could mean their performance would equally be open to scrutiny. Consequently, many goals lack hard metrics and are open to national interpretation with the result that they might be considered only aspirational even if the wording is hardly ambitious. Similarly, the OWG proposed that international follow-up and review arrangements should essentially be voluntary and under the lead of national governments.

The five targets associated with SDG1 differ in kind. The first two, to eradicate extreme poverty and halve poverty in all its forms, relate to outcomes, while the second three loosely concern mechanisms: provision of social protection, equal access and resilience in event of shocks and disasters (Table 3.2). The final two, both means of implementation targets, allude to the possibility of a collective response to national problems and circumstances.

Table 3.2 SDG1: Substantive indicators

Targets (for full specification, see Table 1.1)	Indicators
Outcome	
1.1 Eradicate extreme poverty	1.1.1 Proportion of the population living below the international poverty line by sex, age, employment status and geographic location (urban/rural)
1.2 Reduce by half people in poverty in all its dimensions	1.2.1 Proportion of population living below the national poverty line, by sex and age
	1.2.2 Proportion of men, women and children of all ages living in poverty in all its dimensions according to national definitions
Implementation	
1.3 Implement appropriate social protection	1.3.1 Proportion of population covered by social protection floors/systems, by sex, distinguishing children, unemployed persons, older persons, persons with disabilities, pregnant women, new-borns, work-injury victims and the poor and the vulnerable
1.4 Men and women, in particular the poor and the vulnerable, have equal rights to economic resources	1.4.1 Proportion of population living in households with access to basic services
	1.4.2 Proportion of total adult population with secure tenure rights to land, (a) with legally recognized documentation, and (b) who perceive their rights to land as secure, by sex and type of tenure

(continued)

Table 3.2 (*Cont.*)

Targets (for full specification, see Table 1.1)	Indicators
1.5 Build the resilience to shocks and disasters	1.5.1 Number of deaths, missing persons and directly affected persons attributed to disasters per 100,000 population 1.5.2 Direct economic loss attributed to disasters in relation to global gross domestic product (GDP) 1.5.3 Number of countries that adopt and implement national disaster risk reduction strategies in line with the Sendai Framework for Disaster Risk Reduction 2015–2030 1.5.4 Proportion of local governments that adopt and implement local disaster risk reduction strategies in line with national disaster risk reduction strategies
Means of implementation	
1.a Ensure significant mobilization of resources to provide adequate and predictable means for developing countries,	1.a.1 Total official development assistance grants from all donors that focus on poverty reduction as a share of the recipient country's gross national income 1.a.2 Proportion of total government spending on essential services (education, health and social protection)
1.b Create national, regional and international sound policy frameworks for pro-poor and gender-sensitive development strategies.	1.b.1 Pro-poor public social spending

3.2.1 Outcome targets

Only the outcome targets are truly targets in the sense of specifying the amount of progress that needs to be made.

3.2.1a Target 1.1

The first target, to eradicate extreme poverty, is income-based and defined using the "international poverty line", in 2015 meaning income of less than US$1.25/day. Taken directly from the MDGs, it carries forward the deficiencies already discussed in Chapter 2. That said, the aspiration to eradicate, rather than merely to halve, poverty represents an advance.

This development surely reflects thinking on human rights. While both the MDGs and SDGs have their grounding in the *Universal Declaration of Human Rights*, it was only in 2006 that the United Nations High Commissioner for Human Rights opined that "In a fundamental way ... the denial of human rights forms part of the very definition of what it is to be poor" (HCHR 2006: iii). Furthermore, although the *Guiding Principles on Extreme Poverty and Human*

Rights, approved by the Human Rights Council of the UN General Assembly in 2012, do not define poverty itself as an infringement of human rights, they state that: "A human rights approach provides a framework for the long-term eradication of extreme poverty based on the recognition of persons living in extreme poverty as rights holders and agents of change" (HCHR 2012: 2).

However, the international poverty line has no basis in law and was never defined with respect to any measure of adequacy. Its derivation simply equates to the mean of the poverty thresholds of the 15 poorest countries in 2005 and, therefore, is extreme in the sense that it refers to the poorest of the very poor. To be truly consistent with human rights expectations, a poverty line should be, at very least, adequate to cover the most basic of Maslow's hierarchy of needs: sufficient food, clothing and weatherproof housing. When this is done, taking a "bare bones budget", the international poverty line would appear to be generous, being some 63 per cent above the adequacy threshold measured across 140 countries (Moatsos 2016). However, this budget is costed as the cheapest source of necessary calorific intake and permits no dietary variation. The cost of one metre of linen/per year is allowed for clothing and 5 per cent of the budget for housing.

When these assumptions are relaxed to allow for a degree of food choice, by taking the average of the three cheapest means of achieving the necessary calorific intake, and then adding elements to cover access to improved water, education and basic health care, the international poverty line amounts to just 61 per cent of the adequacy threshold (US$3.10/day). Other estimates similarly suggest that the international poverty line is unsatisfactory. The US Department of Agriculture's *Thrifty Food Plan*, for instance, indicates that the minimum cost of achieving the recommended dietary allowances is as much as US$5.04/day (Reddy & Lahoti 2015) and this makes no allowance for any other expenditures. Likewise, some years ago, when the international poverty line was US$1/day, Peter Edward (2006) estimated that US$2.80 was in fact required to ensure normal life expectancy, US$5.30/day in current terms.

The principal target for SDG1, therefore, is far from ambitious since, even if reached, hundreds of millions of people will still be denied dignity due to their level of income deprivation. While it can be argued that it is best to assist the poorest first since their circumstances are most extreme, and that such a strategy is consistent with the mantra of leaving no one behind, it provides cost-conscious governments with an excuse not to help those who are almost as poor. Moreover, because the poverty gap indicator included with the MDGs has been dropped, it is impossible to establish, within the framework of the SDGs, the extent to which people are left behind. This is important. Between 1980 and 2011, global poverty mostly fell because persons with incomes close to the poverty line moved above it; the living standards of the very poorest scarcely changed while the poverty gap necessarily widened (Ravallion 2016).

Because US$1.25 would purchase varying amounts of goods and services in different countries, the international poverty line is translated into different currencies using the World Bank's purchasing power parities (PPPs). Essentially this involves pricing a large basket of goods and services in all countries and using the variation in total cost to create a substantive, rather than a market, exchange rate. This is an expensive exercise and therefore done infrequently: in 2005, 2011, 2017 and 2021. PPPs for the intervening years are estimated according to national changes in consumer price indices. Alterations between 2005 and 2011 in the precise methodology used to develop the PPPs led to such major revisions in nominal rates of poverty that the World Bank has been advised to retain the 2011 PPPs until at least 2030 (World Bank 2017). Even so, concerns remain about the validity of the PPPs and hence the comparability of poverty estimates across countries. Staple foods vary from one country to another, persons in poverty typically cannot purchase precisely the same goods as the average person used in calculating PPPs, and price inflation differentially affects different groups in different countries, albeit usually having the greatest negative effect on people in poverty. The US$1.25 threshold was increased to US$1.90 in 2017 and, based on the 2021 PPPs, to US$2.15 in 2022.

3.2.1b Target 1.2

Although not all scholars would agree, Northern governments would generally claim to have no citizens living under the international poverty line so that Target 1.1 is relevant only to the developing world (Cai & Smeeding 2020; Ortiz-Ospina 2017). Target 1.2, to halve poverty in all its dimensions, might appear to have universal relevance but the two indicators suggest muddled thinking and do not facilitate meaningful cross-country comparison.

Indicator 1.2.1 (the proportion of population living below the national poverty line) reflects the desire of governments to protect their national policy-making sovereignty and to resist the imposition of standards from outside. Given that, with Target 1.1, the international poverty line was successfully imposed on developing countries, the negotiating power of developed countries would seem to be evident here. Whatever the reason, the result is that there is no basis for comparison because different counties measure poverty in different ways. The United States, for example, sets its poverty line with reference to a fixed basket of goods allowing poverty to be reduced simply by economic growth increasing incomes. In contrast, the European Union uses a relative definition of poverty which means that European countries require an element of positive income redistribution to reduce the poverty rate.

This lack of comparability reflects the different conceptions of poverty discussed in Chapter 1. These have ideological and disciplinary origins. To simplify, the political right prioritizes individualistic over structural explanations of poverty, an absolute definition of poverty and a low threshold to hold down wages and avoid work disincentive effects; the left, in contrast, tends to choose a relative definition that prioritizes social inclusion. Those disciplines that listen directly to people living in poverty and hear about the pain of being excluded from normal life, lean towards relative definitions, whereas scholars who analyse secondary data, as many economists do, tend to favour absolute poverty and to see income inequality as being logically distinct.

The views of economists, the political right and perhaps, if advocates of the OWG process are to be believed, representatives of developing countries would appear to have prevailed with a separate goal, SDG10, addressing inequalities (Kamau *et al.* 2018). However, the lead SDG10 target is more about pro-poor economic growth than inequality:

> 10.1 By 2030, progressively achieve and sustain income growth of the bottom 40 per cent of the population at a rate higher than the national average.

Ironically, the second target, "10.2 By 2030, to empower and promote social, economic and political inclusion of all", takes a standard measure of relative poverty as the first indicator:

> 10.2.1 Proportion of people living below 50 per cent of median income.

Indicator 1.2.2 (the proportion of men, women and children of all ages living in poverty in all its dimensions) simply adds to the conceptual confusion. This indicator distinguishes between men, women and children of all ages, whereas Indicator 1.2.1, like 1.1.1, makes no mention of children but does specify a breakdown by employment status and "geographic location (urban/rural)". While there may be esoteric technical reasons for these differences, it seems more likely that each was negotiated and determined separately without checking for coherence and asking whether, when taken together, the set of indicators was both rational and comprehensive. The indicators were devised separately from targets by the Inter Agency and Expert Group on SDGs (IAEG) and were adopted by the UN General Assembly as late as 6 July 2017. Considered to be purely technical, the reality is that they have substantive implications that are seldom ideologically neutral.

While Indicator 1.2.2 introduces the concept of multidimensional poverty, the dimensions are not defined. Instead, they need to be determined individually by national governments. Comparatively few countries make domestic use of a composite multidimensional measure although many European countries have experimented with "scorecards", separate indicators reflecting different definitions of poverty and/or different dimensions (Walker 2010). While scorecards may reflect a sophisticated understanding of poverty, they cause confusion when used as targets. Governments tend to emphasize indicators that suggest positive change whereas their opponents cite those that are least favourable. China which exceptionally has employed a multidimensional concept for 20 years – described rather enigmatically as "two no worries" (referring to adequate diet and clothing) and "three guarantees" (covering education, health and housing) – appeared in its SDG strategy documents to equate Target 1.2 with its intention to eradicate rural extreme poverty by 2020, thereby creating the impression that no action was required thereafter (PRC 2016).

In the absence of a clear alternative, many countries have adopted the UNDP Multidimensional Poverty Index (MPI), discussed in Chapter 1, as a means of operationalizing Indicator 1.2.2. This follows advice offered by the UN Sustainable Development Solutions Network and other UN agencies (SDSN 2015).

It will be recalled that the MPI was an attempt to operationalize Sen's capability approach to poverty and, as previously noted, many followers of Sen would argue that the SDGs themselves are an institutional manifestation of the capability approach. The 17 SDGs certainly represent domains in which individuals would want to be capable. This, therefore, raises the question why one would want to replicate the exercise within a single SDG.

The UNDP (n.d.) explains that:

> The indicators for the 2010 MPI were drawn from the Millennium Development Goals (MDGs). These original MPI indicators related to MDG indicators: nutrition (MDG 1), child mortality (MDG 4), access to drinking water (MDG 7), access to sanitation facility (MDG 7) and use of an improved source of cooking fuel (MDG 9).

And that the revised MPI

> shows the simultaneous deprivations of people sharing the same household across ten indicators that relate to SDGs 1, 2, 3, 4, 6, 7, and 11. In doing so, it provides a policy tool that can inform policies that seek to address interlinked SDGs and their target.

Indicator 1.2.2, therefore, becomes a composite indicator of individual development, well-being or capability rather than multidimensional poverty defined (as in Chapter 1) as the multiple consequences of a shortage of resources in relation to needs (De Neve & Sachs 2020). The MPI omits many of the consequences of a lack of resources, including limited role fulfilment, powerlessness, stigma, social exclusion and shame.

In summary, the two outcome targets and their associated indicators are deeply flawed, fusing and confusing different concepts of poverty with notions of human development and capability in ways that are counterproductive.

3.2.2 Implementation targets

As is the case for other SDGs, the implementation targets for SDG1 are of two types. The three which appertain to policies that might alleviate poverty are presumed to be largely the responsibility of nation states. The two referring to means of implementation allude to the resources necessary for delivering SDG1, including those provided by the international community.

None of the implementation targets are specific and, while it may be possible to establish a country's direction of travel, it will be impossible to establish whether targets have been met. The targets merely serve to encourage national governments to do better by subjecting them to moral pressure and possible embarrassment if other countries outperform them.

3.2.2a Mechanism targets
Target 1.3 requires governments to have implemented nationally "appropriate" social protection systems by 2030, and to have achieved "substantial coverage" of "the poor and vulnerable". "Substantial" and "appropriate" are weasel words without substantive meaning. However, it is difficult to justify coverage of less than 100 per cent since social security is recognized to be a human right, albeit four billion people remain entirely without any form of protection (ILO 2021a). Hence, the International Labour Organization (ILO 2021b: n.p.) advocates "rapid implementation … of universal access to essential health care and income security at least at a nationally defined minimum level (horizontal dimension) … and the progressive achievement of higher levels of protection (vertical dimension)".

"Basic provision" should, according to the ILO (2021b: n.p.), be made available for all children, older persons and "for persons in active age who are unable to earn sufficient income, in particular in cases of sickness, unemployment, maternity and disability". It is noteworthy that this wording enables governments to support individuals unable to earn sufficient income due to low wages, but it is also salutary to recognize that this guidance is based on a legal framework that is already 70 years old (Social Security (Minimum Standards) Convention, 1952 [No. 102]). "Basic" provision, therefore, is unlikely to meet the human rights criterion of dignity, hence the requirement for progression to higher levels of protection. Regrettably, there is no indicator that assesses the level of provision and so no possibility of measuring change or improvement for countries with full coverage of basic provision. Once again, therefore, the indicators discriminate against the least developed countries allowing governments of high-income countries to do nothing.

A similar pattern of bias or discrimination is repeated with the indicators associated with Targets 1.4 (equal access) and 1.5 (resilience). In the case of the resilience target, the discrimination is indirect. First, the target refers to basic administrative infrastructure and risk reduction strategies which are typically already in place in high-income countries and second, since less developed countries tend to have more agrarian economies, they are more exposed to the consequences of national disasters. Although richer countries may have better provision, the Covid-19 pandemic and the 2021 summer floods in Europe both revealed a lack of necessary prior planning or the political wherewithal to act upon any plans.

The equal access target is somewhat strangely drafted. It refers to "all men and women, in particular the poor and the vulnerable" having "equal rights to economic resources" and "access to basic services" and, additionally, to a heterogenous, arguably random, list of other resources including land, property, new technology and microfinance. The restriction of equal treatment to men and women is perplexing, considerations such as race, ethnicity, age, disability, and sexuality being ignored. It is also unclear whether the target of equal treatment of men and women applies only to those who are "poor and vulnerable" or universally. A further, more radical, reading of the target is that it seeks to ensure that "the poor and vulnerable" have "equal rights to economic resources". Currently people experiencing poverty are, almost by definition, denied such rights.

The two indicators offer little clue as to what the OWG had in mind when drafting this equal access target. A reason for this may be that the indicators were developed separately without involving the OWG. Inexplicably, Indicator 1.4.1 does not require any disaggregation by gender, while 1.4.2 deals with land tenure rights that may be most applicable in low-income agrarian economies. Indeed, both indicators are more challenging for governments of less developed countries. In each case, they refer to "basic" services and elementary legal standards that most developed countries will already have in place.

3.2.2b Means of implementation targets

The two "means of implementation" targets are both aspirational, and arguably, vacuous. Target 1.b nominally imposes obligations on national and supra-national levels of government although the associated indicator, pro-poor public social spending, would appear to operate only at national level. But, while the substantive intent – "sound policy frameworks … based on pro-poor and gender-sensitive development strategies, to support accelerated investment in poverty eradication action" – is undeniably desirable, it is rarely attainable when governments are under-resourced.

Resourcing is the focus of Target 1a which, prioritizing least developed countries, seeks to: "Ensure significant mobilization of resources from a variety of sources, including through enhanced development cooperation … to implement programmes and policies to end poverty in all its dimensions." The reference to "significant" rather than "adequate" mobilization of resources and the failure even to define "significant" illustrate the weakness of this target. It is also both tautological and asymmetrical in that, if a country succeeds in ending poverty in all its dimensions, the mobilization of resources was clearly adequate but that, if not, the failure cannot be directly attributable to insufficient funding (as opposed to, for example, policy intent or corruption). The indicators plot pro-poor national spending and the volume of development aid; while the latter has increased by almost ten per cent in real terms since 2015, only seven of the 38 OECD members have ever matched the UN target of 0.7 per cent of gross national income (GNI) agreed in 1970.

Therefore, while the stated goal is to end poverty, arguably a moral imperative, SDG1 requires much less from most national governments. The least developed countries are expected to eliminate extreme poverty, but other governments are merely invited to halve the poverty that they record, irrespective of the definition used. The presentational advance of SDG1 over MDG1, that it was to apply to all countries, is not replicated in the targets and indicators that are generally not universal and continue to place the greatest demands on low-income countries.

3.3 Conclusion

It is unlikely that anyone committed to a more equal world or to the reduction of global poverty would abandon the SDGs. Resulting from a more transparent style of negotiation, epitomized by the OWG and an unprecedented level of public consultation, they provide a mechanism for nudging the attention of governments towards difficult issues that are of fundamental national and international importance. They have already contributed to the resurgence of national plans and strategies, an approach that had, until around 2015, been denigrated "as a relic of directed economies and state-led development" (Chimhowu *et al.* 2019: 76).

However, others opine that little fundamentally has changed in the domain of global politics (PHM 2017). Inevitably, the goals are a negotiated compromise between different political interests. They also represent an uneasy fusion of different intellectual traditions rather than the product of a coherent theoretical model of sustainable development. Some authors, like Crabtree and Gasper (2020), consider the SDGs to be the culmination of policy development around capability theory and sustainable development leaving only scope for further refinement. Others think them "sprawling and misconceived" or simply "a distraction" (Bond 2015; *Economist* 2015).

Although presented as a package, the goals are not necessarily mutually compatible. SDG8 aspires to sustained, inclusive and sustainable growth and full employment with Target 8.1 requiring the least developed countries, "in particular", to achieve "at least 7 per cent" growth in their gross domestic products, while Target 8.2 demands higher levels of economic productivity. This focus on growth may represent a victory for the G77+China group who were concerned that they would be denied the possibility of catching up economically on account of Northern concerns about climate change. However, economic growth is not always pro-poor, and increased productivity reduces the likelihood of attaining full employment in the short to medium term (Hicks & Devaraj 2015).

Alongside incompatibilities, there are possible complementarities. Kroll *et al.* (2019: 8), for example, conclude that SDG1 has the most synergetic relationships and therefore that:

> Focusing on SDG 1 would ... be the most promising strategy to ultimately start-off a virtuous cycle of SDG progress. For example, a family that no longer suffers from extreme poverty (SDG1) will be able to lead healthier lives for themselves and others, halting the spread of infectious diseases (SDG 3), contributing to a stronger economy (SDG 8), raising the means of implementation through tax payments (SDG 17) which will in turn enable public investments in infrastructure (SDG 9), which will provide education and other important services (SDG 4).

While perhaps true that eradicating poverty is a prerequisite for fulfilling the other goals, the primacy given to SDG1 was primarily political, being "at the insistence of the G77+China (the negotiating voice for developing countries)" (PHM 2017: 17). Unfortunately, because the targets and indicators associated with SDG1 are so theoretically confused and poorly constructed, pursuing this goal offers no guarantee that poverty in any form will be ended nor that the perceived beneficial linkages truly exist.

Moreover, as will become apparent in the next chapter, most of the least developed countries and many others that are still developing economically will find it impossible to achieve SDG1 without support from richer countries. This means that success with respect to SDG1 is conditional on the fulfilment of SDG17, global partnership, which not only requires providing the developing world with financial and technical support, but also fundamental reform of the international finance and trading systems that so advantage developed countries (Chapters 7 and 9).

CASE STUDY 3 AFRICA FIGHTING BACK AGAINST THE MDGs

Focusing on Africa, Durokifa and Ijeoma (2018) analyse the Millennium Development Goals through the lens of dependency theory that attributes the lack of development of "periphery nations" to exploitation by "core nations". They conclude that the MDGs were "not aimed at the deliberate transformation of the social, political and economic structure of the African continent. Instead, the MDGs were designed by Western nations to extend their markets to African countries and have these countries at their mercy" (Durokifa & Ijeoma 2018: 364). They opine that rather than home grown solutions taking account of "African culture and mentality", such as the "having a large family which is often a rational response to poverty", the MDGs were "foisted on developing countries as a path towards development, just like the SAP [Structural Adjustment Programme] had been" (Durokifa & Ijeoma 2018: 360).

They argue that the target of halving the proportion experiencing poverty was insufficiently ambitious and should have focused on halving the number of people who were poor. Equally, they note that the poverty threshold of US$1.90/day was not necessarily appropriate in Africa since, in Uganda, it exceeded the official poverty line and, in Nigeria, it was more than the minimum wage. They insist that African leaders must take ownership of the development agenda based "on the cultures and beliefs of the African people, and that also aligns with the political, economic and social beliefs of Africans" (Durokifa & Ijeoma 2018: 363). They propose "inclusive participation" involving local activists, community leaders and civil societies, and that each country "develop its own yardstick for measuring the actualization of its developmental targets" (Durokifa & Ijeoma 2018: 363, 364).

Analyses akin to Durokifa and Ijeoma's strongly influenced the thinking of the UN Open Working Group, which developed the SDGs in pushing for national autonomy and resisting global standards. Such analyses speak strongly against the concept of a global poverty standard or a minimum standard of living that should be the right of every person on the planet.

Further reading

Durokifa, A. & E. Ijeoma 2018. "Neo-colonialism and Millennium Development Goals (MDGs) in Africa". *African Journal of Science, Technology, Innovation and Development* 10(3): 355–66.

4
PROGRESS SINCE 2015

The title of this chapter may be a little misleading since it is mainly about the enormous challenges that lie ahead if there is to be any hope of achieving SDG1.

To date, progress has been limited. Tacit recognition of this fact was evident when, in September 2019, the UN Secretary-General António Guterres called for a "decade of action". This sought to mobilize three "levels" of action: global "to secure greater leadership, more resources and smarter solutions"; local with new policies, increased budgets and additional legislation; and thirdly, "people ... to generate an unstoppable movement pushing for the required transformations" (UN 2021a). The Covid-19 pandemic, considered in Chapter 5, which began in late 2019, undid much of the limited progress that had by then been made. Consequently, it is generally accepted that the world is now "tremendously off track" in its pursuit of the SDGs. Many would also accept that, the pandemic aside, the reason is poor governance; to cite the UN General Secretary again: "It is time to keep our promise" (UN 2021b).

This is not to say that the period since 2015 has been one of inactivity. There have been innumerable meetings, exchanges, conferences and reports and, as already mentioned in Chapter 3, government plans alluding to the SDGs (Chimhowu *et al.* 2019). Moreover, details of 972 SDG "Good Practice" case studies have been published by the United Nations selected from more than 1,400 submitted for assessment in two waves of consultation. Three hundred and seventy-five of the case-studies address SDG1 and are reviewed in the second part of the chapter alongside evidence on the extent to which SDG1 has been embraced as a core element within national policymaking. However, few of the initiatives are of a scale that could meaningfully address the national targets of eradicating extreme poverty or, indeed, halving poverty as nationally defined. Nor have they generally demonstrated the state-to-state collaboration and level of funding needed to match the intent of Target 1.b: namely, to "create sound policy frameworks at the national, regional and international levels, based on pro-poor and gender-sensitive development strategies, to support accelerated investment in poverty eradication actions".

Ahead of reviewing the policies implemented as part of the 2030 Agenda, it is important to assess the scale of the challenge posed by SDG1 and its component targets. As explained in Chapter 3, the targets and indicators exhibit deficiencies due to having been developed by committees operating in a highly politicized environment; these deficits include ambiguity, inconsistency, partiality and lack of specificity. That said, the outcome targets still offer a basis for calculating the scale of the task upon which the world is engaged, and it is immense. It entails directing life-changing resources to some 2.2 billion people across the world with most concentrated in the Global South. The policy mechanisms required necessitate providing both employment or other income-generating opportunities and instigating transfers within and across nations to boost the incomes of those excluded from employment. Except for global vaccination, this is individualized policy intervention on a scale never previously implemented or even envisaged. The cost is correspondingly large but, when set against national incomes, appears to be quite modest. The implication, therefore, is that only political considerations stand in the way of meeting the SDG1 outcome targets.

4.1 The challenge of poverty reduction

As previously emphasized, SDG1, unlike MDG1, is intended to be a goal applicable to every nation, rich or poor. However, because Targets 1.1 and 1.2 refer to different conceptions of poverty, SDG1 imposes obligations on countries that vary according to their level of economic development.

4.1.1 High-income countries

Target 1.2 – by 2030, to halve the population living below the national poverty line – allows individual governments to specify the concept of poverty used to determine the national poverty threshold. Across Europe, and in many other developed countries, poverty is defined in relative terms. This means that governments cannot rely on economic growth to lift the incomes of people to above the poverty threshold through a process of "trickle down". Instead, they need to implement progressive employment, tax and/or benefit policies than redistribute income from more affluent to less affluent households.

On 17 June 2010, European Union (EU) heads of state and government agreed to reduce the number of people at risk of poverty and social exclusion by 20 million by 2020 (Walker 2010). The language and indicators of poverty adopted in the EU's "2020 Programme" were legacies of much political compromise. In the 1980s, some governments, notably the United Kingdom – then an EU Member State – and Germany, had refused to accept the existence of poverty but eventually agreed to acknowledge that some families could be "at risk" of poverty. "Social exclusion", a term much identified with the French tradition of Social Catholicism, was added to the definition to accommodate those believing that poverty was multifaceted and others wanting to emphasize poverty's structural origins (Atkinson & Davoudi 2000; Byrne 1999). Finally, a measure of employment was included, an acknowledgement of the importance of labour market activation policies that had been promoted by the *OECD Jobs Report* published in 1994.

The resultant composite indicator used by the EU – "at risk of poverty and social exclusion" – adds the number of persons with income less than 60 per cent of national median income to those experiencing material deprivation, and to those living in households "with a very low work intensity". It, therefore, combines a relative definition of income poverty, a measure of deprivation or low expenditure, and employment status – arguably not a measure of poverty but a potential cause.

By 2019, the European Union had managed to reduce the number of people at risk of poverty or social exclusion by a little over 12 million rather than by the 20 million intended (Figure 4.1). However, the reduction was entirely due to falls in the number of people experiencing material deprivation or living in low "work intensity" households; the number of people experiencing relative income poverty actually rose, reaching a peak in 2016. The increase in relative poverty resulted from the fact that economic growth was accompanied by a marginal but measurable increase in income inequality, especially during the middle of the decade.

The inability of European countries to cut relative poverty, even during a ten-year collective policy initiative designed to target poverty reduction, underlines the challenge presented by SDG Target 1.2 for those countries that use relative definitions of poverty. Rather than focusing solely on poverty reduction, many European countries during the 2010s found themselves additionally needing to implement policies designed to prevent poverty from rising. And, as if to stress the vulnerability of even the world's richest countries, the effect of the Covid-19 pandemic was to reverse almost half of the hard-won gains within a single year (Figure 4.1).

At the social summit in Porto in May 2021, the EU agreed to target reducing poverty by 15 million by 2030. This falls far short of the number implied by SDG Target 1.2. Taking solely the number of people living in households with incomes less than 60 per cent of the national median in the 22 countries for which there are data, 36.3 million people would need to be lifted above the poverty line by 2030 to hit the target of halving poverty. Add to that, people experiencing material deprivation and/or low employment and the number rises to 46 million, three times the target agreed in Porto.

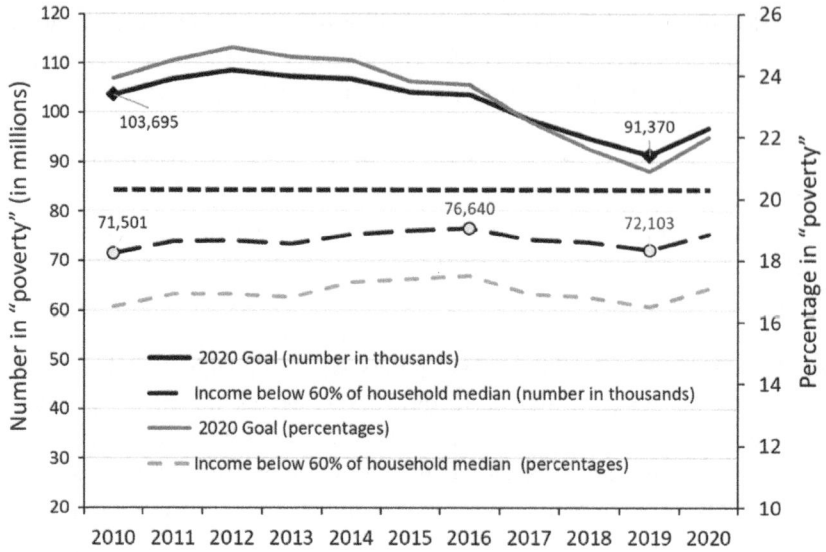

Figure 4.1 Poverty in the European Union, 2010–20
Source: Eurostat for European Union – 27 countries (from 2020).

While experience in Europe speaks to the difficulty of reducing poverty, it is important to determine whether the EU's apparently limited ambition looking forward to 2030 reflects practical constraints or lack of political will. Cost is a key consideration, almost a litmus test to parse the practical from the political. Estimates of what it might "cost" to half relative poverty by 2030 are provided in Figure 4.2. These are derived by simply taking the number of people that must be lifted out of poverty and multiplying this value by the average poverty gap, the amount by which the income of persons living in poverty falls short of the poverty threshold. Therefore, the analysis ignores the cost of the implementational infrastructure necessary to achieve this goal, although this need not be substantial if support is delivered as an unconditional tax transfer. Moreover, the estimates do not take account of the positive stimulus to the economy that would be initiated through transferring resources to people that typically spend a higher proportion of their incomes.

The analysis indicates a fourfold differential in the cost of halving relative poverty across the countries of the European Union. The variation reflects different levels of poverty and income inequality with the "costs" being greatest, as in Italy and Spain, where high poverty rates coincide with much inequality. That said, even in Italy, halving poverty could nominally be achieved by spending little more than 1.6 per cent of annual gross domestic product. If the support were delivered entirely through social protection, this would mean an increase in

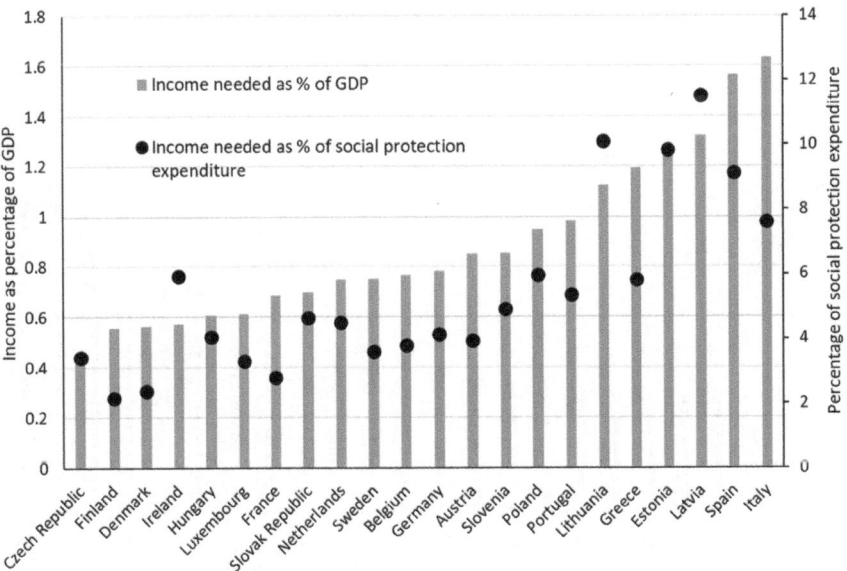

Figure 4.2 The cost of halving relative poverty (defined as 60% median disposable income) in European OECD countries
Source: Calculated from OECD database.

social protection spending varying from about 3 per cent in Finland and Ireland to 11.5 per cent in Latvia.

Target 1.2 focuses on halving poverty but leaves the circumstances of people remaining in poverty much the same as before. The MDGs included an indicator of the average depth of poverty – the poverty gap – that was lost in the move to the SDGs. Adding the objective of also halving the poverty gap for those remaining in poverty increases the total cost of reform by 50 per cent meaning, for example, that the Czech Republic and Italy would respectively need to invest the equivalent of 0.65 per cent and 2.45 per cent of their respective GDPs in reducing poverty (Figure 4.3). At face value, these sums do not appear to be extortionate, suggesting that the root cause of Europe's apparent lack of ambition is political. As will become evident below, much more is expected from countries with far fewer resources.

It is possible to extend the coverage of the analysis to include other OECD countries although not all incorporate a relative poverty line into their domestic policymaking (Figure 4.4). For example, the United States, South Korea and Costa Rica all have poverty lines based on a basket of goods, with that in Costa Rica – which joined the OECD only in 2021 – being as low as US$155/month. South Korea additionally monitors households with incomes lower than 50 per

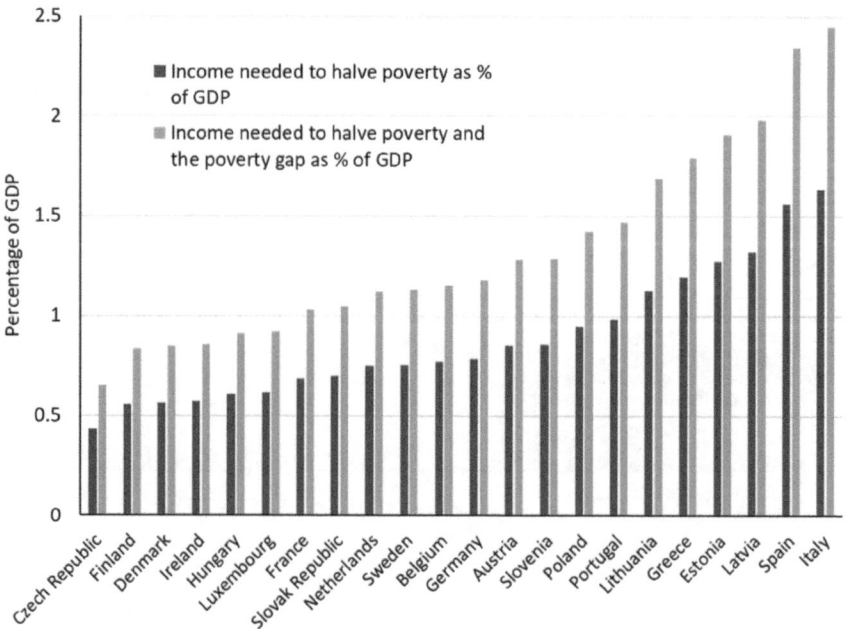

Figure 4.3 The cost of halving relative poverty and the poverty gap (defined as 60% median disposable income) in European Union countries
Source: Calculated from OECD database.

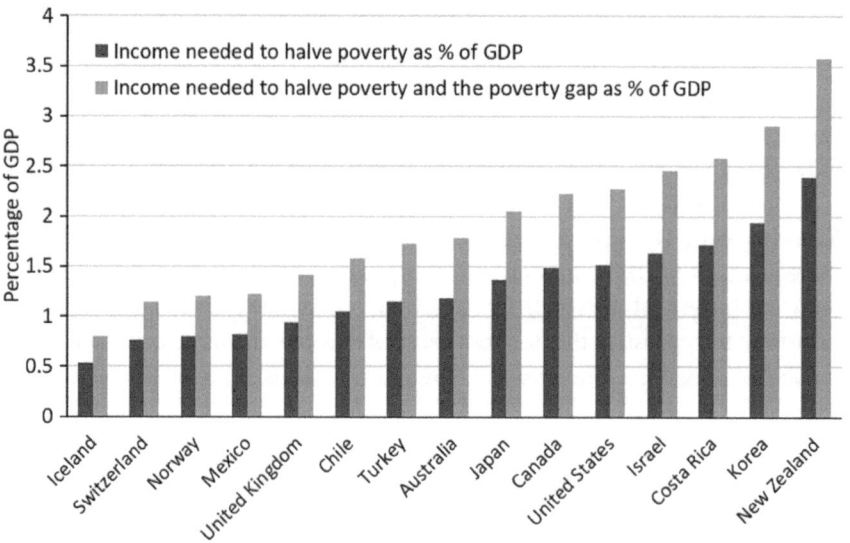

Figure 4.4 The cost of halving relative poverty and the poverty gap (defined as 60% median disposable income) in selected OECD countries
Source: Calculated from OECD database.

cent of the national median and Israel has incorporated this metric into its anti-poverty strategy. In 2015, poverty in Israel was on a downward trend but in 2020, due to Covid-19, it experienced the unusual coincidence of both falling median income and increasing poverty (Jerusalem Post 2021; Ynet 2021). New Zealand does not have an official poverty line, with StatsNZ using a range of indicators including income of less than 60 per cent of the median.

Examining the 15 non-European members of the OECD club of high-income countries for which suitable data are available again indicates that the cost of meeting SDG Target 1.2 is not excessive; it ranges from just 0.53 per cent of GDP in Iceland to 2.4 per cent in New Zealand. This is not to say that the political opposition to achieving this goal would not be consider-able – a greater redistribution of income would be necessary in Israel, Costa Rica, South Korea and New Zealand than anywhere in Europe. Furthermore, countries facing the highest costs are generally those that advocate liberal economics and minimal government intervention; whether these national governments ever anticipated reducing poverty levels when signing up to 2030 Agenda must be open to conjecture.

4.1.2 Low-income countries

Low-income countries pursuing SDG Target 1.1 are required to eradicate pov-erty rather than reduce the poverty rate by half. However, poverty is defined with respect to the international poverty threshold – individual income of less than US$1.90/day – extreme poverty and, in most instances, observed poverty will fall if economic growth is positive and results in increased incomes. This happened in the era of the MDGs but not at a rate sufficient to ensure that, if continued, poverty would be eradicated by 2030 (Table 4.1). Indeed, for extreme poverty to be eradicated by 2030, the rate of poverty reduction needs to increase by a factor of three.

Upper middle-income countries – and, to a lesser extent, lower middle-income countries – were much more successful than low-income countries in reducing extreme poverty in the years before 2015. However, it needs to be recognized that China alone accounted for 85 per cent of the reduction in poverty achieved by upper middle-income countries (a group it only joined in 2011). Sixty-five per cent of total fall in extreme poverty in the East Asian and Pacific region was also attributable to China's development.

In passing, it is worth noting that, while extreme poverty is considered to be very rare in high-income countries, its rarity makes it difficult to measure with confidence. However, World Bank data indicate that extreme poverty rose in high-income countries during the MDG era with notable increases in countries

Table 4.1 The cost of ending US$1.90/day poverty in low-income countries (Target 1.1)

Level of economic development	US$1.90/day % poverty rate 2015	Annual fall in US$1.90/day poverty rate achieved 2000–15 as ratio of that required 2015–30	Cost of ending US$1.90/ day poverty	
			As % of national GDP	As % of GDP of high-income countries
High income	0.7	−0.29	0.0000	
Upper middle income	1.7	13.76	0.0065	
Lower middle income	14.4	1.59	0.1784	
Low income	46.9	0.30	5.3639	0.1036
Region				
Europe & Central Asia	1.5	3.87	0.0039	
East Asia & Pacific	2.1	15.57	0.0104	
Latin America & Caribbean	3.7	2.43	0.0096	
Middle East & North Africa	4.3	−0.19	0.0013	
Sub-Saharan Africa	42.0	0.39	2.1308	
Fragile and conflict affected situations	36.3	0.48	1.5064	

Source: Calculated from World Bank database.

as diverse as Italy, Greece, Spain, Hungary, the Slovak Republic, the United States and Austria.

To return to very considerable challenge posed by Target 1.1 for low-income countries, governments would, on average, need to lift 47 per cent of their populations out of extreme poverty by 2030. In the absence of economic growth, this would require them to direct about 5.4 per cent of their GDPs to the task of ending poverty (Table 4.1). This is six times the proportion of GDP needed by European Union countries to halve relative poverty. Moreover, some low-income countries will need to spend proportionately more with the Democratic Republic of the Congo, for example, required to devote 23 per cent of its GDP to ending poverty (Figure 4.5). It is typically the very poorest countries that must spend most. Leaving Sudan aside, atypical for many reasons, 59 per cent of the variation in the level of expenditure needed to eradicate poverty is arithmetically explicable by differences in per capita GDP.

To summarize, the expectations placed on low-income countries by Target 1.2 – eradicate extreme poverty – are demonstrably disproportionate and arguably unreasonable in the context of richer countries focused on Target 1.2. They appear even more disproportionate when it is recognized that, in theory at least, high-income countries could ensure the elimination of US$1.90/day poverty in

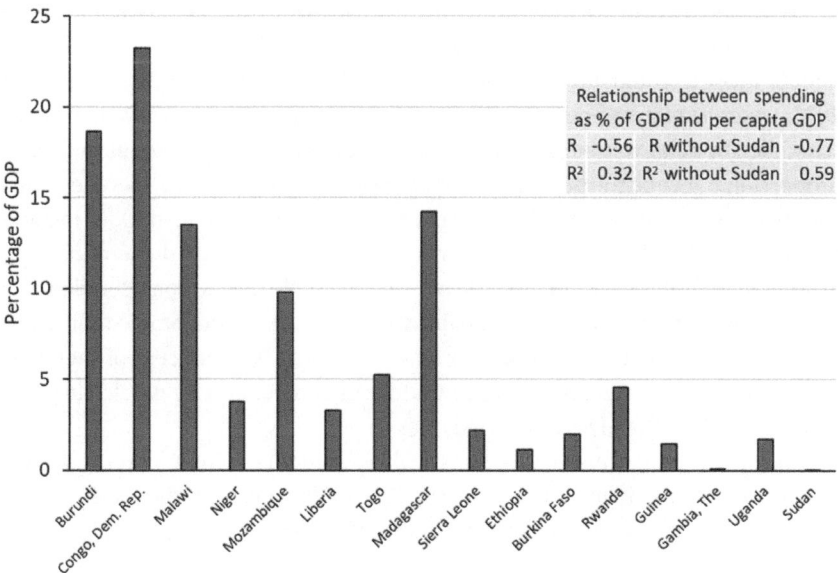

Figure 4.5 The cost of ending extreme poverty (defined as income less than US$1.90/day)
Source: Calculated from World Bank database.

low-income countries through transferring the equivalent of just 0.1 per cent of their collective GDP.

4.1.3 Middle-income countries

As is evident from Table 4.1, countries designated as lower- and upper-middle-income countries typically still harbour extreme poverty but could, in purely financial terms, eradicate it relatively easily. Most countries will do so by 2030 unless the impact of the Covid-19 pandemic turns out to persist (Chapter 5).

In 2016, the World Bank proposed two additional poverty lines – US$3.20 and US$5.50/day – that approximate to the average poverty thresholds adopted by lower- and upper-middle-income countries respectively. The former, as reported in Chapter 3, equates with the minimum required to ensure normal life expectancy and would generally deny people the dignity that human rights considerations would demand. Therefore, US$5.50/day is here taken to be the standard to be adopted for all middle-income countries with the goal of halving the poverty rate by 2030. However, there are good grounds for wanting to ensure that the severity of poverty of those remaining in poverty in 2030 is less than it was in 2015; this is measured by reductions in the poverty gap.

Again, poorer countries confront greater challenges in seeking to reduce poverty (Table 4.2). Based on performance prior to 2015, most low- and lower-middle-income countries will not succeed in halving US$5.50/day poverty by 2030, whereas many upper-middle-income countries could do so well ahead of schedule. To achieve this goal, lower-middle-income countries would need, in proportional terms, to spend 32 times as much as upper-middle-income countries (i.e., 3.92 per cent of GDP rather than 0.12 per cent). Upper-middle-income countries could additionally halve the severity of poverty for those remaining poor at an additional cost of just 0.06 per cent of GDP. Indeed, considered purely in monetary terms, it seems reasonable for upper middle-income countries to eradicate US$5.50 poverty altogether, at a cost of just 0.24 per cent of their collective GDP. More developed upper middle-income countries would find this easier to achieve than less developed ones.

Almost three-quarters of residents in lower middle-income countries have incomes below the higher threshold of US$5.50/day. Even so, the paper cost of halving poverty measured against this threshold – 5.9 per cent of GDP – is only

Table 4.2 The cost of ending US$5.50/day poverty in middle-income countries (Target 1.2)

	US$5.50/day % poverty rate 2015	Annual fall in rate achieved 2000–15 as ratio of that required 2015–30	Cost as % GDP of halving US$5.50/day poverty	Cost as % GDP of halving US$5.50/day poverty and the remaining poverty gap
High income	1.6	0.88	0.000	0.000
Upper middle-income	24.1	3.71	0.123	0.185
Lower middle-income	72.5	0.42	3.919	5.878
Low income	90.9	0.02	28.666	42.999
Region				
Europe & Central Asia	13.9	3.96	0.022	0.033
East Asia & Pacific	34.3	2.94	0.258	0.386
East Asia and Pacific minus China	45.0	1.66	0.409	0.613
China	27.2	4.33	0.164	0.246
Latin America & Caribbean	24.2	1.73	0.145	0.218
Middle East & North Africa	41.8	0.55	0.385	0.577
Sub-Saharan Africa	86.4	0.11	12.150	18.226
Fragile and conflict affected situations	82.8	0.08	9.264	13.896

Source: Calculated from World Bank database.

marginally above that expected of low-income countries to eradicate extreme poverty. However, to attain this more ambitious goal, governments would need to more than double the rate at which they lifted people out of poverty. Low-income countries, however, have little realistic hope of halving US$5.50/day poverty in the absence of unprecedented economic growth. To do so, governments would need to invest 29 per cent of total GDP in reducing poverty. However, as potential donors, the leaders of high-income countries could achieve the same effect by diverting a further 0.55 per cent of their joint GDP to low-income countries.

While Target 1.2 serves to emphasize that Agenda 2030 aims to achieve more than simply the eradication of extreme poverty, the emphasis appears to be lost on certain governments. There is a tendency for the governments of countries that are no longer classified as low-income to continue to focus on extreme, US$1.90/day, poverty. China, for example, the leader in poverty reduction under the MDGs, persistently interprets the multidimensionality referred to in SDG1.2 as appertaining to the various hardships that people experience when living on US$1.90/day poverty (PRC 2021). To do so is to ignore the ambition of the twin targets, SDG1.1 and SDG1.2, and the aspiration underlying SDG1.3 for the "progressive realization" of higher levels of provision as encapsulated in ILO Recommendation 202 on social protection floors

Aspirations aside, while the nominal costs of nations achieving SDG1 are not high, few will manage to be on target taking past performance as the guide. Important exceptions to this generalization are the upper-middle-income countries; with continued economic growth, most should eradicate extreme poverty by 2030. But the most striking observation is that, with modest transfers from the richest countries, extreme poverty could be eradicated everywhere. This implies that eradication of extreme poverty is a matter of political choice.

4.2 Policy responses to ending poverty

Having defined the challenge of eradicating poverty by 2030, it is next appropriate to consider whether the actions taken by governments are equal to the challenge. SDG Targets 1.3, 1.4, 1.5 and 1.1.b were intended as guidelines, if not a blueprint, for governments to follow.

4.2.1 SDG Target 1.3: Social protection

The UN Secretary-General's report on progress towards the Sustainable Development Goals in July 2021 was understandably much preoccupied by the impact of the Covid-19 pandemic. In this context, it stressed the importance of social protection and the limited progress made with respect to SDG Target 1.3, noting that "by 2020, only 47 per cent of the global population was covered effectively by at least one social protection cash benefit, leaving 4 billion people unprotected" (UN 2021c: 4).

It will be recalled from Chapter 3 that SDG Target 1.3 is full of weasel words and lacks precision. It is also contradictory. It proposes universal coverage with "nationally appropriate social protection systems and measures for all" but merely "substantial coverage of the poor and the vulnerable" to be achieved by 2030. This discrimination against "the poor and vulnerable" is arguably incompatible with human rights legislation. Additionally, much of substance rests on the interpretation given to "nationally appropriate".

Since 2016, the ILO has run a "Flagship Programme" to assist governments to develop social protection schemes (ILO 2021c, 2021d). The ILO acknowledges that one reason for initiating the programme was to leverage additional funding to support the ILO's work on social protection (a telling indication of the underfunding of UN agencies). Originally involving 21 "target" countries, coverage was extended to 50 countries in 2021. The programme is based on a linear model of policy development involving strategy, programme design and improved operations. The ILO claims that by 2020, the programme had succeeded in extending coverage of social protection by 30 million people and ensured "better access to 130 million". However, only ten of the 21 participating countries developed the strategic plan expected of them, while 16 sought to improve operations (against a target of seven). The focus on operations is as understandable as it is disappointing. It is much easier to focus attention to existing provision and to consider how it might be improved than to ask what provision is needed and how it could be delivered.

The evaluation of the first phase of the Flagship programme additionally revealed that low-income countries and those nations "facing a socio-economic, humanitarian or environmental crisis" would be unable to mobilize sufficient resources from domestic sources to provide adequate systems of social protection. It, therefore, concluded that there was a need to develop "an international mechanism to complement and support the domestic financial efforts of these countries" (ILO 2021c: 97).

Social protection is a very effective defence against poverty, but it is only well developed in high-income countries where coverage of most groups is almost universal (Figure 4.6). It should, therefore, be no surprise to find that in low-income countries, where extreme poverty is most prevalent, social protection is almost non-existent except for retirement pensioners. Provision is similarly minimal in lower middle-income countries where it only reaches a privileged minority, while that in higher middle-income countries prioritizes elders, workers, and maternity services.

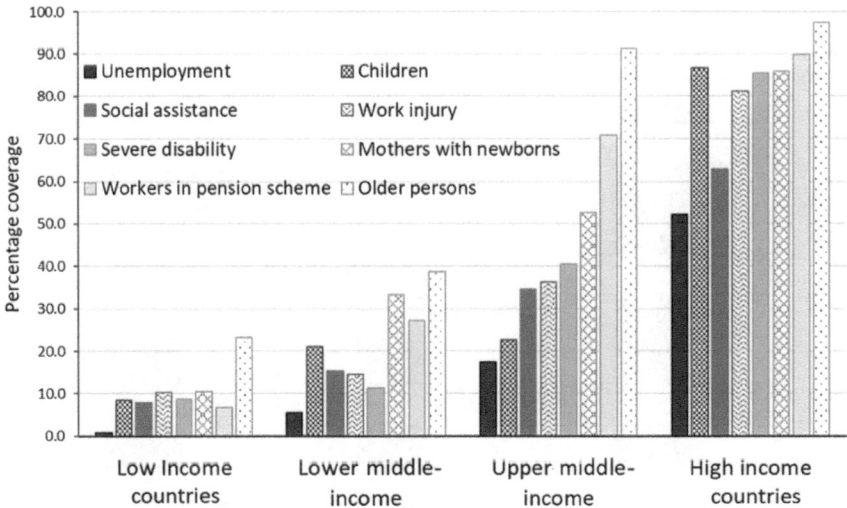

Figure 4.6 Coverage of social protection, 2020
Source: Calculated from ILO database.

The exceptions to universal social protection coverage in developed countries, mostly unemployment benefit and social assistance, are instructive. (Social assistance typically provides the final safety net for needy persons without other means of protection.) They reflect political concerns about the possibility of work disincentives created by the provision of welfare benefits but also point to stigma towards those in poverty and to the limited political voice of the most disadvantage. In the 1990s, to cite an extreme example, the United States removed its universal safety net by imposing time-limits on the receipt of certain social assistance benefits. Elites in some developing countries, notably in Sub-Saharan Africa, have raised similar concerns about the creation of dependency that have curtailed even basic provision (Seekings 2019).

For a variety of reasons low-income countries are less likely than lower middle-income countries to have participated the ILO Flagship Programme for developing social protection. The resource constraints faced by the governments of low-income countries remain formidable; on average, they would need to devote 8.5 per cent of their GDP to providing the minimum level of social protection consistent with ILO Recommendation 202 (Figure 4.7). Covering the current shortfall would cost the equivalent of 45 per cent of their existing tax takes, whereas the relative costs for lower- and upper-middle-income countries are much less (Durán-Valverde *et al.* 2020).

The Flagship Programme apart, there is no evidence of a consistent and comprehensive expansion of social protection since 2015 (Figure 4.8). While coverage increased in Sub-Saharan Africa and much of Asia (Central Asia excluded), it fell

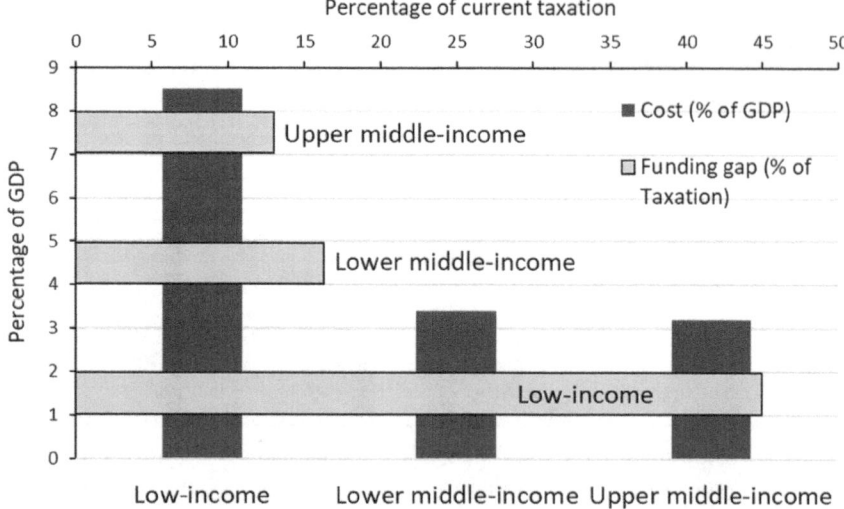

Figure 4.7 Cost of providing minimum social protection (children, maternity, disability, old age), 2019
Source: Adapted from Durán-Valverde *et al.* (2020).

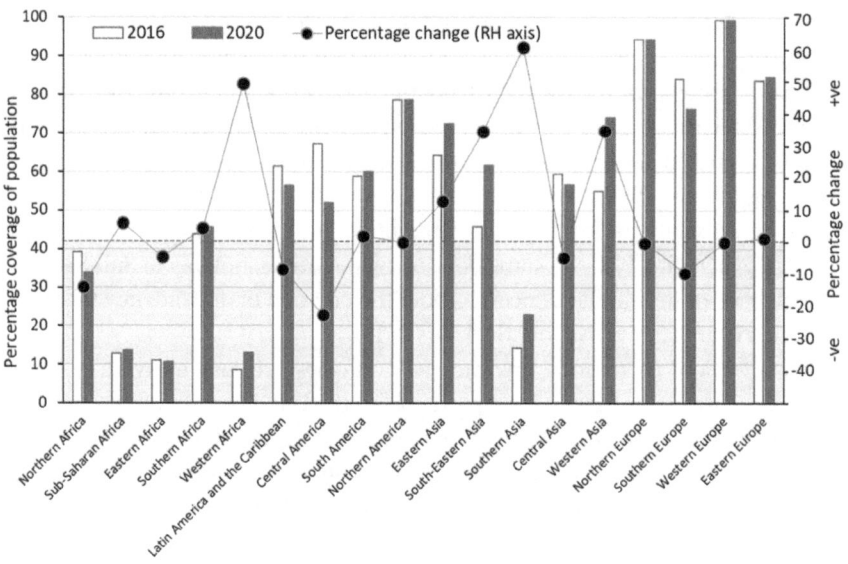

Figure 4.8 Change in the coverage of social protection, 2016–20
Source: Calculated from ILO database.

in Latin and Central America (notably in Costa Rica and Argentina), Northern Africa and Southern Europe. The advent of Covid-19 served to demonstrate the vulnerability of populations and the protective power of social security and assistance with 1,600 new measures being introduced in 2020 by 209 countries and territories. However, all but 5 per cent of the measures were temporary underlining the fact that social protection for all – Target 1.3 – remains a very long way off (ILO 2021e). In the immediate future, there is need to determine what a "suitable" level of social protection should mean for people living in low- and lower-middle-income countries. The social protection floor promoted by the ILO with an emphasis on *basic* provision is considered over generous by many African leaders and an imposition of Western values (Seekings 2019)

4.2.2 Targets 1.4, 1.5 and 1.b: creating sound policy frameworks

A system of National Voluntary Reviews (NVR) was established in 2016 to provide a basis for monitoring the effectiveness of the SDGs and to encourage national governments to integrate the SDGs into their domestic policymaking. By 2020, 168 countries had submitted at least one NVR with 46 countries subsequently reporting in 2021, several for the second or third time. The United Nations considers that participation in the NVR system demonstrates the "continued commitment to the implementation of the 2030 Agenda and its SDGs" (UN 2020b: 5).

The reality is that it is very difficult to ascertain whether national policies were prompted by the existence of the SDGs or merely packaged to be part of the 2030 Agenda for reasons of international presentation. It might be that the pressure to report encourages governments repeatedly to consider the SDGs. Equally, it is conceivable that NVRs are produced after the event by comparatively junior officials far removed from strategic policymaking.

An additional problem in evaluating the NVRs is that there is seldom a one-to-one match between a policy and a particular SDG. This reflects the inter-connectedness of the SDGs which some see as a virtue given that reality is seamless. However, it means that the same policy may appear under several goal headings, thereby potentially exaggerating the extent of policy innovation or coverage. This is particularly problematic when considering SDG1, given that some analysts consider it to be the most interconnected of all the SDGs (Kroll *et al.* 2019). Unfortunately, the SDGs, being products of political negotiation and compromise, are not underpinned by a coherent and comprehensive theory of change which adds to the challenge of implementation as much as to evaluation. Indeed, the United Nations 2020 synthesis report concluded that governments generally gave little explicit consideration to the interactions and trade-offs between SDGs that could have improved policy targeting (UN 2020b).

During the early years of NVR reporting, considerable attention was paid to describing the institutional architecture being developed to integrate the SDGs into national policy. This was still the case in the 2020 reports despite the UN concluding that "countries [had] significantly progressed with the integration and localization process of the 2030 Agenda" (UN 2020b: 18). A little surprisingly, some governments were continuing to review the SDGs and to identify priority targets and indicators even five years into the 2030 Agenda.

Some governments had embarked on institutional reform and were implementing legislative change, but others were simply mapping the SDGs onto national priorities rather than instigating substantive change. Most countries claimed that they operationalized the SDGs principally through their national development plans, although some referred to mainstreaming SDGs at sectoral level and others to integrating the goals at subnational level. Integrated national financing frameworks were often absent as was the ability to undertake the medium-term budgetary forecasting necessary to ensure financial viability of any policy innovation.

Only five of the 43 NVRs submitted for 2021 made explicit references to SDG1 that were taken forward by the UN secretariat for inclusion in their compilation of main messages. Three reported falls in US\$1.90/day poverty, including China meeting the Target 1.1, "10 years ahead of schedule". The Thai government noted its intention to develop a multidimensional measure of poverty while Niger's NVR focused on the increase in poverty linked to Covid-19. Indeed, many of the NVRs submitted to date dwell on the challenges that governments face in addressing SDG1. They emphasize the concentration of poverty in rural areas, the reliance on low productivity agriculture and the task of delivering decent employment opportunities in situ to prevent the unregulated growth of cities. Many also refer to the high incidence of poverty among children with its long-term consequences, and to persistent unemployment among young people. They acknowledge, too, the weaknesses of government, especially in the context of underdevelopment: limited budgets; an absence of adequate data to monitor and evaluate policy; and a lack of infrastructure that made it difficult even to reach some concentrations of poverty.

The specific policy strategies highlighted by governments with respect to SDG1 fall under four headings: infrastructure development; human capital investment; employment creation; and social protection. The first two were typically developmental and long-term, the latter two focused on individual support and were more immediate. Algeria and Pakistan stressed the role of structural investment to promote employment with anticipated positive effects on poverty. Brunei Darussalam, Gambia, Slovenia and the United Kingdom all highlighted reforms linked to employment and employment activation, sometimes alluding to the need to break "the cycle of poverty", a phenomenon the importance of which is much questioned in the academic literature (Hirschman 1961; Shildrick *et al.* 2012). Algeria, Georgia, Panama, Turkey and New Zealand detailed social protection reforms, as did Burundi, Ghana, Malawi and Nepal, countries involved in the ILO Flagship Programme. There was relatively little mention of gender (Target 1.4) in any of the NVRs, or resilience (Target 1.5) other than that associated with the Covid-19 pandemic.

The annual analysis of policy implementation presented by the Sustainable Development Solutions Network (SDSN) effectively reduces the 17 SDGs to just six based on the premise that "all 17 SDGs can be achieved through six major societal transformations, focused on: (1) education and skills, (2) health and well-being, (3) clean energy and industry, (4) sustainable land use, (5) sustainable cities, and (6) digital technologies" (Sachs *et al.* 2021: 44).

This premise lacks independent empirical justification and has the unfortunate effect that the SDSN's annual report cannot be used to assess progress towards meeting SDG1.

4.2.3 Target 1.a: Mobilization of adequate and predictable resources

Target 1.a draws attention to the need for adequate funds to eradicate poverty raised domestically by nation states and from overseas donors. The latter, overseas development assistance, rose annually in US dollar terms between 2015 and 2020 more quickly than during the 15 years of the MDGs. Moreover, the NVRs of the high-income countries are replete with references to their financial support of countries in the developing world. The British government, for example, emphasized spending that enabled developing countries to increase the coverage and sustainability of their social protection systems. The NVRs of Austria, Estonia, Finland, Morocco and Slovenia all reported funding poverty reduction through international and regional development cooperation. Reflecting its geopolitical interests, New Zealand's report focused on assistance to vulnerable small island states, the least developed countries and fragile and conflict affected states. The Kuwaiti government, in its 2019 NVR, listed as many as 2,018 projects conducted under the rubric of SDG1 that had benefited 316,701 families experiencing poverty (although the time over which this had been achieved is somewhat opaque) (Kuwait 2019).

SDG Target 17.2 also concerns global partnership and is more specific than Target 1.a in encouraging donor countries to match the level of development assistance specified in a United Nations resolution in 1970. By agreement this was "to be reached by 1975 and in no case later than in 1980". However, even by 2020, when spending on international development assistance reached its highest level, it represented just 0.32 per cent of the combined GDP of donor nations, less than half of the 0.7 per cent target (OECD 2016, 2021b; Pearson 1969). Moreover, much of the 3.5 per cent increase in overseas development assistance witnessed between 2019 and 2020 was a response to the Covid-19 pandemic and took the form of bilateral sovereign lending. It may, as in the case of increased spending on social protection, prove to be temporary (OECD 2021a). Furthermore, while many donors increased spending in real terms, others reduced it – often for reasons linked to the pandemic including higher domestic expenditure. Reductions were notable among Anglo-Saxon nations – Australia, New Zealand and the United Kingdom. South Korea, Israel, Saudi Arabia and the United Arab Emirates were other governments reducing development assistance at the time of the pandemic.

Some measure of the overall priority given to mobilizing additional resources can be gauged from the response to calls for examples of best practice issued by the UN Department of Economic and Social Affairs in 2018/19 and 2020/21. A total of over 1,400 submissions were received from which 977 were selected for online display. Thirty-eight per cent of the submissions displayed relate to SDG1. Examples of "best practice" clearly cannot be taken as representative of all the activities being undertaken as part of Agenda 2030, but they may hint at underlying patterns. Forty per cent of initiatives were reported to address all 17 SDGs, which points to the interconnectedness of the goals or, possibly, to attempts to make the submissions look attractive. Five of the selected projects were a response to the implications of the Covid-19 pandemic.

One hundred and fourteen of the 464 successful submissions in 2020/21 embraced both SDG1 and SDG17 and might therefore be expected to contribute to ensuring adequate and predictable resources for developing countries. Thirty-one per cent of these were funded by, or involved, the European Union or national or local governments, of which about one in three entailed cross-border support. A further 27 per cent of projects had input from UN agencies meaning that just 40 per cent of all the best practice projects selected in 2020/21 entailed North–South or South–South collaboration in relation to SDG1.

The projects described in the submissions were very heterogenous both in scale and purpose with some aiming to create a global asset, others entailing regional investment such as in the redesign of major cities and yet others providing services for no more than tens of individuals. Only a fifth of the projects offered a theory of change focused on improving the lives and life-chances of people experiencing poverty. These included public works programmes, cash transfer schemes, educational provision for disadvantaged youth, food and nutrition initiatives and clinical support for disabled children. Clearly, technical assistance, a very broad category of support that aptly described more than a third of the projects, might indirectly enhance the lives of those living in poverty while also bringing benefits to others. Another third of the projects were to support administration of the 2030 Agenda itself. Of these, two out of three offered direct administrative support connected to the SDGs ranging from online data resources to offers of publicity. The others were largely concerned with increasing public awareness of the SDGs and/or mobilizing support among various interest groups.

In sum, there is yet little evidence of a global partnership strong enough to mobilize sufficient resources to achieve SDG1. Indeed, the best practice case studies reveal the gulf between the scale of project and the enormity of the task of eradicating poverty. The role of international development assistance is stressed in the NVRs of donors and, indeed, marginal increases would be sufficient to eradicate extreme poverty in low-income countries. Moreover, while significantly more assistance would need to be forthcoming to eliminate poverty throughout the developing world, the cost would not be prohibitive proportional to the wealth of donor countries. However, as explained in Chapters 6 and 9, there is little sign of donors changing their current priorities in response to the SDGs.

4.3 Conclusion

There is little doubt that extreme poverty could be eradicated and other forms of poverty much reduced by 2030. The financial resources already exist and yet, even before the Covid-19 pandemic, it was apparent that progress toward reaching SDG1 was inadequate. The reason is political: the world's leaders lack sufficient commitment and/or are constrained by political structures.

The two outcome targets, 1.1 and 1.2, were intended to signal that poverty is not just a problem of the developing world, while the implementation targets emphasize the international partnership necessary for the outcome targets to be met. As explained in Chapter 3, the outcome targets relate to different conceptions of poverty that are potentially divisive: Target 1.1 for the developing world; Target 1.2 for other countries. However, while Target 1.2 refers to poverty in all its dimensions according to national definitions, very few countries have fully integrated multidimensionality into their domestic agendas. Moreover, those that adopt the UNDP Multidimensional Poverty Index, which adds poor health and low education to living standards, risk confounding SDG1 with SDG3 and SDG4. While there are strong arguments to expand the dimensions of poverty better to reflect the true experience of poverty, these have yet to be taken on board by policymakers (Bray *et al.* 2020).

For the most part, distinctions relating to multidimensional poverty are immaterial since governments tend to rely on measures of income poverty. With this as the focus, different obstacles confront countries at varying levels of economic development. For rich countries, the problem is not one of finance, but lack of political courage in the face of interest groups that benefit from income inequality. There is little evidence that this situation is about to change. While it is true that the Covid-19 pandemic demonstrated both the need for enhanced social protection and the ease with which this could be provided, the enhanced provision was generally temporary and served mostly to protect the interests of the privileged (see also Chapter 5).

There are, however, reasons for some optimism. Based on the policy performance achieved during the era of the MDGs, and hence discounting the impact of the Covid-19 pandemic, extreme poverty (less than US$1.90/day) should be eradicated in all middle-income countries by 2030, if not before. However, the experience in high-income countries is salutary; while extreme poverty in these countries is very rare, it has been shown to have increased noticeably in the years before 2015. If extreme poverty is to be eradicated from low-income countries, there can be no excuse for permitting it to re-emerge in high-income ones.

Upper-middle-income countries should readily be able to half US$5.50/day poverty by 2030, although lower middle-income countries will find this noticeably more difficult. The reason is not predominantly financial. Rather, recent history indicates that poverty reduction policies have not been prioritized to the extent that they need to be if SDG1 is to be attained. This suggests, therefore, a lack of political will to ensure pro-poor growth or to implement pro-poor resource redistribution. A similar lack of focus on poverty reduction has been evident among high-income countries, many of which had witnessed increases in relative poverty even prior to the Covid-19 pandemic.

If politics and political structures explain lack of progress in combatting poverty, economic growth very largely explains why poverty has fallen to the extent that it has. The economic transformations required to achieve clean energy (SDG7) and sustainable cities (SDG11), to stem climate change (SDG13) and to foster environmental improvement (SDGs 14 and 15) create uncertainties as to whether economic growth will – or, indeed, should – continue at past rates (Hickel 2021; Raworth 2017). It is also unclear whether these global transformations will be pro-poor and/or benefit the developing world. Left to the market, they are unlikely to be either and there is little evidence yet, despite the hopes enshrined in Agenda 2030, that rich governments will unite to ensure that the interests of poorer nations are considered first. Moreover, at the time of writing, the Covid-19 pandemic is not over nor are its long-term ramifications well understood.

However, the critical weakness of SDG1 is that, like MDG1, it imposes the greatest financial burden on – and hence the biggest political challenge for – the least developed countries. In proportional terms, the resources necessary for low-income countries to eradicate absolute poverty are six times greater than those needed by high-income countries to half relative poverty. Without international financial support to low- and to some lower-middle-income countries, extreme poverty cannot be eradicated. This illustrates very clearly the interrelatedness of the SDGs. If SDG17 – global partnership – is not met, SDG1 will not be.

The solution once again is not financial but political. Arithmetically, extreme poverty could be eliminated by high-income countries transferring another 0.1 per cent of their collective GDP to low-income countries. The chances of this happening are not high, as evidenced by the fact that governments have mostly reneged on the agreement brokered over 50 years ago to commit 0.7 per cent of national income to international development assistance.

CASE STUDY 4   CANADA'S RESPONSE TO SDG1

Figure CS4   Canada's 2018 strategy

In August 2018, Canada's Liberal Party government, under Justin Trudeau, introduced the nation's "first poverty reduction strategy", *Opportunity for All*. While emphasizing "Dignity: Lifting Canadians out of poverty by ensuring basic needs are met", the strategy document also spoke to the majority middle class with references to "Resilience and security: Supporting the middle class by protecting Canadians from falling into poverty", and to "Opportunity and inclusion: Helping Canadians join the middle class by promoting equality of opportunity" (ESD 2018: 6).

It set two policy targets directly referenced to the 2030 Agenda and the SDGs: (1) "a 20 percent reduction in poverty by 2020", and (2) "a 50 percent reduction in poverty by 2030, which, relative to 2015 levels, will *lead to the lowest poverty rate in Canada's history*" (ESD 2018: 7, emphasis in original).

It also, for the first time, defined an official poverty line "based on the cost of a basket of goods and services individuals and families need in order to meet their basic needs and achieve a modest standard of living in communities across Canada" (ESD 2018: 65). Fixing the targets against this absolute measure rather than the Low-Income Measure (LIM), a measure of relative poverty set at 50 per cent of median household income that had been widely used for several years, has led critics to accuse the government of limited ambition.

Indeed, given that the strategy included no additional resources or policies beyond those which were already in place (e.g., Canada Child Benefit) or proposed (e.g., the new Canada Housing Benefit), *Opportunity for All* would appear to have had more to do with politics and presentation than with policy or commitment. That said, the strategy was opposed even within the Liberal Party. Bill Morneau, the finance minister at the time, has accused the Trudeau government of investing too much energy on finding ways to redistribute Canada's wealth rather than on means to generate it.

Further reading

Blatchford, A. 2022. "Morneau unleashes on Trudeau's economic policies". *Politico*, 1 June. www.politico.com/news/2022/06/01/morneau-critiques-trudeau-government-policies-00036606.

ESD 2018. *Opportunity for All: Canada's First Poverty Reduction Strategy*. Ottawa: Employment and Social Development Canada.

5

THE IMPACT OF COVID-19

A signature characteristic of the Covid-19 pandemic has been its unpredictability. While sophisticated epidemiological models have proved invaluable in short-term planning and national leaders have very publicly relied on "the science" to justify policy responses, politics has necessarily driven the choice and timing of interventions with less predictable outcomes. Moreover, the ability of the virus to mutate into more virulent and contagious variants has undermined the value of horizon projections of the diffusion of the disease. Furthermore, attempts to assess the likely economic impact of the pandemic have been hindered by the prevalence of equilibrium models used in forecasting and the difficulty of accounting for disruptive events such as a pandemic. This has left forecasters scrambling to draw lessons from previous economic shocks of equivalent scale and from earlier pandemics most of which occurred in a noticeably less integrated global economy.

Writing anything about the implications of the pandemic while it continues is, therefore, full of attendant risks. To accommodate the uncertainty, the chapter is divided into two sections with a brief postscript included in the conclusion. The intention is to assess the impact of the first two years of the pandemic, although many of the necessary facts are unavailable. The lack of evidence is mostly due to the inevitable delay in assembling comparable information necessary for global analysis but is sometimes a result of the pandemic disrupting the collection of reliable statistics. Even so, the accumulation of evidence points to the very inequitable impact of the pandemic discussed in the first section, and to a sizeable increase in poverty which is considered in the second.

5.1 Covid-19 and income inequality

From the very earliest days of the pandemic, the expectation was that it would most disadvantage people who were already poor. That, after all, was the experience with previous pandemics (Alfani 2020; Furceri *et al.* 2020).

The Huanan Seafood Wholesale Market in Wuhan, where the first cases appeared to be clustered, was frequented more by migrant workers than by Wuhanren with urban residency. The Wuhan lockdown initially hurt daily labourers, denying them income. Then, when the lockdown was quickly extended nationally in China, poorer migrant workers who were caught at home because of the New Year festival were prohibited from returning to work in the cities. The media portrayal of Covid-19 – it being associated with eating animals, dirtiness and poverty – meant that Wuhanren rapidly became ostracized. In Chinese social media, they were described as "backward" and "Southern" (Walker & Yang 2021).

In India, urban migrants were locked out of work in the cities and forced to return home. Images of migrants on the long painful walk back to their villages were broadcast globally and announced to the world the hardships caused by the pandemic. High-income countries responded by boosting public spending to protect their economies, jobs and people's finances, but few governments in the Global South were able to do likewise. By early 2021, most Western economies had typically begun to recover but less developed economies generally lagged behind.

While such generalizations are true in the sense of being stylized facts and are important for understanding the likely impact of the Covid-19 pandemic on poverty globally, the reality is inevitably nuanced and often surprising. The effect of the pandemic on inequality, and hence on poverty, was not initially as expected.

5.1.1 Inequality between countries

Global inequality is the product of inequality both within nations and between them. With income comparatively easy to measure, this form of inequality attracts most attention. Prior to the pandemic, there was no clearly discernible trend in within-country income inequality, but between-country inequality was steadily declining. As measured by the mean log deviation (MLD), it fell by 34 per cent between 1993 and 2017 for multiple reasons. Economies in Southeast Asia grew rapidly early in the period, were then followed by some in South Asia and latterly by others in parts of Sub-Saharan Africa. While economic growth was an impact factor in reducing between-country inequality, almost half of the reduction occurred between 2008 and 2013 when the Great Recession curtailed economic growth more in richer countries than in poorer ones (Yonzan *et al.* 2021). The Covid-19 pandemic appears to have stemmed this decline in between-country inequality and, indeed, may have reversed the gains of the previous four years. Its impact, however, has varied during the pandemic.

The human and economic consequences of the first year of the pandemic defied expectations in that mortality was concentrated in high-income countries. While it is possible that deaths were under-recorded in low-income countries, this is unlikely to have been the full story (Deaton 2021; Troesken 2015). Low-income countries tend to be less densely populated than developed ones, to have younger populations, to enjoy warmer climates and, in some cases, to attract fewer overseas visitors. These characteristics may have provided protection against the spread of Covid-19. It is also possible that communal values associated with traditional cultures encouraged individuals to prioritize the interests of the community more so than in advanced economies characterized by a strong commitment to personal liberty.

During the first year of the pandemic, the negative impact on economic activity was greater in high-income countries than in developing ones, which served to reduce global income inequality rather than to increase it. Confronted by high initial death rates and public pressure, governments with the resources to do so were able to impose economic lockdowns, requiring people to stay off work and imposing social distancing while simultaneously supporting incomes. In the absence of lockdown, high rates of sickness reduced output.

However, a different story emerges when account is taken of differences in population size, in effect shifting the focus from countries to people. Viewed through this lens, inequality increased with the relationship between national per capita income and economic growth turning slightly positive (Yonzan *et al.* 2021). The reversal reflects the contrasting experiences of China and India. The former, although still characterized by its leaders as a developing country, now has much higher per capita income than India. Successfully containing the pandemic, China experienced few deaths and an early return to economic growth. In contrast, the death rate in India was disproportionately high and it experienced a 10 per cent decline in national income. Taking account of the trajectories of India and China, which together account for 36 per cent of the world's population, indicates that people with incomes above the global average were less badly affected by the pandemic that those with lower incomes. The pandemic halted a trend towards greater income equality that had begun around 1993.

The second year of the pandemic appears to have reinforced the growth in income inequality. At this point, it is necessary to rely on complex simulations to estimate how variations in national growth rates affected household incomes (Yonzan *et al.* 2021; Lakner *et al.* 2020). In 2020, the first year of the pandemic, the incomes of the richest and poorest 20 per cent of the world's population appear to have fallen by similar amounts, by 5 per cent and 6 per cent respectively. By 2021, the incomes of the richest fifth were already recovering following the peak period of national lockdowns; they regained almost half of the income lost in the previous year, while the incomes of the poorest fifth continued to fall

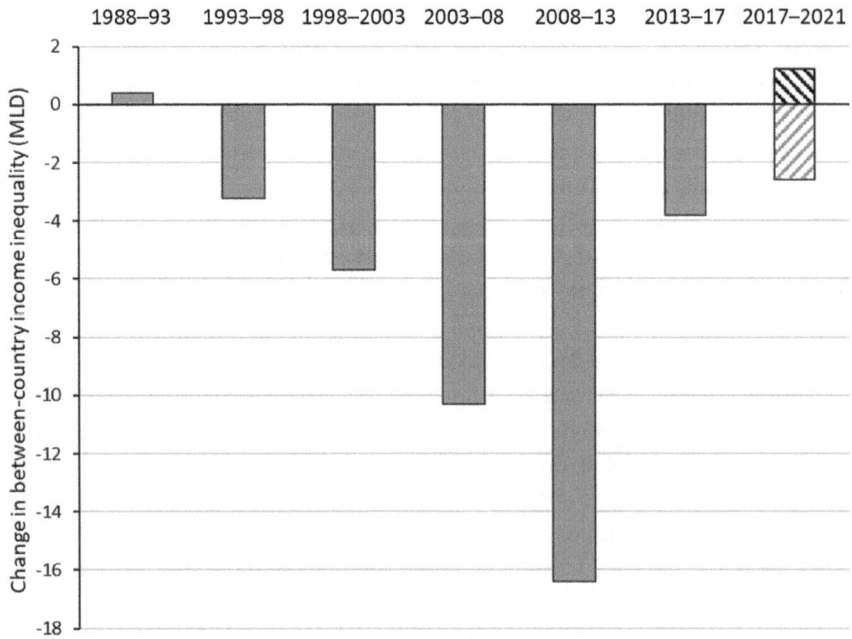

Figure 5.1 Change in between country income inequality, global, 1988–2021
Source: Adapted from Yonzan *et al.* (2021).

by another 5 per cent. This increase in inequality in 2021 is apparent irrespective of whether the focus is on countries or individuals.

To summarize, while the first year of the pandemic reduced incomes everywhere, the recovery in the second year was much more selective. Taking the two years together, the pandemic increased global income inequality. By the end of 2021, global inequality had risen by 1.2 per cent whereas it had previously been projected to fall by 2.6 per cent (Figure 5.1)

5.1.2 Inequality within countries

Analysis of within-country income inequality is usually dependent on administrative records and face-to-face household surveys and data takes many months to become available. However, in response to the Covid-19 pandemic, the World Bank has been sponsoring high-frequency telephone surveys since May 2020. These have been conducted every four to six weeks in some 72 countries providing uniquely up-to-date information. Inevitably telephone surveys have some limitations over face-to-face surveys. Telephone ownership, for example, is less among the least well-off while poor response rates are frequent among the most prosperous. As another innovation triggered by the pandemic, ongoing panel surveys in Europe (in which the same people are repeatedly interviewed) have been co-opted to monitor the impact of the pandemic with additional questions added.

Both sources of information are drawn on, together with official statistics on infection and death rates, in assessing the impact of the pandemic on within-country inequality

5.1.2a Inequality in developing countries

While deaths were heavily concentrated among the elderly in high-income countries, this was much less so in the developing world. This was the case even after accounting for different age structures and, where possible, identifying excess deaths that were clearly related to the pandemic. Taking age-corrected death rates by way of illustration, just 59 per cent of deaths officially recorded to be the result of Covid-19 in lower middle-income countries occurred among people aged 65 and over, compared to 73 per cent in upper-middle-income countries, and 89 per cent in high-income countries (Demombynes *et al.* 2021; data are not yet available for low-income countries). The United States stands out as an exception among high-income countries; with 27 per cent of excess deaths occurring among those aged under 65, it resembles Chile in the age distribution of Covid-19-related deaths.

There are several potential reasons for these differences. Fewer people in less developed countries may have been able to work from home or afford to give up work. As a result, younger people would have been more at risk of catching Covid-19 and to dying from it; the chance of death among people contracting Covid-19 is estimated to be between 1.3 and 2.5 times higher in the developing world than in high-income countries (Nepomuceno *et al.* 2020). A second possible factor is that older people in high-income countries may have been less well than their counterparts in poorer countries. This would be due to better health care enabling persons to survive into old age despite underlying health conditions. Older people in richer countries could also have been more susceptible to infection because they more were often living in residential care – 46 per cent of excess deaths in England recorded through to May 2020, for example, occurred in care homes (PHE 2020).

The implications of the different profiles of age-related deaths may be long-lasting. The greater prevalence of deaths among people of working age in poorer countries is likely to result in a proportionately greater loss of household income. It will also have a greater impact on the well-being of children; estimates suggest that, globally, some 1.1 million children were orphaned by Covid-19 between March 2020 and April 2021, with 1.6 million losing at least one parent or custodial grandparent (Hillis *et al.* 2021).

In assessing the extent of the negative consequences of the pandemic, it is salient to note that perhaps only one in seven cases of Covid-19 in Africa are reported (Burki 2021). However, the World Bank's high-frequency telephone surveys provide insight into the immediate impact of Covid-19 pandemic on the lived experience in developing countries during the first year of the pandemic (Bundervoet *et al.* 2021). While losses through morbidity and death were very real, the other negative consequences of the pandemic were largely iatrogenic; that is, the result of policy measures designed to control the spread of the infection through lockdown and social distancing. According to the Oxford Stringency Index, these containment measures peaked in April 2020 in the 34 countries in which high-frequency telephone surveys were being conducted and had halved in their average intensity by the October. At the peak of Covid-19 containment, 46 per cent of respondents had stopped work in the 11 upper-middle-income countries covered by surveys. Almost as many (41 per cent) were off work in the 14 lower middle-income countries considered. The situation was markedly different in the seven low-income countries surveyed where just 19 per cent of respondents had stopped working on account of lockdown measures; nevertheless, the number reporting loss of income due to the pandemic, 68 per cent, equalled that in upper-middle-income countries.

The substantial differences in job losses and reduction in working hours were no doubt driven by diverse labour market conditions but also, statistically, by variation in the stringency of containment policies pursued by national governments (Bundervoet *et al.* 2021). The employment structure in low-income countries is dominated by agriculture and own-account working. For farmers and others working for themselves in these countries, giving up work was neither necessary nor financially viable. Likewise, casual traders in urban areas would have needed to continue trading, although their incomes were likely to have been reduced due to a lack of customers. While countries differed in the employment consequences of the pandemic, the groups most negatively affected were very similar. Women, older and younger workers (those aged above 60 or below 30), and those without tertiary education were all more seriously affected. So, too, were persons working in manufacturing, services and in agriculture-related industries. In addition, families with school-aged children were more likely than other people to report a fall in income, although not to lose their jobs.

The differential impact on children was not limited to falls in household income. School closures, social distancing in educational settings and the move to home learning all had detrimental effects on children. Moreover, children from disadvantaged homes, especially those located in rural areas where poverty in the developing world is often concentrated, more frequently found themselves on the wrong side of the digital divide and unable to participate in online teaching.

The evidence is that many children failed to continue with schooling during the pandemic with the possible double jeopardy of falling behind educationally.

The experience of children speaks to the longer-term implications of the pandemic. So, too, does that fact that the groups who lost employment in largest numbers – the young, the old and the less well educated – have subsequently found most difficulty in returning to work. While the prospects of the pandemic having cross-generational consequences are very real, these and other possible long-term consequences for inequality cannot yet be determined.

5.1.2b Inequality in high-income countries

The evidence is that increased income inequality in high-income countries arising from the pandemic was short-lived (D'Ambrosio *et al.* 2021; Clark *et al.* 2021). According to panel studies conducted in Greece, Italy and Spain, income inequality, as measured by the Gini coefficient, rose between January and May 2020 at the start of the pandemic, but then fell to levels in January 2021 that were below those in January 2020.

The reason seems to be that the immediate loss of income caused by early lockdowns occurred before compensatory social protection measures were fully in place. This was especially true of Italy, the European country hit first by the pandemic, whereas Germany responded more quickly with social protection measures and, there, income inequality fell steadily between January 2020 and January 2021. The initial loss in income was mostly sustained by the self-employed and those with lower pre-pandemic incomes. Unfortunately, it is impossible to identify any gender differentials because in the panel studies income was measured at the level of households. However, people living alone who could not benefit from income sharing were seen to suffer disproportionate income losses.

While directly comparable information is not available for the United Kingdom, the evidence points to a somewhat more sustained increase in income inequality than in the four continental European countries discussed above, Germany, Greece, Italy and Spain. As in these countries, lockdowns in the United Kingdom triggered unprecedented falls in employment between February and April 2020. Those employed in hospitality were the most badly affected with only 40 per cent doing any work during April 2020, but the loss in employment was also substantial in the manufacturing, wholesale and retail sectors. As in the European countries, the self-employed were badly affected but persons employed on zero-hours contracts fared even worse – 60 per cent had no work at all in April 2020. Employment levels had largely recovered by September 2020, when almost 90 per cent of the labour force were back working, but additional lockdowns in November 2020 and January 2021 further disrupted employment patterns. As late as March 2021, employment was still only around

80 per cent of pre-pandemic levels with just 60 per cent of those on zero-hours contracts doing any work during the month.

The impact of reduced employment on incomes in the United Kingdom was mediated by the March 2020 introduction of a furlough scheme for those laid-off due to the pandemic and by a £20 per week increase in the main social assistance benefit. Those furloughed, 32 per cent of the workforce in May 2020, had 80 per cent of their wage paid for by government subject to a prescribed maximum income (Görtz *et al.* 2021).

By August 2021, 11.6 million jobs in 1.3 million businesses had been furloughed; furloughed employees typically experienced a 17 per cent drop in income (Davies *et al.* 2021). The workers who were most protected by the furlough scheme were those with the lowest qualifications. People in low-status processing occupations were almost twice as likely as their managers to be furloughed, and three times more likely than those in professional occupations. However, it should be recognized that many people in higher-status occupations were able to continue working from home and therefore suffered no drop in income.

The initial lockdown had a disproportionately negative effect on minority ethnic groups who were also more likely to become unemployed rather than to be placed on furlough. Young people were similarly badly affected initially, although employment levels for them, as for ethnic minorities, had returned to their pre-pandemic levels by March 2021. Recovery was noticeably slower for older workers.

Contrary to expectations, average weekly wages in the United Kingdom appear to have risen at an exceptionally high rate during the first year of the pandemic. However, the statistics are distorted because those losing their jobs and therefore no longer included in the figures were disproportionally low paid (Cribb *et al.* 2021). Nevertheless, wages in the public sector peaked during the first lockdown, presumed to be due to overtime paid to frontline health care staff dealing with the pandemic. Private sector wages, in contrast, fell sharply during and after the lockdown, coinciding with the peak of furlough, with sharp increases in the proportion saying that they were behind with bills. However, wages had typically recovered within three to four months, and it was only among the self-employed that significant numbers reported financial difficulties running into the first quarter of 2021 (Crossley *et al.* 2021).

The median earnings of those continuously in employment grew steadily during the pandemic and at the same rate as in previous years. Moreover, with reduced opportunities for spending, savings ratios almost doubled among those in the top half of the income distribution. Yet, at the same time, significant proportions of people experienced sustained falls in earnings. A fall in wages of a fifth or more between January 2020 and March 2021 was most prevalent among individuals in households with low pre-pandemic incomes, potentially pushing them into poverty (Figure 5.2). However, falls of this magnitude were also more frequent than average among individuals from the top income quintile. The fact that sustained increases in earnings were also most common among low-income households serves as a reminder of the instability of low incomes and the fact there is no true counterfactual to the pandemic, that is knowledge of what would have happened to incomes in its absence.

While the Covid-19 pandemic was more severe and long-lasting in the US than was generally the case in Europe, it seems to have added little to inequality. As in Britain, average wages rose through 2020 and into 2021 with the increase being exaggerated due to increased unemployment among the previously lowest paid (Kochhar & Bennett 2021). While the median income of the lowest wage quintile appeared to drop to zero in the first quarter of 2020 – the assumption made being that those becoming unemployed in the peak of the pandemic received no wage – it had fully recovered by the second. In contrast to Britain, where no differences were observed by gender, women in the US were more affected by unemployment than men during the early part of the pandemic. However, they returned to work more quickly. Indeed, the only demographic group to suffer sustained losses were Asian Americans whose unemployment rate more than

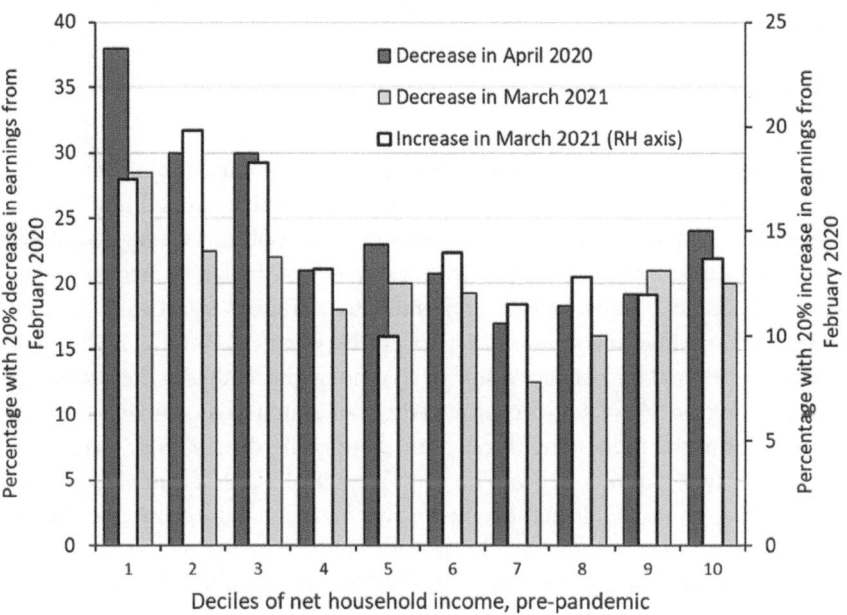

Figure 5.2 Change in UK earnings by income decile
Source: Adapted from Crossley *et al.* (2021).

doubled between 2019 and 2021 to 5.6 per cent but remained below the national average. It is unclear whether this increase was due to growing prejudice; certainly, China was the presumed source of the virus and there were abundant reports of racial stereotyping during the early stages of the pandemic. This could have been fuelled by President Trump's overt criticism of the Chinese government and by the impartiality of the US media (Walker 2021).

Despite the US being much criticized for its weak social safety net, people losing their jobs due to the pandemic were nominally entitled to unemployment insurance or to support under the Coronavirus Aid, Relief, and Economic Security Act that provided a form of furlough to certain sectors of the economy. It is not yet clear how much support people actually received by way of the government financial assistance, which expired by September 2021.

The pandemic seems likely, therefore, to have increased between-country income inequality, with higher-income countries faring better than others, and to have increased within-country inequality across the developing world but only briefly in high-income countries. A crucial distinction is that richer countries were better able to put in place compensatory measures often building on pre-existing social protection schemes. Where social protection was rudimentary or absent, the pandemic will have most hurt the economically weakest, thereby widening inequalities. Longer term, it may be that children will have suffered most given the importance of good nutrition and schooling to human development.

5.2 Covid-19 and poverty

The differential impact of the Covid-19 pandemic on inequality both within and between countries helped to determine the numbers that slipped into poverty and the likely duration of the poverty experienced. Without survey-based evidence, only available at the end of 2022, estimates of the fall in income coincident with Covid-19 must be based on simulations. These suggest an average fall in global household incomes of 4.6 per cent between 2019 and 2021 but with declines of 6.6 and 6.7 per cent respectively among households in the lowest two quintiles (Figure 5.3). While the onset of the pandemic and the initial lockdowns led to substantial reductions throughout the income distribution, incomes in the lowest two quintiles showed no improvement in 2021 against substantial recoveries for households in the top two. This means that the economic costs of the pandemic have already been borne more heavily by the poorer sections of the global community and raises the possibility that its differential impact will prove to be long-lasting.

Estimates of the global impact of Covid-19 on poverty offered by the World Bank have been subject to repeated revision as the pandemic has evolved (Mahler *et al.* 2021). In April 2020, based on economic growth forecasts from the 2020 *World Economic Outlook*, the expectation was that the pandemic would increase the numbers with incomes below the US$1.90/day poverty line by 62 million worldwide. However, by January 2021 the estimate had risen to 124 million based on the current *Global Economic Prospects* analysis. This figure, however, was subsequently revised downwards to 97 million in June 2021, an estimate that was still current in October 2021 (Table 5.1).

The 97 million people estimated to have been drawn into extreme US$1.90/ day poverty equates to almost the combined population of Germany, Austria and Switzerland. Seventy per cent of newly poor individuals were to be found in lower middle-income countries, mostly located in South Asia and Sub-Saharan Africa (Hills *et al.* 2021). However, the largest percentage point increase in extreme poverty (3.3 per cent) occurred in low-income countries. This was, no doubt,

Table 5.1 Regional and income group estimates of poverty increases due to Covid-19 (nowcasts for 2021)

	Poverty level					
	US$1.90/day			US$5.50/day		
	Millions increase	Percent point change in poverty rate	Years of progress lost	Millions increase	Percent point change in poverty rate	Years of progress lost
Regions						
East Asia & Pacific	7	0.3	1–2	37	1.57	1–2
Europe & Central Asia	1	0.11	1	4	0.43	2–3
Latin America & Caribbean	2	0.31	6–7	12	1.84	5–6
Middle East & North Africa	8	1.23	*	14	2.15	*
Rest of the world	0		+	1		3–4
South Asia	50	2.69	–	82	4.42	-
Sub-Saharan Africa	29	2.55	2–3	15	1.32	6–7
Income groups						
Low-income	22	3.31	8–9	9	1.35	2–3
Lower-middle-income	69	2.07	4–5	119	3.57	2–3
Upper-middle-income	6	0.24	5–6	34	1.35	3–4
High-income	0		2–3	1	0.08	2–3
Global	**97**		**3–4**	**163**		**2–3**

Notes: *Poverty has been increasing in MNA; – Not reported due to great uncertainty because of lack of data for India; + Poverty negligible.

Source: Hill *et al.* (2021) plus author's own calculations.

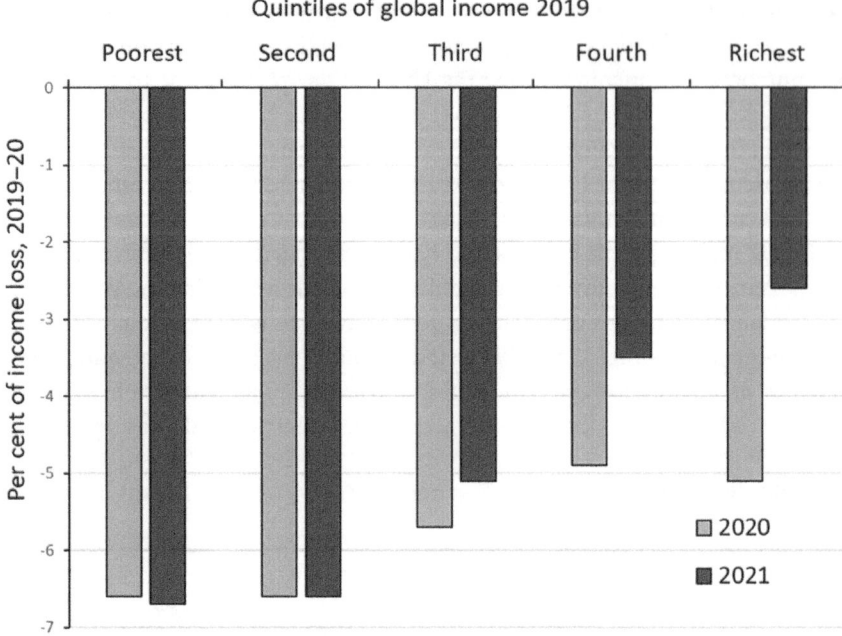

Figure 5.3 Percentage of income loss by global income quintile due to Covid-19
Source: Adapted from Hill *et al.* (2021).

because a greater fraction of the populations in these countries were living just above the extreme poverty line and were thus more susceptible to a drop in income taking them across the threshold and into poverty. The implications of this are profound. As explained in Chapter 4, low-income countries are not only less likely to have effective social protection schemes but also to be less able to reduce poverty through economic growth. Given this, and the greater proportional increase in poverty, the impact of the pandemic has been particularly pernicious for low-income countries. The World Bank estimates this setback to be equivalent to eight or nine years of normal progress, almost twice that experienced by lower-middle-income countries.

It is likely that, globally, most of those who were pushed into extreme poverty by the pandemic were already poor according to the US$5.50/day threshold. In addition, the World Bank calculates that another 163 million, equivalent to the population of Bangladesh – the world's eighth most populous nation – have become poor according to the US$5.50 poverty standard. Again, most of the people affected live in lower-middle-income countries with about half residing in South Asia. The effect has been to add 3.6 percentage points to the poverty rate – 4.4 percentage points in South Asia – taking poverty levels back to where they were in 2017/18. The 1.4 percentage point increase in US$5.50 poverty in low-income countries, although less, may well ensure that over 90 per cent of the population in these countries will remain poor for some years to come.

The World Bank modelling suggests that the pandemic may have increased the number of people in high-income countries experiencing US$5.50/day poverty by one million. Proportional to population, this increase is miniscule, but for those affected, given the extremely low level of the threshold in relation to median incomes, the level of deprivation experienced will be very severe. Official poverty thresholds in high-income countries, where they exist, are generally set much higher than US$5.50/day, averaging US$21.70/day. As explained in previous chapters, poverty in high-income countries is typically defined in relative terms and, while data on the true increase in poverty attributable to the pandemic are not yet available, the simulated estimates available for European Union are instructive (Figures 5.4–5.7).

Relative measures of poverty can generate perverse results during economic recessions if fixed as a proportion of median disposable income. If median income falls during a recession, the poverty threshold will also fall, thereby reducing the number of persons counted as being poor. Median income derived from earnings fell noticeably in Europe between 2019 and 2020 with, at the level of the individual, the biggest falls occurring among those with already low earnings (Figure 5.4).

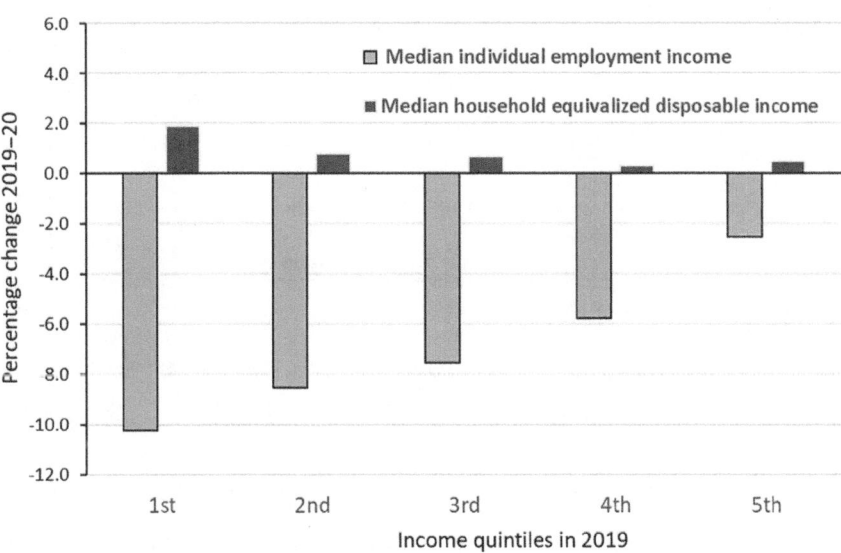

Figure 5.4 Median employment income vs median disposable income in the EU, 2020 (% change compared with 2019, income by quintile)
Source: Eurostat.

However, median household income, the datum against which poverty is assessed, held steady for Europe as a whole; indeed, it marginally increased due to targeted reductions in taxation and to benefit schemes introduced by governments to compensate for reduced working hours and layoffs. Of course, the same was not necessarily true of all member states and the fall in median household income between 2019 and 2020 was significant for Cyprus, Italy, Belgium and Greece.

Correspondingly, the change in poverty between 2019 and 2020 associated with the pandemic was far from uniform across Europe (Figure 5.5). The impression to be drawn from Figure 5.5 is that poverty drifted upwards across two-thirds of Europe and that the increase was statistically significant in Spain, Croatia, Italy, Slovenia and Greece. However, for the Europe Union as a whole, the change was not significantly different from zero; indeed, poverty fell significantly in Estonia, Lithuania, Romania, Czech Republic, Germany and Finland. It is important to recognize that these changes cannot be directly attributed to the pandemic since there is no counterfactual, an indication of what poverty would have been in the absence of the pandemic. Moreover, the values presented in Figure 5.5 are based on national median household incomes in 2020 and therefore understate the increase in poverty in those countries in which median income fell.

A notable surge in poverty among children and young people aged under 18 occurred in nine countries between 2019 and 2020. Some of the youths

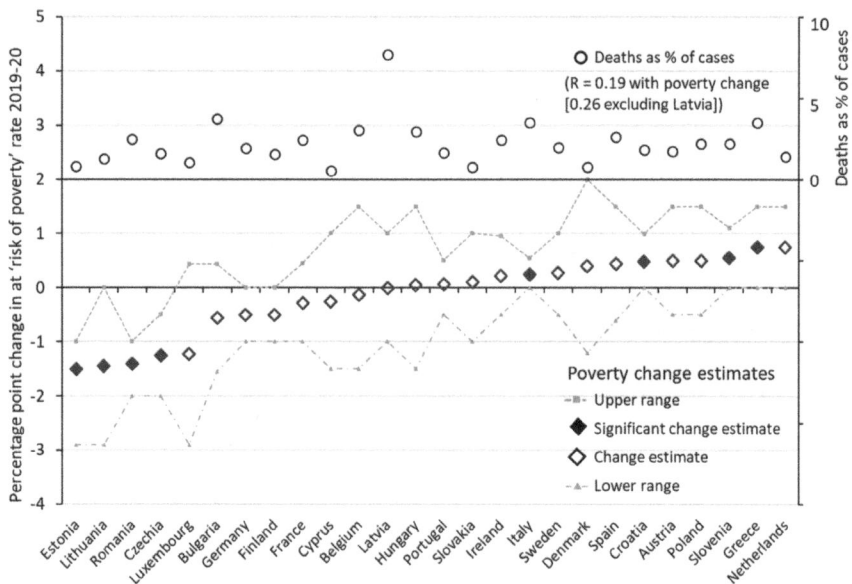

Figure 5.5 Changes in the "at risk of poverty rate", 2019–20
Source: Adapted from Eurostat and Our World in Data.

affected may have been casualties of the widely reported layoffs among new appointees as employers adopted a "last in, first out" principle. Additionally, children will have been disproportionately affected by job losses and wage reductions experienced by their parents. Poverty among under-18s, however, fell in Luxembourg, Lithuania and Germany. The European Commission attributes this fall to deliberate policy action including higher wage compensation for reduced worked hours for employees with dependent children and additional lump-sum payments of child benefit.

Poverty among persons aged 65 and over also fell significantly between 2019 and 2020 in half of European countries. This is unlikely to have been due to the grim statistical artefact that impoverished elderly were more susceptible to dying from Covid-19. Rather, it appears to be the continuation of a secular change in which younger cohorts of elderly retire with better pension provision than previous ones. The elderly, however, were also less affected by the labour market consequences of lockdowns that might have contributed to the statistically significant increase in poverty among people of working age experienced by nine member states.

While recognizing that the estimates presented in Table 5.1 cover two years whereas those recorded in Figures 5.5 and 5.6 relate to only one, the increases in

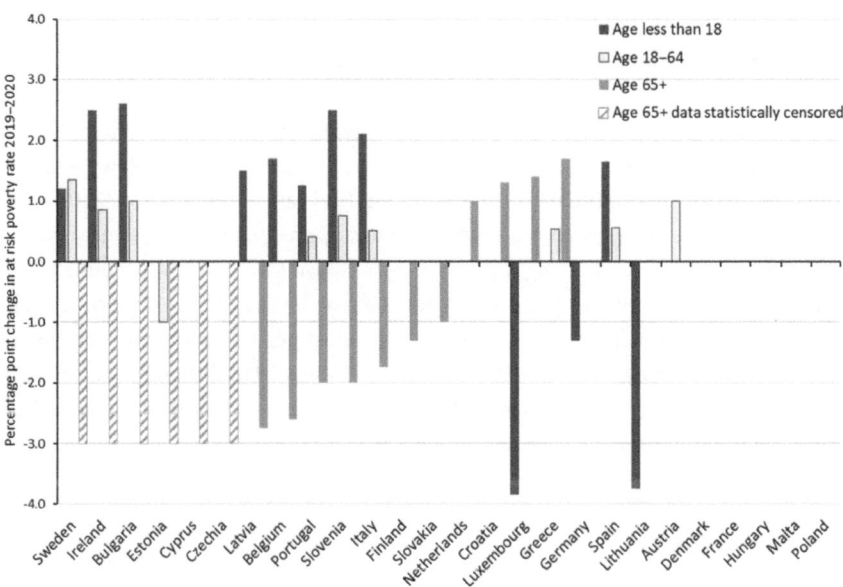

Figure 5.6 Statistically significant changes in the at risk of poverty rate 2019–20 according to age (mid-point estimates)
Source: Adapted from Eurostat.

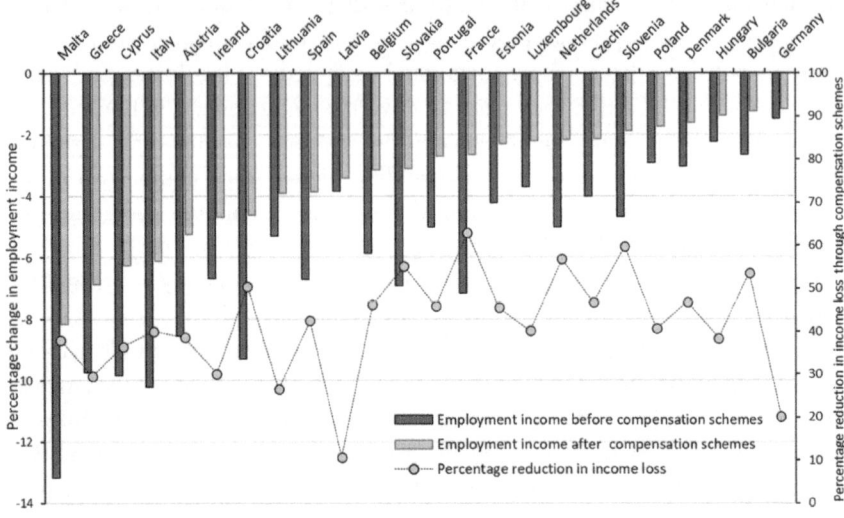

Figure 5.7 Impact of compensation on employment income, 2019–20
Source: Adapted from Eurostat.

poverty experienced across Europe were noticeably less than in developing countries. Partly a consequence of differing definitions, this difference is also likely to
have been due to the various temporary income protection schemes implemented
in all European countries in recognition of the negative consequences of social
distancing measures. The wage compensation schemes (before payment of taxes)
succeeded in reducing average losses in earnings to less than 5 per cent in all but
five member states with the degree of protection afforded against falling wages ranging from 11 per cent (in Latvia) to 63 per cent (in France) (Figure 5.7). Although
it is important to recognize the complex interactions of the polices introduced
by some governments, the slight positive correlation (R = 0.26) between level of
protection and the increase in poverty hints at the level of support being driven
by the seriousness of the rise in poverty. The modest positive correlation between
increases in poverty and high deaths rate due to Covid-19 (although negative with
infections) similarly suggests policy chasing events in some countries despite the
overall success in limiting increases in poverty.

5.3 Conclusion

While the effects of the Covid-19 pandemic were first felt by richer countries, briefly
reducing global between-country inequality, this effect was short-lived. During the
first two years, the economic fallout from the pandemic increased pre-existing

inequalities with the same inevitability as water erodes the cracks in pervious lime-stone. Throughout much of the world, youth, older workers, the unskilled and the marginalized appear to have been most negatively affected during the early stages of the pandemic. Moreover, the pattern to date is that the inequalities opened by the pandemic have proved resistant to closure as the groups most badly affected were left behind during the economic recovery of late 2020 through 2021. At a national level, too, poverty increased more in the poorest parts of the world not least because governments lacked the fiscal space to implement the temporary social protection schemes that, in the Global North, managed to protect family incomes and keep businesses afloat to take advantage of the post pandemic opportunities.

As a postscript, it is important to note that the Delta and Omicron variants of Covid-19 added their own dynamics to the pandemic, the effects of which have yet to be determined. The Delta variant, first named in May 2021 and thus later than most of the statistics presented above, seems to have emerged in India in around November 2020. It tended to produce more severe symptoms than earlier strains, which led governments to impose new lockdowns but, by February 2022, it had been superseded by the Omicron variants which were much more transmissible but less severe. Omicron caused the number of confirmed new infections to peak in late January 2022 at a level over four times greater than the previous high in April 2021. Deaths, however, peaked later in mid-February 2022 at a lower rate (1.39 deaths/million) than in late January 2021 (1.88 deaths/million) which remains the apogee for mortality.

The statistics reproduced in Figure 5.8 suggest that Covid-19, and especially the Omicron variant, was most virulent in high-income and, to a lesser extent, upper-middle-income countries, although it remains unclear how much of the apparent difference is attributable to differential reporting. Nevertheless, given the importance of economic growth in reducing poverty in the developing world, the fact that, largely because of the pandemic, global GDP fell by 3.4 per cent in 2020 instead of growing by 2.9 per cent is likely to have a lasting impact on the extent of world poverty (Szmigiera 2022). The resultant loss of US$5.4 trillion to the global economy is the equivalent to taking US$693 from every person on the planet; it could have funded a payment of US$1.90 daily to everyone for an entire year.

Moreover, neither the pandemic nor its consequences are yet history. The negative global economic dependencies revealed by the pandemic have united elements of the political left and right against globalization. The calls for pro-tectionism and home production, if followed by policy, are likely to curtail employment in developing economies. Inflation has been fuelled by government borrowing and by a shortage of raw materials due to attempts to engineer a rapid post-pandemic recovery. This will probably most hurt families with lowest incomes since they need to spend a higher proportion of their incomes. And, at the time of writing in spring 2022, China has begun locking down cities and

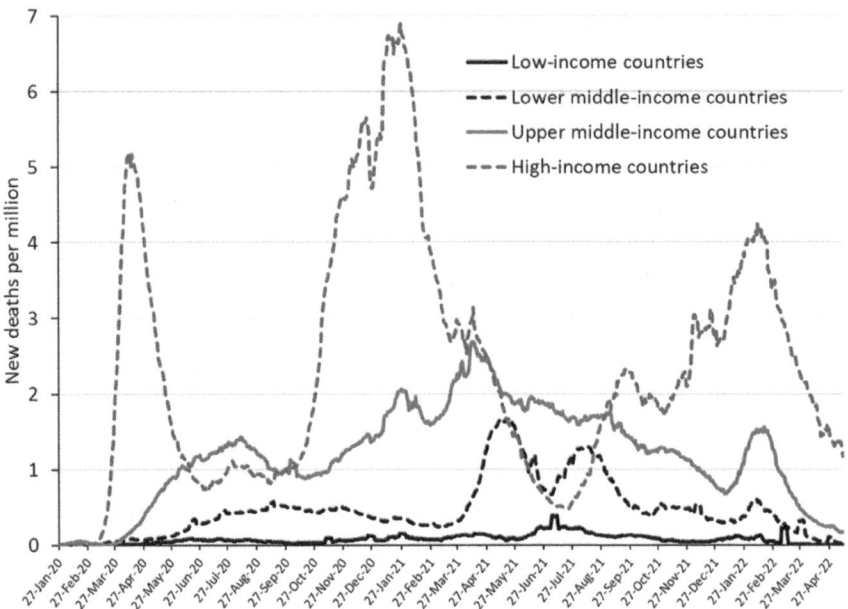

Figure 5.8 Updated history of the Covid-19 pandemic
Source: Our World in Data.

closing urban economies to restrain the advance of Omicron with an immediate impact on the livelihoods of millions of migrant workers. China's success in containing the pandemic and maintaining its levels of production has hitherto been a major element in minimizing the global economic impact of the pandemic. If China's policy of zero-tolerance in controlling the pandemic fails, the negative economic ramifications of the pandemic could be severely magnified.

CASE STUDY 5 COVID-19: 1 IN 386 MILLION

Radhu, a widow aged about 50, lives in a semi-rural part of Bangladesh. She earns a living as a casual worker in the local market carrying water, sorting onions and loading goods for a group involved in extortion, threatening store holders with disruption. Even in the best of times she rarely earns the equivalent of US$1/day. When the pandemic arrived in April and May 2020, she was unable to work, prevented from attending the market by police and fear. Her income dropped precipitously.

She had managed, through stringent budgeting, to accumulate savings but these were for her yet-to-be-married daughter. She therefore cut her spending, especially on food. This she accomplished by receiving food through private

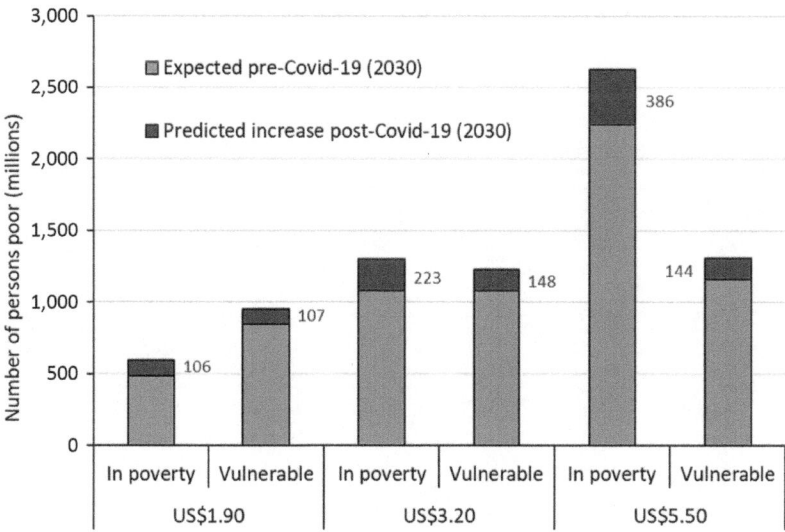

Figure CS5 Long-term impact of Covid-19 on global poverty
Source: Adapted from Lara and Mendez-Ramos (2021).

donations and public relief, but also by working in return for food for her sisters-in-law with whom she lived. While her income increased in June and July, her spending remained low. This was because she continued working for food rather than cash but also because she increased her rate of saving for her daughter's dowry.

Like others in her community, Radhu somehow managed to survive despite large income losses and significant financial hardship although not without anxiety. She suffered lower earnings for some time after the height of the pandemic.

Globally, the impact of the pandemic is likely to be felt long-term with, in 2030, over 100 million more people likely to be living in extreme poverty than had previously been predicted and 386 million more living on less than US$5.50/day. The number of persons with incomes only a little above the poverty line, and thereby vulnerable to falling into poverty, are similarly likely to remain above pre-pandemic levels.

Further reading

Lara, J. & F. Mendez-Ramos 2021. "Poverty vulnerability: the role of poverty lines in the post pandemic era". *Economics Bulletin* 41(4): 2690–96.
Rönkkö, R., S. Rutherford & K. Sen 2022. "The impact of the COVID-19 pandemic on the poor: insights from the Hrishipara diaries". *World Development* 149: 105689.

6

TACKLING THE ROOT CAUSES OF POVERTY

This chapter marks a turning point. The origins of the Sustainable Development Goals, their form, and the disappointing progress to date have been documented in Chapters 1 to 5. In addition, in Chapter 4 it was established that it is perfectly feasible, in terms of global financial resources, both to eradicate extreme poverty and halve poverty in all its forms – that is to reach Targets 1.1 and 1.2 by 2030. Indeed, it is a humiliating failure of international governance that these targets have yet to be achieved. In this and the remaining chapters, therefore, attention shifts to explore how more rapid progress can be made and whether this is likely. The fundamental causes of global poverty are first considered before discussing the kinds of policies that need to be pursued if poverty is to be eliminated.

6.1 On the causes of inequality and poverty

Poverty, whether conceptualized as being absolute, relative or multidimensional, results from the unfair primary and secondary distribution of resources. The primary distribution is market-driven. It takes place within and between countries through the production and sale of goods at home and/or abroad which generate income in the form of wages and returns on assets and investments.

The secondary distribution is that engineered by governments through taxation and transfers which determine the resources that populations can access and deploy. For the most part, the secondary distribution currently takes place within nation states but does occur between national states in the form of overseas development assistance (ODA), discounted loans made available by the International Monetary Fund and the World Bank, and charitable aid dispensed by non-governmental organizations.

The distributions are unfair to the extent that they lead to, or do not prevent, poverty. In a narrow quasilegal sense, this is the case because it has been internationally agreed that poverty should be eliminated or, at least, reduced by half or more. The distributions may be unfair in the wider sense of structuring patterns of well-being that cannot be justified with respect to commonly accepted moral criteria. Given the context, the focus in this chapter is on unfairness narrowly defined.

Inequality and poverty are being reproduced every day due to market forces and because of the failure of governments adequately to alter the primary distribution of income. But today's pattern of inequality has its origins deep in history. To illustrate, differences in the per capita GDP of countries in 1870, that is before the first wave of globalization associated with colonization, explained 50 per cent of the variation in national incomes as recently as 2008 (Michalopoulos & Papaioannou 2017). Equally remarkable is the increase in the scale of inequality witnessed in the twentieth century and subsequently. In 1870, per capita incomes in Western Europe were about four times those in Africa; by 2008, this difference in incomes had tripled.

In is important, therefore, to consider the history of inequality before addressing the current processes of reproduction.

6.1.1 Historical legacies

This persistence in the rank ordering of countries and the growing dispersion has variously been attributed: to initial geographical endowments; to cultural traits including religion, beliefs and norms; to historical institutions including precolonial political systems and colonial extractive rules; and to historical "accidents" such as the national borders drawn across Africa in the late nineteenth century (Acemoglu & Robinson 2012). Bhattacharyya (2016), echoing Mackinder's environmental determinism of a century earlier, proposes a unified framework prioritizing geography, disease, trade and institutions which he uses discursively to explain the greater success of Western European countries, and later North America, relative to Africa, Latin America and Russia (Mackinder 1904, 1910).

Helpful though a unified framework might be in providing an overview, constraints on development are complex and the legacy of colonialism is strong (Glaister et al. 2020). Acemoglu and Robinson (2017: 84) make a distinction between those colonial institutions based on the control and extraction of rents from indigenous peoples that have left a legacy of poverty, and those that were inclusive and created positive incentives and opportunities. While recognizing that European colonization did not reach everywhere, they calculate that its legacy nevertheless accounts for "a third of income inequality in the world today".

The hierarchical underpinnings of global inequality were already self-evident in 1950 as the disruption caused by the Second World War dissipated, the United Nations began to function, and the Bretton Woods organizations started to look beyond reconstruction (Chapter 2). Some 90 territories were administered as colonies or other forms of formal dependency. Many Latin American countries, although independent, were disadvantaged by being economically dependent on the export of primary products and the import of added value manufactured goods. However, the American and British administrations, positioning themselves as global leaders after the wartime victory, viewed economic development simply as a process of catch-up by "undeveloped" countries. The presumption was that through trade, initially as colonies and later gaining independence, all territories could become modern, mass consumption, liberal democracies. The Bretton Woods organizations, as agents of the victorious powers, inevitably took a similar view.

However, many Latin American governments, together with some leaders of newly independent countries, sought to break these historical economic dependencies. They did this through stimulating the development of local industries and protecting them with tariffs. They sought, too, to build social cohesion through employment generation and other social reforms. Made voiceless in the Bretton Woods institutions by voting arrangements that privileged rich countries, new groupings were created to increase their bargaining power. The Non-Aligned Movement (NAM) was established in Belgrade in 1961 (the name only being adopted in 1976), and the G77 intergovernmental voting bloc within the United Nations was founded in 1964. Both groupings gained influence as the Cold War intensified, but progress was slow (Phillips 2020). Between 1950 and 1980, per capita GDP in Latin America only increased from 113 to 125 per cent of the global average.

Elsewhere different forces were at work. Average per capita GDP in East Asia rose from 29 to 45 per cent over the same period – 1950 to 1980 – primarily due to spectacular growth in incomes in Japan – in part the result of US financial support to create a bulwark against a communist Asia (Figure 6.1). Income from oil-rich states lifted per capita GDP in the Middle East and North Africa region area from 117 to 173 per cent of the global average during the corresponding period, although the development was uneven (Chancel & Piketty 2021). In marked contrast, however, per capita GDP in Sub-Saharan Africa (excluding South Africa) fell further behind, from 56 per cent of the global average in 1950 to just 39 per cent in 1980.

In the context of the Cold War, international development policies were overtly political and certain developing countries were able to exploit competition between the ideological power blocks. In the 1970s, the non-aligned countries succeeded in building momentum for reform around the multifaceted notion of a New International Economic Order (NIEO) (Gilman 2015). Aimed to give developing countries more influence, advocates of the new order primarily sought greater economic sovereignty. Some, however, wanted to create a "socialism of nations" and pressed for the United Nations General Assembly to be given powers to enact

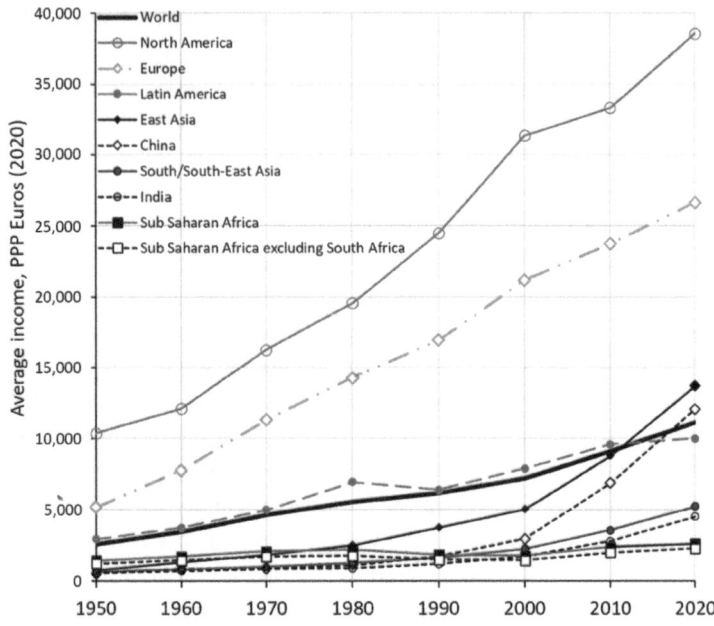

Figure 6.1a Average per capita incomes, 1950–2020

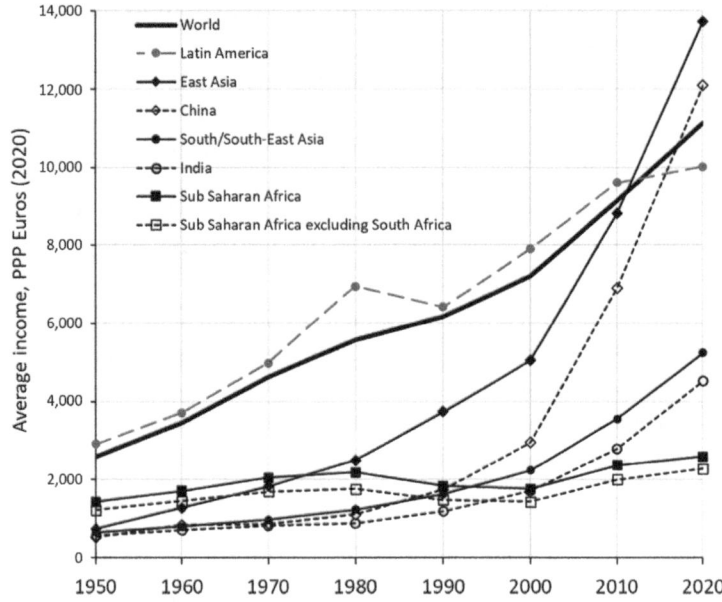

Figure 6.1b Average per capita incomes, developing world, 1950–2020
Source: World Income Database.

international laws. However, the 1980 publication of the Brandt Report proved the apogee of the movement for, while demonstrating that some Western politicians were prepared to listen, the turn to neoliberalism was about to happen.

6.1.2 Neoliberalism and globalization

The ending of fixed exchange rates, the escalation in oil prices in the 1970s, and massive increases in liquidity in international financial markets led, in combination, to increased indebtedness among developing countries pursuing a policy of import substitution. This was to provoke economic crises in Latin America and Africa in 1982 by which time the newly elected President Reagan had declared – at the Cancun Economic Summit in 1981 – that USA would not countenance any reform of global economic institutions. With UK Prime Minister Margaret Thatcher in support, the neoliberal agenda advocated small government, strong private property rights, free markets and free trade. Financial assistance from the World Bank and the IMF became conditional on policy reform – "structural adjustment". This typically included the privatization of state-owned enterprises, deregulation of the economy, trade liberalization, "competitive" exchange rates and the elimination of barriers to foreign direct investment. Developing countries were therefore obliged to engage in globalization and to do so from a position of economic weakness.

By the 1990s, there was clear evidence of the failure of structural adjustment programmes, with measurable falls in real incomes in Latin America and Sub-Saharan Africa (Figure 6.1b). However, this failure was interpreted by the World Bank and IMF as being due to weak national institutions. Therefore, under the rhetoric of "good governance" and "anti-corruption", governments seeking financial assistance were obliged to modernize through fiscal and tax reform and to implement policies that enhanced labour flexibility. The aim, thereby, was to create model neoliberal states. This broad approach, which encourages the free flow of trade and capital, has survived both the Asian financial crisis of the late 1990s and the Great Recession in 2007–09 that revealed the dangerous volatility of global capital flows (Moreno 1998).

There is little evidence that the mechanisms of structural adjustment, "good governance" and open borders that have fostered globalization, have benefited countries outside North America and Europe (Wade 2017a). China and a few smaller economies in East Asia prospered during this period but most probably did so because they did not pursue a neoliberal agenda (see below). Between 1980 and 2020, the world's richest 1 per cent of inhabitants – some 77 million people, seven million fewer than the population of Germany – enjoyed 23 per cent of all the global income growth, whereas the poorest 50 per cent (3.8 billion) received just 9 per cent (Chancel et al. 2021). Indeed, 56 per cent of countries, mostly in the developing world, experienced a fall in real per capita GDP between 1980 and 2000 (Wade 2017a). Moreover, whereas incomes in North America in 1980 averaged nine times those in Sub-Saharan Africa, by 2020 the differential had increased to 17 (Figure 6.1a).

While richer countries have undoubtedly gained from globalization, it is important to recognize that the national benefits have not been equally shared by all their citizens. With a global workforce to choose from, labour employed in the developing world partly substitutes for that in the Global North, creating unemployment, holding down wage growth and increasing inequality within Northern countries. Whereas the share of income enjoyed by the top 10 per cent fell both in Europe and North America between 1950 and 1980, it rose between 1980 and 2020 to higher levels than in 1959 (Figure 6.2).

The neoliberal agenda and structural adjustment policies failed to produce a pattern of primary income distribution that benefited developing countries relative to developed ones. At the same time, conditional international lending to developing countries restricted the ability of recipient governments to enact a secondary distribution of incomes that favoured those experiencing poverty. The measures promoted by international lenders were those intended to stimulate market-driven, pro-poor economic growth rather than social protection, which, it was argued, blunted financial incentives. Pro-poor redistribution declined in Sub-Saharan Africa, Asia and the Middle East from levels that had already been very low in 1980 (Figure 6.3). Redistribution similarly fell in Latin America until the 1990s when the neoliberal idea of making cash transfers conditional on pro-market behavioural change took hold (Millán *et al.* 2019; Papadopoulos & Velázquez Leyer 2016).

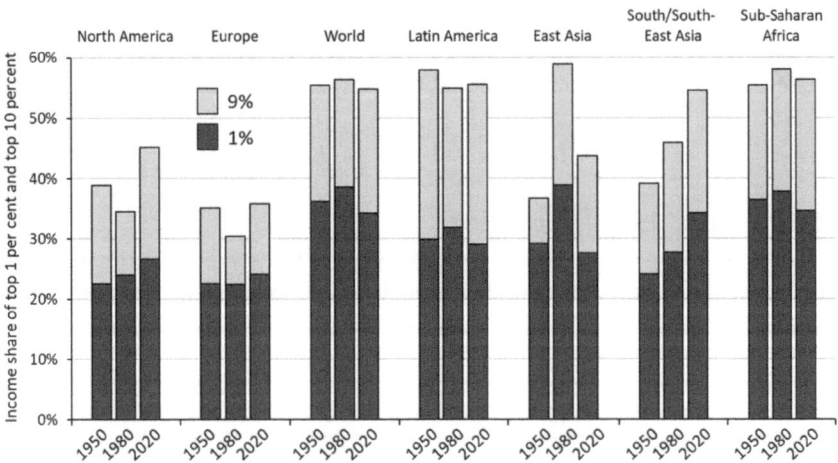

Figure 6.2 Income shared of the richest 10 per cent, 1950–2020
Source: World Income Database.

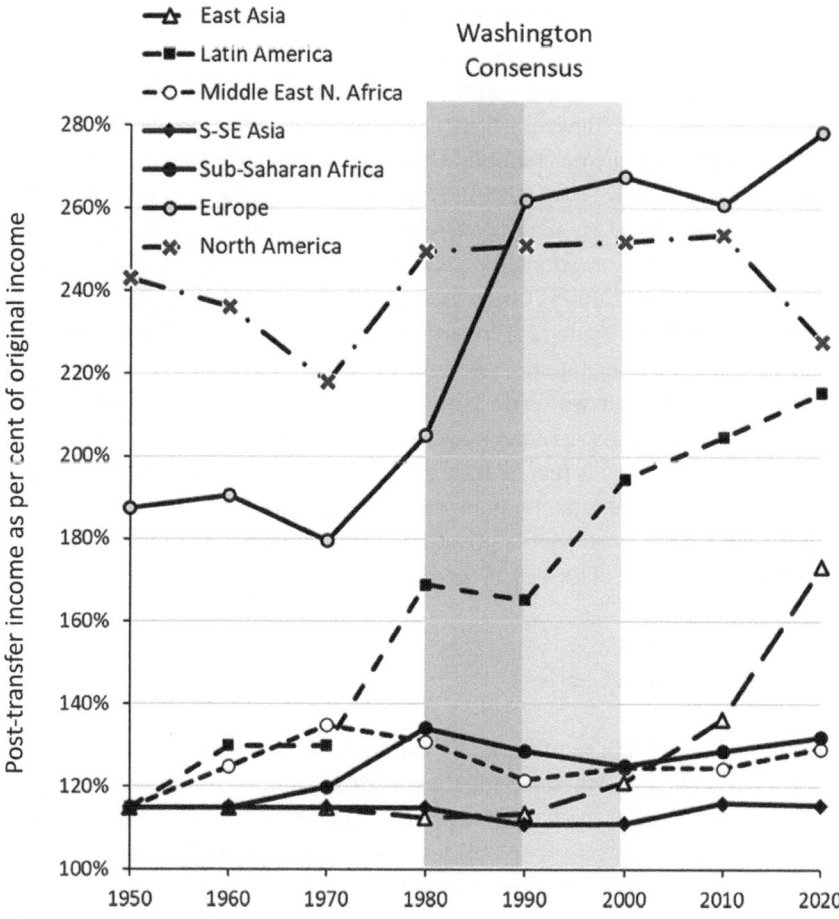

Figure 6.3 Income transfers, 1950–2020
Source: World Income Database.

There was no corresponding reduction in redistribution in North America during the same period, albeit little expansion. In Europe, by way of contrast, the 1980s witnessed a marked increase in social protection reflecting aspirations for a partial upward harmonization of welfare policies. Thereafter, however, with the expansion of Europe eastwards and neoliberal arguments articulated by Britain, the European Bank for Reconstruction and Development, the accession states and the OECD, welfare retrenchment became a dominant theme during the 1990s and 2000s (Lødemel & Moreira 2014).

The neoliberal framework that shapes the global economic order most benefits high-income countries and the United States in particular. The order – comprising an economic centre located in North America and Europe and a periphery – is largely fixed; only nine economies classified as low- or middle-income in 1970 had become high-income by 2010, and seven of those doing so were small, European and had already achieved upper-middle-income status by 1970. The exceptions were South Korea and Taiwan, which, like Japan in an earlier era, both benefited enormously from US financial support to contain the threat to the economic order posed by communism (Wade 2018). Ironically, in pursuing a developmentalist rather than a neoliberal agenda with state-directed investment and strategic tariffs, South Korea and Taiwan adopted policies that were analogous to those pursued very successfully by mainland China following the partial opening of its economy in the 1980s. Indeed, Wade (2017b) argues persuasively that, beneath neoliberal rhetoric, the US has long pursued developmentalist policies that were first focused on the military and then, within the past three decades, expanded to cover directed federal investment across a broad range of new technologies. Where the US perhaps differs from China is that its state investments in research and development are not set in a venture capital framework that enables the state to benefit directly from its investment. Instead, the private sector takes large profits while the state carries most, if not all, of the risk of innovation.

6.1.3 Corporate beneficiaries

Elsewhere, Wade (2020) identifies global corporate power as being the main beneficiary of the neoliberal orthodoxy and the controlling influence on macroeconomic policy. It gains from "as open a global playing field for profit maximization as possible; and want[s] to shape state policies to privilege their profit making" (Wade 2020: 346). It is aided by an international monetary system based on the US dollar as the principal international currency and by many procedural details, such as the fact that many bilateral agreements signed by developing countries allow foreign corporations to sue host governments for actions that threaten their expected future profits. Consequently, the wealth extracted from developing countries by Western businesses is worth far more than the development assistance that they receive, which often is itself formally or informally tied to trade. Between 1970 and 2012, for example, capital income flowing out of African countries exceeded the international aid received by a factor of three (Chancel *et al.* 2021).

Wade (2020: 347) concludes that governments, North and South, are captive to business interests:

> The business community in the West, with its enormous resources, dominates the public debate about world economic order. It commissions studies, endows think tanks and university chairs, and broadcasts appropriate findings ("political" science) with fanfare.

The main political parties depend on the business community for finance, not on members, and present what is good for business as what is good for the nation – centre-left parties almost as much as those of the right.

Recent research has further emphasized how closely the interests of business and government have become intertwined. Mizuno *et al.* (2020) analysed the ownership holdings in 49 million companies in 2016 distinguishing between direct and indirect power and influence (Table 6.1). Direct power derives from direct ownership. Network power is based on equity ownership and the potential to defragment dispersed power through proxy voting. Network control reflects the fact that intermediaries can exert a degree of influence, while the potential for control through network share ownership lies solely in the ability to divest shares and is constrained by performance of the financial markets. While financial institutions and energy companies dominate in terms of direct power, certain governments can exert network power and a degree of influence through share ownership.

Table 6.1 Global corporate control in 2016: rank order on indices of power

Shareholders	Country	Direct ownership	Network power	Network control	Network share-ownership
BlackRock Inc	US	1	31340		
Vanguard Group Inc	US	2	360167		
SASAC	China	3	-	8	
Fujitsu Ltd.	Japan	4	-	5	
State Street Corp.	US	5	3297262		
Royal Dutch Shell PLC	The Netherlands	6	-	2	
Capital Group Co Inc	US	7	3		
China National Petroleum Corporation	China	8	-		
China Petrochemical Co., Ltd.	China	9	-		
Fidelity Management and Research LLC	US	10	4262527		
Bidvest Group Ltd	South Africa	11	-	9	
Walton Family	US	12	14	4	
Government of Norway	Norway	13	2		2

(continued)

Table 6.1 *(Cont.)*

Shareholders	Country	Direct ownership	Network power	Network control	Network share-ownership
Exxon Mobil Corp	US	14	30	12	
Government of Saudi Arabia	Saudi Arabia	15	28	14	
JPMorgan Chase & Co	US	16	1989990		
China Petroleum & Chemical Corp	China	17	-		
ENGIE	France	18	35	20	
Toyota Motor Corporation	Japan	19	-	13	
Allianz SE	Germany	20	23		
Government of China	China	272	1	1	1
Wellington Management Group LLP	US	33	4		4
Government of South Africa	South Africa	627	5		9
Vanguard Index Funds	US	432469	6		5
Sun Life Financial Inc.	Canada	50	7		
Government of the Russian Federation	Russia	84	8	3	13
Johnson Family	US	10717	9		3
Sumitomo Mitsui Trust Holdings, Inc	Japan	96	10		
Mitsubishi UFJ Financial Group Inc	Japan	88	11		
HSBC Custody Nominees (Australia) Ltd	Australia	89	12		
Vanguard Bond Index Funds	UK	666167	13		11
Familien Porsche/ Piech	Germany	2049428	15	7	
Dimensional Fund Advisors LP	Germany	26	16		
Government of France	France	40	17	17	16
Government of South Korea	South Korea	62	18		12
Government of Singapore	Singapore	498	19		15

Table 6.1 *(Cont.)*

Shareholders	Country	Direct ownership	Network power	Network control	Network share-ownership
TIAA Board of Overseers	US	598	20		14
BP PLC	UK			6	
Vitol Holding II SA	Luxembourg		29	10	
Wesfarmers Ltd	Australia		-	11	
Glencore PLC	Switzerland		-	15	
Daimler AG	Germany		-	16	
Berkshire Hathaway Inc	US		751045	18	
E.ON SE	Germany		34	19	
Everwin Company Limited	??		6319		6
Japan Trustee Services Bank Ltd	Japan	22			7
Mr. David Booth	US		11832429		8
Master Trust Bank of Japan Ltd	Japan		25		10
Government of Qatar	Qatar		37		17
BNP Paribas	France		33		18
Capital World Investors	US		31		19
Geode Holdings Trust	US	11832460			20

Source: Adapted from Mizuno *et al.* (2020).

In 2016, 42 companies were listed among the top 20 on one or more of the four criteria of economic power. Fourteen were American, ten European, six Japanese, two Australian and one was Canadian. The lack of representation of low-income countries is to be expected but also emphasizes their vulnerability – and that of most of the world's poorest populations – in the global market. The pre-eminence of the rich-world companies is only counterbalanced by one South African company, SASAC, China's state asset holding agency, and three Chinese state-owned petroleum companies. Of the eight governments appearing in the list, three – including the Norwegian government – are petroleum states, while the governments of Russia, Singapore and South Korea, like that of China, have all operated outside the neoliberal economic model.

The pattern of economic ownership and influence captured in Table 6.1, which ensures that business interests will always trump those of people in poverty everywhere, also hints at the geopolitical cleavages that impede progress towards eradicating poverty. American and European power is represented in the list by commerce, that of the developmentalist and petroleum states by their governments. President Trump made public longstanding elements in US policy when calling the European Union "America's 'biggest foe'" and declaring a trade war on China (Roth *et al.* 2018). Although the European Union has been pushed into adopting some neoliberal policies, it does not share American values but instead seeks, in the European Social Model and much else, to balance the interests of governments, employers, employees and civic society (Bertin *et al.* 2021). More immediately, Europe, like China, is seen as an economic competitor to the US, albeit not one that is first thought of as being an ideological rival.

Clearly, however, the economic success of China has unsettled America, not least because it demonstrates that the neoliberal model is not without alternatives. Furthermore, its ownership of global assets means that, theoretically at least, China can disrupt the smooth running of the economic order that has served American geopolitical interests. Indeed, some argue that China's growth was inadvertently the cause of the 2008 financial crisis that temporarily made neoliberalism look vulnerable; America and the American public succumbed to the temptation to live beyond their means on cheap credit as global interest rates were held down by high savings rates in China (Mees 2012).

The crisis was overcome by a rare example of international collaboration and Keynesian-like demand management policies (Wade 2020; Helleiner 2014). However, with neoliberalism rescued and the anarchy of international competition restored, the system will – without proactive intervention – continue to deliver "development for the few and under-development [and poverty] for the many" (Frank 1967; Phillips 2020: 382). SDG17 has yet to deliver the partnership required for proactive intervention.

6.2 Global partnership and intergovernmental action

As shown, while the origins of global poverty may lie in the unequal geographic distribution of marketable resources and the lasting effect of colonial exploitation, the concentration of corporate ownership allows poverty to be reproduced on a daily basis by a global economic system that favours rich countries and their corporate interests (see also Chapter 7). Therefore, the challenge in eradicating poverty, short of nihilistic revolution, is to disrupt this system without destroying it. This would still be, to borrow the words of the Agenda 2030 Declaration, "supremely ambitious and transformational". It means, first, engineering a less unequal primary distribution of income and, second, ensuring a redistribution that substantially lessens, if not removes, remaining inequalities.

Reform requires much more than increasing the level of development assistance since poverty is continuously being produced in all countries as a by-product of the economic world order. Moreover, the post-colonial world in which rich countries in the Global North provided charitable aid to countries in the Global South has been superseded by a more complex globalized political economy. Once-poor countries are wealthy enough in be investing and supporting others in South–South transactions, while some commercial enterprises have more resources than national governments.

Given this new context, the term "global public investment" is gaining currency with a team of self-appointed experts currently working diligently to give it substantive meaning (Glennie 2021; EWG 2022). Aspirational at present, the underlying argument is that international aid should be seen not as charity but as "a public investment in our common global good, the price of a better world" with a focus, less on poverty relief, and more on a global convergence of living standards (Glennie 2021: 4). It follows that, like national public expenditure, the investment is continuous, not destined to end or to be replaced by other sources when targets are reached. It implies a global partnership with public investments at global, regional and national levels. Moreover, the scale and continuity of investment required means that it must be public – government organized – and be funded as a global partnership with countries probably contributing according to their ability. The European Regional Development Fund (ERDF), which aims to correct economic imbalances between European regions, might serve as a regional model.

Carrying forward the notion of global political investment but focused on SDG1, a useful model is provided by the well-developed national welfare state (Figure 6.4). National economies are variously managed, and markets regulated, to maximize incomes. Thereafter, excessive inequalities in market incomes are countered by progressive taxation that simultaneously raises revenue to support the incomes of those who are disadvantaged with respect to the labour market. By analogy, world trade should be regulated to maximize global incomes, global taxes raised and used to boost incomes in poorer countries and to reduce global inequalities. The role of the national state remains central, but their actions are supported by the global partnership.

Implementation of this model first requires reform of trade regulation and measures to expand the fiscal space available to governments for strategic investment and to respond meaningfully to the needs of their populations. This should enable individuals and nations to be more sustainably productive, thereby boosting incomes and useable assets. Second, it is necessary to reduce the global inequalities that serve to inhibit productivity and perpetuate the persistence of poverty. Measures that have been proposed include various forms of progressive global taxation that simultaneously reduce inequality and release funds for social investment and the supplementation of intergovernmental social transfers.

Figure 6.4 A welfare state model of global partnership

6.2.1 Instigating trade reform

Trade in 2017 contributed 48 per cent to the GDP of developing countries compared to 34 per cent in 1990 (Engel *et al.* 2021). However, the trade stimulated by globalization and fostered by the neoliberal agenda benefits some, disproportionately residing in the Global North, at the expense of the many, mostly living in the South. This distribution must be corrected if poverty is to be eradicated.

The ways in which trade impacts on inequality and poverty are context-specific, differing even from firm to firm (Pavcnik 2017: 65; Irwin 2019). The losses tend to be concentrated on sectors exposed to overseas competition, while the benefits will be more diffuse (Engel *et al.* 2021). Moreover, the scarring effects of opening an economy can be long-lived because those persons negatively affected cannot easily move between economic sectors or cross administrative and regional boundaries to secure new employment. Children taken out of school when parents lose their livelihoods may extend the transition costs across generations (Pavcnik 2017).

This benefit–cost asymmetry, which is pertinent to countries in both the Global North and South, has been linked in the former to the shift in popular opinion against globalization (Rodrik 2020). However, a comparison between the US and Europe is telling in this regard since the more generous social protection available in Europe means that increased inequality arising from, for example, more trade with China, is less pronounced than in the US (Dorn *et al.* 2021). Because social protection is understandably less well developed in the poorest countries, the social divisions opened by increased exposure to world trade can be extremely damaging for these societies.

World Trade Organization (WTO) rules discriminate against developing countries, thereby magnifying the inequities created by neoliberal globalization. Developing countries face peak tariffs across a disproportionate number of exports – illustrated by US tariffs of over 150 per cent on peanuts and sugar. The system of tariff escalation – with higher tariffs imposed on processed goods than on raw materials – serves to prevent exporting countries from developing viable domestic processing industries (Stewart 2021). Moreover, the proportion of trade covered by import restrictive measures has increased by 27 per cent since 2012 (UN 2020c).

Developing countries are also often inequitably affected by the compliance costs of non-trade measures such as health and quality control procedures and certification (de Melo & Nicita 2018). These have increased as formal tariffs have been reduced and apply disproportionately to agricultural produce on which developing countries frequently depend. Additional certification is sometimes demanded on goods simply because they originate in developing countries presumed to lack adequate health controls.

All this is well known and, from 2001 until 2015, a sequence of negotiations was conducted by the WTO – the so-called Doha Agenda – designed to address many of the inequities built into the existing trade system which disadvantage developing countries and perpetuate poverty. SDG Target 17.10 makes clear the importance of these negotiations: "Promote a universal, rules-based, open, non-discriminatory and equitable multilateral trading system under the World Trade Organization, including through the conclusion of negotiations under its Doha Development Agenda." Yet, in the year that the SDGs were agreed, the Doha process was abandoned. More is said about the failure of the Doha Round of negotiations in Chapter 7, but, essentially, rich countries were unprepared to make the concessions necessary to reach agreement (Fry 2021; Nègre 2021).

The World Bank was still stressing the importance of pursing the Doha aspirations in 2020. While not naming countries, it seemed to be speaking directly to the USA:

- Meaningful outcomes may be possible if the major developing country traders engage as equal partners and even leaders instead of seeking special and differential treatment; if the large, advanced countries continue to place their faith in rules-based negotiations instead of resorting to unilateral protection; and if countries together define a negotiating agenda that reflects both development and business priorities.

• Sustaining openness to trade and global value chains (GVCs) requires cooperation beyond trade policy on taxes, regulation, competition policy, and infrastructure.

(World Bank 2020: 219, 238)

With the failure of the global community to address the trade inequities as agreed under the SDGs, the World Bank has subsequently shifted responsibility for protecting populations negatively affected to individual countries (Engel *et al.* 2021). Applied to developing countries, this is tantamount to blaming the victim. It recommends: "adjustment assistance and active labour market programs" "while also maintaining a broad-based unemployment benefit system"; "targeting incentive programs such as tax credits or wage subsidies directly to lagging regions" "combined with broader regional development policies to improve the competitiveness of the local economy"; "boosting productivity by strengthening capabilities, improving managerial and organizational practices, innovation competencies, and worker skills"; "better infrastructure"; "good access to quality seaports and air connectivity"; and creating "a business-friendly environment" (Engel *et al.* 2021: 90, 83, 85, 86, 82).

There is much to commend this list as a second-best to trade reform. However, the implication is that governments in low-income countries are wilfully failing to implement such policies whereas the reality is that they lack the finance to do so. To the extent that these measures are necessary for countries successfully to engage in global trade to help facilitate sustainable growth, they are clear examples of the need for global public investment and the global partnership envisaged for the SDGs. This means substantial financial support by high-income countries. Similar arguments hold with respect to co-funding the generous social protection needed to reduce the social costs of the globalization – as demonstrated by the comparison of Europe and the USA (Dorn *et al.* 2021).

6.2.2 Increasing fiscal space

Trade alone will not make low-income countries rich even with supportive trade rules. Resources are required for necessary investment in human, social and physical capital. The SDGs, like human rights, are inherently indivisible; all goals must be simultaneously addressed (Chapter 4). Additional spending required for education, health, roads, electricity, water and sanitation averages around 4 per cent of GDP in emerging economies and 15 per cent in low-income countries (Benedek *et al.* 2021; Gaspar *et al.* 2019). International action is required as is acknowledged in SDG17.

Sachs *et al.* (2021) propose four mechanisms through which international action could facilitate this necessary expenditure. The first is to enable developing countries to borrow on the same scale and terms as high-income countries: borrowing by advanced economies in 2020 averaged 120 per cent of GDP, compared to 64 per cent for emerging economies, and less than 50 per cent for low-income countries. Many developing countries are denied access to loans because of low credit ratings or deterred from borrowing by high interest rates. Both obstacles could be relieved by the IMF extending Special Drawing Rights based on need rather than, as at present, being fixed in relation to a country's IMF quota which means that most of the facility is directed towards high-income countries. Drawing rights were extended in 2021 in response to the Covid-19 pandemic but, being based on quota shares, only one-third went to developing countries and just US$15 billion out of US$650 billion reached the least developed countries. Central banks could also establish swap-lines which would allow developing countries to receive internationally traded currencies in return for their own currencies. Currently, unable to borrow cheaply, developing countries are being punished for historical defaults that do not reflect their current financial circumstances.

A related strategy is to empower the multilateral development banks to increase their lending to developing countries since banks can borrow at low rates of interest. Banks can also lever complementary lending from the private sector by lowering the latter's operational and default risks. Sachs *et al.* (2021) suggest that this lending should be at least tripled.

A third approach is to implement and scale up the provision contained in SDG Target 17.4, which encourages the global community to use debt relief and debt restructuring to enable developing countries to progress towards the Sustainable Development Goals. Finally, Sachs *et al.* (2021) advocate increasing the tax taken by governments in developing countries: at 15 per cent and 18 per cent of GDP for low-income and emerging economies respectively, this is much lower than the median of 26 per cent of GDP for advanced economies. Clearly taxing people below the poverty threshold is unacceptable and constrains the capacity of low-income countries to raise taxes. Even so, Akanbi *et al.* (2021) suggest that, on average, countries in Africa could reasonably increase their tax take by between 27 and 38 per cent. This, however, would require international support in removing tax havens in which elites currently hide their incomes, in increasing corporate taxes and in finding better ways of counteracting the creative tax accounting of many global companies.

State, and state-directed, investment in infrastructure can simultaneously enhance life quality, foster future development and create employment directly in the short term and indirectly in the long term. Khanna (2022) argues, in the context of the US, that strategic investment in IT, which is more footloose than in earlier investment cycles, might reduce regional inequalities by bringing dignified employment to people at home rather than people needing to migrate to find work. China is making much use of e-commerce to revitalize rural economies and it remains to be seen whether this model is generalizable.

6.2.3 Taxing unfairness

Trade encourages economic growth. It also increases global inequality that, in turn, constrains the beneficial effects of trade in reducing absolute and relative poverty. The rational global response should be, as within national welfare states, to enact post-market income redistribution. Overseas development assistance (ODA), of course, achieves this to a limited scale and, if implemented as intended with national contributions equivalent to 0.7 per cent of GDP, would be sufficient to eradicate poverty in low-income countries (Ortiz *et al.* 2018). As an addition, even as an alternative, several authors have suggested the implementation of global tax systems with hypothecation to address poverty or to fund progress towards meeting all SDGs (Piketty 2014, 2022; Chancel *et al.* 2021).

A global wealth tax has been popularized by Piketty (2014, 2022). It is premised on two aspects of unfairness: first, wealth is typically taxed less than income; and second, asset prices have moved ahead of wages, fuelling growing global inequality. Estimates of the yield of a global wealth tax vary according to the level and progressivity of the tax schedule chosen but indicate that revenue equivalent to between 0.3 and 3.3 per cent of global GDP could be raised without eroding the tax base (Chancel *et al.* 2021; Grimalda *et al.* 2021; Oxfam 2022; see Table 6.2). While being heavily criticized as being unworkable and "leaving everybody worse off" by those on the political right (Cowen 2014; Schuyler 2014), the proposal continues to be rationally discussed and advocated (Advani *et al.* 2021; Brumby 2021; Tippet 2020). Making a wealth tax global would prevent capital flowing to low tax venues but would require international agreement and, subsequently, an ongoing exchange of information between international agencies. The 2021 agreement negotiated by the OECD to impose a minimum corporate tax rate of 15 per cent on large companies demonstrates a willingness of countries to collaborate on fiscal policy when united by a common goal (Laudage & von Haldenwang 2021). The OECD agreement involved 136 countries and was successful because it was seen to be of direct benefit to all nations. Accommodating national self-interest is likely

Table 6.2 Estimates of revenue from global taxes

	Level	Minimum rate	Maximum rate	Yield % of global income*
Global Wealth Tax				
Sachs *et al.* (2021)		2% on wealth over US$1b		0.30
Chancel *et al.* (2021)	Low	1% on wealth US$1m–10m	3.5% on wealth over US$100b	1.60
	High	1% on wealth US$1m–10m	10% on wealth over US$100b	2.10
Oxfam (2022)		2% on US$5–50m	5% on wealth over US$1b	2.65
Grimalda *et al.* (2021)		2% for US$1m–1b	3% on wealth over US$1b	3.30
Financial Transactions Tax				
Pekanov and Schratzenstaller (2019)		0.01% on derivatives transactions	0.1% on trading of stocks/ bonds	0.43
Grimalda *et al.* (2021)		0.1%		7.00
Carbon Tax				
Jacob *et al.* (2016)				1.69
Grimalda *et al.* (2021)				1.90

*GDP except GNI for Chancel *et al.* (2021).

to be essential even if the goal of a global wealth tax is to achieve progressive international redistribution.

A wealth tax could raise substantial sums even in low-income countries. For example, a progressive annual tax schedule of 2 per cent on wealth over US$5 million, 3 per cent on wealth over US$50 million and 5 per cent on wealth over US$1 billion would enable health expenditure in Nigeria to be doubled and that in Kenya to be increased by 36 per cent (Oxfam 2022). However, the extreme concentration of global wealth in rich countries means that the USA and Canada could raise 118 times more in wealth taxes than would be possible from the whole of Sub-Saharan Africa (Chancel *et al.* 2021). A graduated wealth tax, increasing from 1 per cent on wealth between US$1 million and $10 million to 10 per cent for that above US$100 billion, might yield the equivalent of 3.5 per cent of GDP in North America but only 1.3 per cent in Latin America, 1.0 per cent in South and South-East Asia and just 0.4 per cent in Sub-Saharan Africa. The diplomatic challenge and necessity would therefore be to maximize the secondary redistribution of the revenue raised in favour of lower income countries.

A tax on financial transactions (FTT) offers another potential source of global revenue that, while probably less lucrative, might attract fewer opponents given the consensus that the financial sector is relatively under-taxed. The ideal FTT would be global – thereby reducing the scope for avoidance – and comprehensive, covering equities, bonds and derivatives. This would enable the tax rate to be kept low while complementing national schemes that are currently mostly narrow in their coverage. Given a tax rate of 0.1 per cent on the trading of stocks and bonds and 0.01 per cent on the transaction of derivatives, a global FTT might be expected to raise some US$327 billion (or 0.43 per cent of global GDP) after allowing for estimated evasion (Pekanov & Schratzenstaller 2019). The tax would be progressive since those involved in financial transactions tend to be relatively wealthy, but revenues would reflect variations in the relative importance of the financial sector in each economy. Yields might be as high as 4.5 per cent of GDP in Singapore, 3.8 per cent in Hong Kong and 2.9 per cent in the UK. The IMF and European Union have both discussed introducing a FTT but without agreement. The reason appears to be concern about the complexity of reconciling a global scheme with national ones already operative in more than 20 countries (IMF 2010; EC 2011).

A third form of global revenue generation, a carbon tax, is primarily discussed as a means of facilitating the transition to a low-carbon economy since it serves to penalize practices that release carbon into the atmosphere (Pirlot 2021; WEF 2021). However, it has the potential to raise substantial resources, at least initially before companies and countries respond as intended by reducing carbon emissions. Assuming a graduated tax regime ranging from US$25 per metric tonne of carbon dioxide for low-income countries to US$75 for high-income ones, the tax might generate sums equivalent to about US$1.6 trillion (1.9 per cent of global GDP) (WEF 2021; Jacob *et al.* 2016). Most attention has been given to emissions trading systems, but global taxation is both simpler and more efficient in that the rate would not be volatile (as a market determined rate would be [WEF 2021; Nordhaus, 2006]). Since both carbon pricing and taxation can be regressive – within and between countries – compensatory measures would be required such as targeted carbon dividends to low-income families and differential rates for low-income countries. In addition, the revenues generated by a carbon tax would be highest for economies that are heavily dependent on carbon-dirty industries; a tax might generate revenues as high as 2.8 per cent of GDP in South Africa, 1.75 per cent in China, 0.6 per cent in the USA and just 0.4 per cent in Sub-Saharan Africa (WEF 2021).

The three sources of global revenue introduced above could potentially benefit all countries. This avoids the perception of a zero-sum game that sometimes attaches to overseas development aid. However, as demonstrated, each scheme would generate different levels of national revenue that would need to be reallocated on grounds of both fairness and efficiency. This takes international collaboration further than the OECD-sponsored agreement on minimum corporate taxation which included no provision to share the tax yield and served to benefit developed countries much more than developing ones (Laudage & von Haldenwang 2021). Lysandrou (2019; City University 2018: 1) argues that to achieve this post-tax redistribution, there is the need for a global body "vested with the power of authority in the realm of taxation". He envisages that such a body would comprise tax experts nominated by national governments. Approaching the same need to offer more support to low-income countries, albeit from a different perspective, De Schutter and Sepúlveda (2012) propose a global fund for social protection to mobilize resources and foster reliance (De Schutter 2021) (Chapter 9).

6.2.4 Global basic income or something less

Advocates of the model of global public investment view development assistance as inherently paternalistic. Aid is allocated based on discretionary decisions made by donor governments, their executive agencies or the multilateral development institutions through which the finance is channelled. Eligibility for receipt is determined with respect to gross national income as assessed by the World Bank and countries that attain high-income status become ineligible. As such, it smacks of charity and dependency even though the focus on development was deliberately to prevent this (Hynes & Scott 2013). Grimalda *et al.* (2020: 3) additionally argue that intergovernmental institutions "suffer from a perceived lack of legitimacy" because they "embody the interests of rich countries and multinational companies".

There is a strong case, therefore, for rethinking how development assistance is distributed. Indeed, this would be a practical necessity if global taxation were to be pursued since the revenue raised would need to be disbursed. Development assistance should neither be viewed as a gift nor as charity. Rather, it is a necessity to compensate for the inequities generated by global trade that are, in turn, a legacy of an uneven distribution of natural resources and the history of colonialism (Piketty 2014). A global basic income scheme could be an efficient means of achieving a global redistribution.

There is overwhelming evidence that cash benefits paid to individuals are a very effective way of delivering assistance (ILO 2021a; Walker 2005). Much discussed and piloted of late, basic income schemes ensure that all citizens receive a regular income from government irrespective of their labour market status or income level (Crocker 2020; Ortiz *et al.* 2018; Standing 2017). They are simple and cheap to administer, and effective in tackling poverty (van Parijs

& Vanderborght 2017; Stern & Kravitz 2016). Grimalda *et al.* (2020, 2021: 10) suggest introducing a global citizen's or basic income as "a cornerstone for global social citizenship". This "would grant every individual, in each society at a given moment, the material set of resources that is necessary to lead a dignified life". They aspire to global coverage providing a benefit equivalent to US$3.20, the World Bank's poverty line for lower middle-income countries, that they calculate could be funded through the three forms of global taxation discussed above (Figure 6.5). As an interim measure, they suggest a benefit of US$1.90 covering India and all countries poorer than India at an estimated cost of $600 billion.

The Grimalda proposal is largely compatible with the requirements of ILO Recommendation 202 on social protection floors (ILO 2012): the payment is adequate and predictable; socially inclusive; includes informal employment; and the funding could be non-regressive. Basic income schemes have been costed by the ILO based on providing benefits equivalent to national poverty lines but were deemed to be too expensive, partly because poverty thresholds in high-income countries average around US$21/day (Ortiz *et al.* 2018). However, the Grimalda proposal seeks only to guarantee the abolition of absolute poverty with payments supplementing existing provision, the prime intention being to make demonstrable the individual benefits of global citizenship.

While critics of basic income schemes emphasize the possibility of infla-tion, work disincentives, dependency and tax evasion (IMF 2017; Daruich &

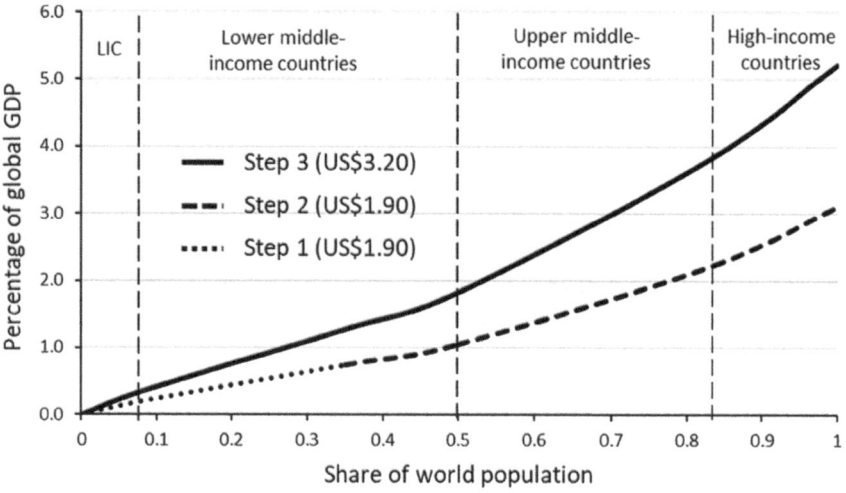

Figure 6.5 Cost of a Global Citizen's Income
Source: Adapted from Grimalda *et al.* (2021).

Fernández 2021), the empirical and experimental evidence suggests that such fears are overstated (Ortiz *et al.* 2018; Kela 2020; Kangas *et al.* 2020). More fundamentally, Standing (2017) and Crocker (2020) view universal basic income as a viable solution to fundamental defects in global capitalism: unemployment and excess production. Investment in labour saving technology is perpetual, driven by the desire to reduce labour costs, boost sales and maximize profit. This temporarily lowers labour demand and, with the advance of robotics and artificial intelligence, may do so permanently. Increased unemployment, growth of the precariat, depressed wages and increased poverty all reduce aggregate demand and result in excess production. A basic income removes poverty, eases labour supply, holds up wages and maintains demand while enhancing freedoms and promoting dignified work based on aptitude and choice.

While the symmetry of the Grimalda proposal is attractive, linking global benefits and taxation to foster a sense global citizenship, the disbursement of global taxation could, of course, be selective, directed disproportionately to developing countries on the basis of need. Governments could then determine how best to spend the additional resources subject to transparent accountability for the use of global resources.

6.3 Conclusion

Although short, this conclusion is fundamental to all that follows. In earlier chapters, it was demonstrated that, while the extent of poverty is both daunting and increasing, global finances are adequate to enable poverty to be eradicated and for SDG1 to be successfully attained. In this chapter, it has been shown how the necessary finances can be marshalled and effectively used to achieve SDG1.

However, this optimistic scenario must be tempered by practical realities. The origins of poverty have been shown to be structural, the product of historical inequalities and exploitation that was largely undertaken by countries in the Global North. Moreover, poverty is daily being reproduced by an economic system that continues to be exploitative, benefiting rich countries and the businesses domiciled in them at the expense of poorer ones.

While the policy mechanisms described for addressing poverty could substantially reduce global suffering, enhance individual rights and enrich moral well-being, they will lessen the competitive advantages of rich countries and the companies that fund their governments. Based on past evidence, therefore, the reforms are likely to be strongly resisted by the most powerful groupings on the planet.

How to overcome such resistance is the focus of subsequent chapters.

CASE STUDY 6 ODA AS NATIONAL SELF INTEREST

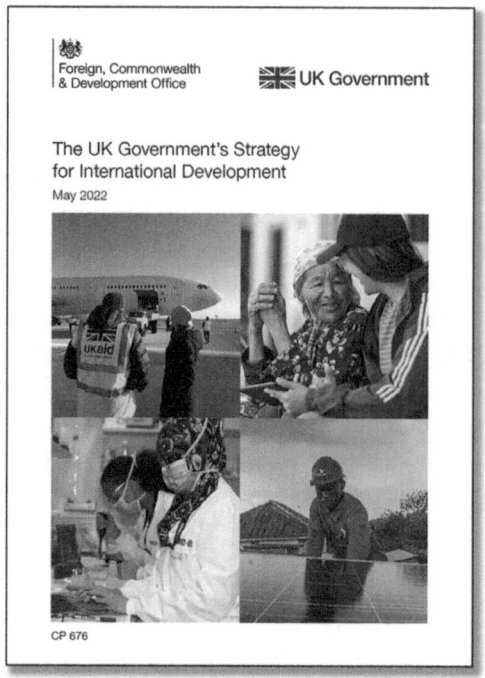

Figure CS6 Britain's 2022 ODA strategy

In May 2022, the UK government presented its strategy for international development. Laudably transparent, the Foreign Secretary explained the purpose of international development: "In an increasingly geopolitical world, we must use development as a key part of our foreign policy" (Landale 2022: n.p.).

The strategy illustrates some of the obstacles to achieving a fairer world and eradicating global poverty. Its critics might assert that it also demonstrates how politicians in powerful countries exploit global poverty for (party) political ends.

In 2021, UK spending on ODA was reduced from 0.7 per cent to 0.5 per cent of GNI, representing a monetary cut of 27 per cent over 2019. Even in 2019, 67.5 per cent of ODA had been bilateral, not channelled through multilateral organizations, and this proportion is planned to rise to 75 per cent by 2025. Against the efficiency gains of multilateral assistance, the strategy emphasizes that bilateral agreements can be used to "focus funding on UK priorities and control exactly how taxpayers' money is used to support these" (FCDO 2022: 22).

These priorities include bringing "more countries into the orbit of free-market economies" which "will help low and middle-income countries become our trade and investment partners of the future" (Landale 2022: n.p.). Additionally, the then Foreign Secretary explained that "Malign actors treat economics and development as a means of control, using patronage, investment and debt as a form of economic coercion and political power. We won't mirror their malign tactics, but we will match them in our resolve to provide an alternative" (Landale 2022: n.p.).

The BBC's diplomatic correspondent, James Landale (2022), suggests that "malign actors" is a reference to China. However, critics might argue that the Foreign Secretary's definition of malign behaviour accurately describes the stated aims of Britain's new ODA strategy.

Further reading

FCDO 2022. *The UK Government's Strategy for International Development*. London: Foreign, Commonwealth & Development Office.
Landale, J. 2022. "Foreign aid: UK cuts funding to UN in change of strategy". *BBC News*, 17 May, www.bbc.co.uk/news/uk-61466163.

7
GLOBAL GOVERNANCE AND ITS LIMITATIONS

While poverty is continuously being generated by the global economic system that simultaneously produces great wealth, the biblical notion that "the poor are always with you" does not need to be true. The world is rich enough to eradicate poverty and the policies introduced in Chapter 6 provide means of doing so.

Even so, the United Nations is correct to stress that the SDGs and eradication of poverty offers the world a "supremely ambitious and transformational vision" (UN 2015a: para. 39). They require national governments to accept "primary responsibility for [their] own economic and social development" but also call for "a global partnership" to "work in a spirit of global solidarity, in particular solidarity with the poorest". Without the proactive support of richer nations, the least economically developed states will not attain SDG1 and eradicate extreme poverty, while some lower middle-income countries will have difficulty halving poverty with the threshold set at poverty US\$3.20/day (Figure 7.1).

While the composition of any global partnership needs to be wide-ranging and to include civil society and representation from labour and employers, the scale of the venture, as explained in Chapter 6, needs to be driven by intergovernmental organizations. Only they have the resources and authority to support national governments and the ability to cajole or even to direct them. Moreover, as nation states were necessarily the sole signatories to 2030 Agenda, the United Nations General Assembly resolution establishing the SDGs in 2015, the required global partnership can only be achieved by national governments working together through existing intergovernmental organizations or ones that are specially created.

Returning to the metaphor of the national welfare state introduced in Chapter 6, there is no international equivalent to central governments with the authority to affect the primary distribution of incomes through market regulation or to influence the secondary distribution by means of taxation and spending. Insofar as the necessity of curbing the inequality generated through the symbiotic relationship between powerful firms, financial institutions and states is recognized, it falls to a host of international organizations to achieve it (Cimadamore 2016).

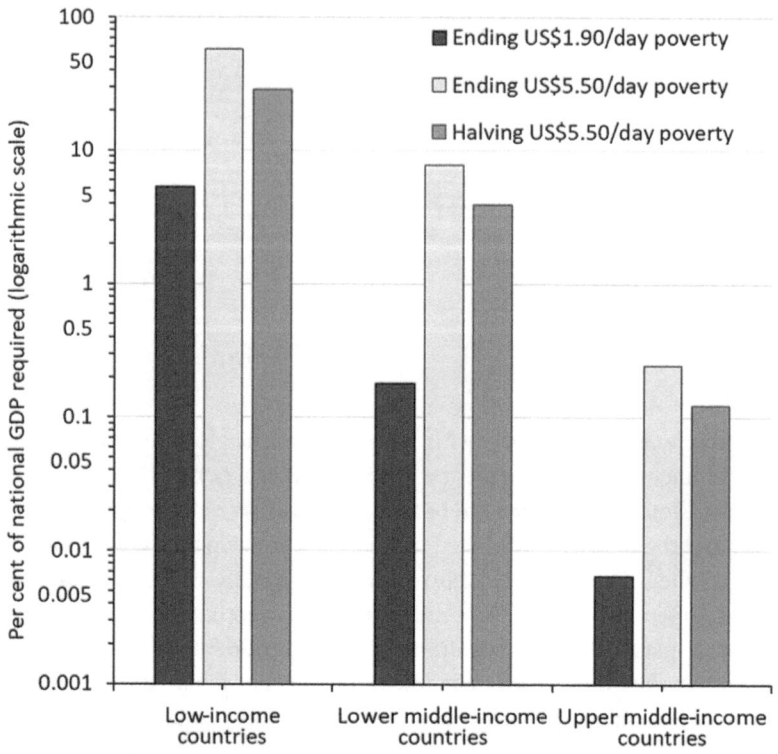

Figure 7.1 National cost of implementing a social protection floor (as a percentage of GDP)
Source: Calculated from World Bank database.

Some 340 officially recognized intergovernmental organizations together represent global governance (Eilstrup-Sangiovanni 2020). While the United Nations is the largest such organization and the custodian of the SDGs, it is not the best placed to arrest and reverse the inequality resulting from unfettered market and international competition that is necessary if global poverty is to be eliminated. Far more important are the World Trade Organization (WTO) that effectively controls access to global markets, and the IMF, World Bank and the OECD that can directly redistribute resources to nation states, applying varying degrees of conditionality to the financial support on offer.

Given that these are the principal intergovernmental organizations that constitute the global partnership now charged with assisting national governments to fulfil the SDGs, it is essential to understand why they have previously failed to eradicate poverty. It will become clear that intergovernmental organizations have no authority beyond that agreed by their member states and that their strategic direction is invariably determined by a cabal of their most powerful members, typically comprising the richest nations. While global development may be a nominal goal, this is realized only to the extent that it is perceived to be in the interests of the already developed world. This is particularly evident in the gulf between the rhetoric of all important SDG17, to "strengthen the means of implementation and revitalize the Global Partnership for Sustainable Development" and its substance.

7.1 Intergovernmental organizations

The WTO, IMF, World Bank and the United Nations represent attempts to curb the chaos that arises from unregulated markets and to bring order to the anarchy that neorealist scholars consider to be the natural state of international relations (Meibauer 2021; Gold & McGlinchey 2017). Their comparative ineffectiveness in reducing poverty is largely because they are controlled by strong nations that gain from anarchy and chaos. The strong employ their brute power rather than needing protection from laws and regulations.

7.1.1 The WTO

In the aftermath of the Second World War and the Great Depression that preceded it, sensitized to the destructive forces of protectionism and trade barriers, it was hoped that peaceful coexistence could result from international collaboration. The original intention was to establish an International Trade Organization within the newly created United Nations. However, although a founding document was signed by 56 nations, US President Truman refused to seek Congressional approval, fearing that American influence would be too limited. Instead, the United States established the General Agreement on Tariffs and Trade (GATT) with seven other signatories, and this subsequently became the de facto international trade organization. By 1986, GATT had 123 members at which point a new round of negotiations commenced which were to lay the foundations for the WTO, launched in 1995.

The ostensible goal of the WTO is therefore to impose order on unregulated international trade. Trade is an important mechanism by means of which developing countries can grow their economies. However, the benefits of trade are not universal and, just as buyers and sellers in an unregulated street market can lose out to malpractice, so weaker trading nations can suffer if international trade is not well regulated. From the beginning, however, GATT and the WTO have been controlled with geopolitical and business intent by the US and its allies.

The negotiations preceding the formation of the WTO, the so-called Uruguay Round (1986–94), were the first to involve developing countries and were ostensibly to consider their needs especially in relation to textiles and agriculture. An important outcome was the introduction of the "single undertaking" principle, namely that countries should adhere to all aspects of any deal rather than selectively choosing to implement only those that were nationally advantageous. However, the Round took twice the anticipated time to reach agreement and left unresolved a host of issues relating to agriculture and to market access that had long disadvantaged developing countries. Hence, the ill-fated "Doha Development Round" of negotiations was launched at the WTO's Fourth Ministerial Conference in Qatar in November 2001 with 32 additional members including China (joining in 2001) and Russia (in 2012).

When the Doha Development Round was abandoned in 2015 without progress on key issues, it meant that, although 96.7 per cent of world trade is now covered by WTO rules, these continue to favour high-income countries (Chapter 6; Martin & Mercurio 2017). There are conflicting views about the failure of the Doha process, some arguing that it sought to achieve too much and others that it was insufficiently ambitious (Fry 2021; Charlton 2006). However, while there were sometimes disagreements among developing countries during the negotiations, it is generally accepted that the United States and Europe, under pressure from their domestic lobbies, were unprepared to make the concessions necessary to reach agreement (Fry 2021; Nègre 2021).

While nominally promoting free-trade, the developed world has sought to protect its industries by insisting that high-import tariffs be retained on goods produced by lowly paid workers in low-income countries. Faced with high tariffs and to retain competitiveness, low-income countries are forced to further lower labour costs, thereby perpetuating in-work poverty. While international trade can facilitate development, opening a low-income economy carries many risks. Local producers, for example, can be forced out of business by higher quality but cheaper imported goods, while within-country income inequality may be increased as the wage returns to education rise (Olarreaga et al. 2020; Koopman et al. 2020). In fact, most developed countries – including those recently developing such as South Korea and China – initially protected their commerce and industry behind tariff walls, lowering them only when considered wise to do so (Wade 2020).

China joining the WTO has had significant implications for world trade and for the WTO itself. Emerging and developing countries have generally benefited significantly from the growth in China's trade by being able to export increased volumes of primary goods to China, although the direct impact of this on poverty is unclear (Zhou & Latorre 2021). However, countries in East Asia have been deleteriously affected because, while being intermediate suppliers for China, they have been displaced in other markets by Chinese exports. Japan and Europe have lost out to China in some sectors but exported more in others, while the USA – despite declaring a trade war – has been one the countries least affected by China's rise.

As the custodian of trade rules, the WTO has offered a judicial system to resolve trade disputes. However, this has mostly been used by the US and European Union, both offensively and defensively, with China being the target in an eighth of cases. The judicial process has therefore been used to protect the interests of the richest countries in a system that already favours them. Even so, in 2018, the US, having failed to win certain disputes, began refusing to approve new arbiters bringing the judicial system to an end. Bown and Keynes (2020: 816) conclude that this decision was "not based on a reasoned cost-benefit analysis … [but] simply to achieve more US policy space to access trade remedies". In effect, the US reneged on the "single undertaking" principle.

While WTO rules impose some degree of order on global anarchy, the rules are stacked against developing countries with the effect of perpetuating poverty. Where concessions have been made – as, for example, in ending the Multifibre Arrangement that imposed import tariffs solely on developing countries – they have been offset against the retention of other discriminatory practices (Heron 2006). Until rich countries agree to include a multilateral "social clause" in trade agreements that protects labour standards, developing countries will continue to be expected to compete in the global economy based on low labour costs and high poverty rates. However, for the most part, the abortive Doha Round being evidence, the rich world simply refuses to consider relinquishing its privileges.

7.1.2 The International Monetary Fund (IMF) and World Bank

When founded in 1944, at the Bretton Woods Conference, geographical distance mattered greatly and so the IMF and the World Bank were both located close to American political power in Washington DC rather than in New York where the United Nations might seek to represent international interests (McQuillan 2021). The original goal of the IMF was to stabilize currency exchange rates, and to avoid competitive devaluations and extreme balance of payments deficits, by enabling countries to borrow funds when needed. Initially, countries fixed the value of their currencies relative to the US dollar that was, in turn, linked to the value of gold fixed at US$35 per ounce. However, in 1971, US President Nixon unilaterally ended this system by refusing to sell gold at the agreed price. Without the ability to regulate exchange rates, the IMF turned to loaning money to developing countries.

The World Bank similarly did not begin with a focus on economic development but on postwar reconstruction. Whereas history records that the IMF was founded as an Anglo-American institution, not least because of the influence of the economist John Maynard Keynes, the World Bank was a US creation; all 12 presidents have been American citizens proposed by the US government. The US has a de facto veto on changes to the Bank's statutes.

Robert McNamara, who headed the World Bank from April 1968 to June 1981, is credited with refocusing the bank's mission towards poverty and income inequality by permitting loans to be given for health and welfare initiatives. Under the next president, A. W. Clausen, in the context of the Latin American debt crisis and with the US neoliberal Reagan administration, the Bank and the IMF imposed fresh conditionality on loans and developed the policies of structural adjustment (Chapter 2). These effectively forced recipient countries to implement free-market reforms including the privatization of state assets and the reduction of barriers to foreign capital, an agenda that is still recognizable today.

The IMF and World Bank can and do override national sovereignty and, as such, constitute a form of global governance rather than the association which characterizes the United Nations. For IMF loan approval, countries are obliged to submit a letter of intent listing quantitative performance criteria and structural benchmarks that embrace macroeconomic policy reforms. Similarly, to receive World Bank Development Policy Financing, governments need legally to commit to "Prior Actions", that is "policy and institutional actions deemed critical to achieving the objectives" of programmes for which funding is sought (World Bank 2022a). While such conditionality might be viewed as a requirement of probity, it also constrains the policy space open to recipient governments.

Voting rights in the World Bank are weighted according to the shares in the bank that a country owns. The IMF similarly applies a weighting formula comprising measures of GDP, openness of the economy, variability of current receipts and net capital flows, and international reserves. These weighting systems mean that rich countries have more influence than poorer ones and, as a block, can easily outvote developing countries. To illustrate, the USA has a voting quota within the IMF of 17.4 per cent, the source of its veto since most decisions require an 85 per cent majority. Similarly, the G7 countries (with a quota of 43.4 per cent) can outvote all developing and emerging economies (42.4 per cent) (BdF 2022; Truman 2018). High-income countries have a quota of 57.6 per cent compared to just 4 per cent for all low-income countries.

While powerful vis-à-vis countries seeking assistance, the IMF and World Bank are weak in relation to their powerful members. America delayed for six years reforms originally proposed in 2010 to update the IMF voting system to take account of the growing economies of emergent nations and has held out against further reforms since then. The IMF ignored its own rules in 2010 to bail out the Greek economy, in effect, supporting the European countries whose loans to Greece were at risk (Wroughton *et al.* 2015). Toussaint (2020) documents numerous occasions when the World Bank has been co-opted in pursuit of American foreign policy such as denying support to the socialist Allende regime in Chile but supporting Pinochet after the 1973 coup. In 2017, when the World Bank was in crisis mode with the US threatening to reduce its financial commitment, it reputedly succumbed to pressure from China, altering its ranking in the *2018 Doing Business Report* from 85th to 78th. It similarly made changes to the 2020 report seeking to "reward Saudi Arabia for the important role that it played in the Bank community" (Machin *et al.* 2021: 10). Exposed, these irregularities led to resignations, but hint at the intensity of global competition, the importance of the World Bank as a conduit for business finance, and the vulnerability of underfinanced intergovernmental organizations.

If together the IMF and World Bank constitute a form of global financial governance, which they do, it is scarcely democratic or meaningfully accountable to all its members. Day-to-day decisions are left to technocrats, and governments in need of financial support are vulnerable to coercion with little right of appeal. While the *raison d'être* of both organizations might reasonably be to protect weaker economies and their populations, there is no assurance of this or counter to the accusation that the organizations act only when in the interests of richer, more powerful members.

7.1.3 The Organisation for Economic Co-operation and Development (OECD)

The OECD was founded in 1948 as the Organization for European Economic Co-operation (OEEC) to administer the European Recovery Program (or "Marshall Plan") funded by the US and Canada. The Marshall Plan mainly comprised direct appropriations rather than loans (as available from the World Bank), enabling the US to avoid the problem of surplus capacity after the war or embroiling Europe in long-term debt. Originally open to all European countries, the Soviet Union and its satellites chose not to participate, and the Plan rapidly became part of the fabric of the Cold War.

In 1960/61, the OEEC was reconstituted as the OECD with the US and Canada as members. It now has a membership of 38 countries, 26 being European, and a self-described remit to inform, influence and set standards to create better policies for better lives. The direct successor to the OEEC can be found in the Development Assistance Committee which, as explained in Chapter 2, was instrumental in the design of the MDG indicators, many of which were carried forward into the SDGs. Technical and advisory, the OECD has been a major proponent of neoliberalist economics.

The DAC's current mandate is "to contribute to implementation of the 2030 Agenda for Sustainable Development" and "to a future in which no country will depend on aid". While motivated by good intent, the aspiration to rid the world of the need for aid smacks of rich countries handing out charity. It simultaneously serves to stigmatize recipient countries, to downplay the virtues of a global community, and to deny the interconnectivity that makes rich countries rich (Alawattage & Elshihry 2017). It contrasts with the explicit reciprocity of global public investment while interpreting the global partnership advocated for the SDGs as a one-way transaction.

7.1.4 The United Nations and the ILO

If the Bretton Woods organizations and the WTO clearly reflect and perpetuate global inequality in incomes and geopolitical power, the United Nations Charter insists on the sovereign equality of all its members. This, however, is both its main strength and weakness. To preserve national sovereignty, decisions reached in the General Assembly have the status of recommendations rather than international law. Moreover, some nations are more equal than others since the Security Council, comprising five permanent members each having a veto and ten countries elected for periods of two years, can act as well as recommend. Whereas 79 per cent of high-income nations have been elected to the Security Council, this is true for only 60 per cent of low-middle-income countries and for 71 per cent of all others.

The UN Charter established the Economic and Social Council (ECOSOC) with an initial remit that nominally covered all the non-security functions of the United Nations. This might have developed as a necessary counterweight to the Security Council but has never done so. Three factors prevented this transformation: first, a lack of clarity about its role vis-à-vis the working committees of the General Assembly; second, the financial autonomy of the IMF and World Bank; and third, a lack of funding to secure its role in economic development (ECOSOC 2012; Rosenthal 2018). Apart from being the UN's interface with the Bretton Woods organizations, and more generally with civil society, ECOSOC has largely taken forward recommendations from UN Summits and now supports the High-Level Political Forum that reviews progress on the 2030 Agenda. The suggestion of transforming ECOSOC into an Economic Security Council with a decision-taking, rather than a deliberative, remit has repeatedly been resisted (ECOSOC 2012).

Real power, therefore, rests with the Security Council and the five permanent members, victorious allies in the Second World War. However, with the founding of the People's Republic of China (PRC) in 1949, and then the Korean War, the victors quickly became foes amid Western fears of communist expansion, fears heightened within the United States by anti-communist hysteria during the McCarthy era. The Security Council therefore became a place of veto rather than consensus.

UN funding is raised from membership contributions based on national GDP and population size, making the US the principal funder. With decolonization and a growing membership, the US found its influence waning, especially during the 1970s when increasing numbers of non-aligned countries sought to avoid taking sides in the Cold War. It, therefore, began systematically to withhold funding as a form of leverage, a strategy continued under various administrations that has added to the chronic underfunding of the United Nations. Under President Reagan, for example, the US argued that the UN was the propaganda arm of the Soviet Union while President Trump declared that it was an ally of China. While China's financial contribution to the UN has risen with its economic growth, it is still much less than that of the United States; it was, however, up to date in its payments at the end of 2020 (the latest available date) whereas the US was not (UN 2020d).

The International Labour Organization (ILO) was adopted into the United Nations as its first specialized agency in 1946. It had been founded as part of the League of Nations in 1919 as a bulwark against communism. Whereas the UN General Assembly does not have the power to make law, the ILO does. ILO conventions, which establish labour standards, are international treaties that are ratified by member states and, uniquely, are subject to a supervisory system designed to ensure that countries implement the conventions once ratified. The ILO is also the UN's lead agency on social protection. In 2012, the non-binding ILO Recommendation 202 was approved and offers guidance on building comprehensive social security systems and social protection floors to cover "the unprotected, the poor and the most vulnerable, including workers in the informal economy and their families" (ILO 2012). This was incorporated into SDG1.3 and, as noted in Chapter 4, the ILO has sought funding to establish a Flagship Programme to assist developing nations in implementing social protection schemes in accordance with the recommendation.

Since the 1980s, under the neoliberal hegemony, the ILO has been criticized by some for moving towards "soft law" – recommendations – rather than hard law – conventions (Jakovleski et al. 2019; La Hovary 2015; Seekings 2019). However, the ILO has largely avoided capture by the governments of high-income countries. This is because it has a tripartite governance structure comprising states and representatives of workers and employers that has proved robust for over a century. States are held responsible for the implementation of international labour standards and, in the decision-taking Governing Body and the International Labour Conference, have votes equal to employers and workers (2:1:1). However, in working groups, they can be outvoted 2:1 if employers join with workers. Eighteen of the 28 nation states represented on the Governing Body are elected; the others participate as "states of chief industrial importance".

Other UN agencies, including those principally responsible for tacking poverty such as the United Nations Development Programme (UNDP), are much affected by the rivalries between the five permanent members of the Security Council. The UNDP was created in 1966, largely at the insistence of the developed world, by merging two UN development programmes. It initially had no clear mandate other to avoid the duplication that was considered previously to exist. The US, especially, was keen to keep development funding within the auspices of the World Bank since it was fearful that a UN development agenda would be usurped by developing countries (Stokke 2009; Bhouraskar 2013). Strategic considerations similarly shaped the foundation of the United Nations Volunteers (UNV), which the United States wished to model on the US Peace Corps. Initially the idea was opposed by the Soviet Union, worried that young Americans dressed in UN uniforms would be globally spreading Western values (Pastor 1974). Subsequently sponsored by Iran, and drawing support from some developing countries and the UNDP, the US sought to make its funding of the UNV conditional on the appointment of Americans to key roles.

Like many UN agencies, the UNDP has had to occupy the space between national sovereignties. Memories of colonialism inform attitudes of many developing countries, while donors generally seek to retain influence by prioritizing bilateral relationships. Attempts, in the 1980s, to part-fund the UNDP through assessed contributions, partly to compensate for substantial reductions in US funding, were overturned in favour of voluntary contributions. This left the UNDP needing to beg for funding and susceptible to colonization by funders' interests.

The UNDP has created space for multilateralism and some independence with its promotion of the annual *Human Development Report*, the human rights agenda and the MDGs and the SDGs. However, it remains vulnerable to ideological capture. This is illustrated by its attachment to good governance as part of the rehabilitation of the neoliberal agenda and in its commitment to democratic government (UNDP 2010). The latter orientation, which emerged in the 1990s as the Soviet empire disintegrated, is contentious and was never comprehensively discussed (Missoni 2014). It goes beyond the UN Charter, which makes no mention of democracy, carefully remaining neutral with respect to forms of governance. In 2021, the US Biden administration used the "Democracy Summit" aggressively in its war of words with China, inviting Taiwan but not the PRC to attend (Wintour 2021).

While the UNDP, as its website asserted in March 2022, "plays a critical role in helping countries achieve the Sustainable Development Goals", the UN Department for Economic and Social Affairs (DESA) simultaneously claims to be "the home of the Sustainable Development Goals", where "each goal finds its space and where all stakeholders can do their part to leave no one behind". Within the DESA, the Division for Sustainable Development Goals provides the secretariat for the SDGs, while the Office of Intergovernmental Support and Coordination for Sustainable Development supports the work undertaken on sustainable development by the General Assembly, ECOSOC and the High-Level Political Forum (HLPF). Within a remit that spans support, analysis, knowledge management and capacity building, the DESA divisions have sought to foster partnerships with government, civil society, business, foundations and academia in support of implementation of the SDGs. In March 2022, 6,231 organizations were listed on the Partnership Platform of which 1,106 mentioned SDG1 among their goals. A further partnership, the Sustainable Development Solutions Network of knowledge-based institutions, launched under the auspices of the UN Secretary-General in 2012, seeks to "mobilise global scientific and technological expertise to promote practical solutions for sustainable development" (SDSN n.d.).

Without the legal leverage of the WTO or the ILO or the coercive power of financial incentives wielded by the World Bank and IMF, the modus operandi of most UN agencies is that of persuasion based on moral authority, branding and partnership as an expression of multilateralism. Whereas the Bretton Woods organizations can act independently, the United Nations is invariably dependent on the support of other organizations including civil society. Partnership, therefore, is central to the United Nations' mission; essential for getting things done, it also strengthens its legitimacy. The assault on poverty since 2000 has proved to be a successful catalyst for developing supportive partnerships and has given the UN a sustained non-security role and, through the MDGs and SDGs, a global public presence. However, as reported in Chapter 3, while the UN secretariat attempted to steer the content of the SDGs, the goals, targets and indicators were the asymmetrical outcome of negotiations between a small number of more powerful developed countries and larger numbers of less powerful developing ones.

Global governance is, ironically, much weaker than its national equivalent and its legitimacy and accountability are less. Not surprisingly, therefore, its achievements in controlling the primary and secondary distributions of global income are much more limited than would be expected of individual governments managing national economies. Furthermore, although tackling poverty is important in the mission of each intergovernmental organization, other objectives often take precedence, not least because they have greater saliency for the principal funders. Global security, a buoyant economy and seamless world trade all tend to favour poverty reduction but, as explained above, they bring disproportionately greater rewards to the richest countries. While most conceptions of justice include provisions to protect the weak, the agents of global enforcement are controlled by the most powerful countries.

7.2 SDG17: evidence of global partnership?

While out of necessity the United Nations is reliant on building partnerships, the ambition of the SDGs is such that global governance must take the form of a global partnership in which richer countries assist poorer ones. SDG implementation targets, such as Target 1.a concerning the mobilization of resources, speak to this global partnership but SDG17, which aims to "strengthen the means of implementation and revitalize the Global Partnership for Sustainable Development", defines its form and establishes the basis of accountability.

SDG17, therefore, provides a model of global partnership and one specifically focused on the goal of eradicating poverty. It is considered here not as a blueprint of what partnership should be, but as an indication of what global partnership currently is. To the extent that it is flawed, and it most definitely is, it offers an opportunity to understand why international partnership is so difficult to achieve and to consider how a better partnership for attaining SDG1 might be built.

SDG17 has 19 targets – more than for any other goal (Table 7.1). The targets, which embrace finance, technology, capacity-building and trade, arguably establish the foundations and the infrastructure for meeting the SDGs. They additionally address such systemic issues as policy and institutional coherence, multistakeholder partnerships, monitoring and accountability. Given the importance of SDG17, it is understandable that more time was spent developing the associated targets than for any other goal. However, the reality is that much of discussion time was consumed by richer countries resisting the demands of the G77 block and China, which they largely succeeded in doing (Kamau *et al.* 2018).

7.2.1 Negotiations

As described in Chapter 3, the SDGs were developed by the UN Open Working Group (OWG). Some developed countries in the group believed that the SDGs should not reference the means of implementation. Their argument was that

Table 7.1 Goal 17 – Strengthen the means of implementation and revitalize the Global Partnership for Sustainable Development

Targets	Indicators
Finance	
17.1 Strengthen domestic resource mobilization, including through international support to developing countries, to improve domestic capacity for tax and other revenue collection	17.1.1 Total government revenue as a proportion of GDP, by source 17.1.2 Proportion of domestic budget funded by domestic taxes
17.2 Developed countries to implement fully their official development assistance commitments, including the commitment by many developed countries to achieve the target of 0.7 per cent of gross national income for official development assistance (ODA/GNI) to developing countries and 0.15 to 0.20 per cent of ODA/GNI to least developed countries; ODA providers are encouraged to consider setting a target to provide at least 0.20 per cent of ODA/GNI to least developed countries	17.2.1 Net official development assistance, total and to least developed countries, as a proportion of the Organization for Economic Cooperation and Development (OECD) Development Assistance Committee donors' gross national income (GNI)
17.3 Mobilize additional financial resources for developing countries from multiple sources	17.3.1 Foreign direct investment, official development assistance and South–South cooperation as a proportion of gross national income 17.3.2 Volume of remittances (in United States dollars) as a proportion of total GDP
17.4 Assist developing countries in attaining long-term debt sustainability through coordinated policies aimed at fostering debt financing, debt relief and debt restructuring, as appropriate, and address the external debt of highly indebted poor countries to reduce debt distress	17.4.1 Debt service as a proportion of exports of goods and services
17.5 Adopt and implement investment promotion regimes for least developed countries	17.5.1 Number of countries that adopt and implement investment promotion regimes for developing countries, including the least developed countries
Technology	
17.6 Enhance North–South, South–South and triangular regional and international cooperation on and access to science, technology and innovation and enhance knowledge- sharing on mutually agreed terms, including through improved coordination among existing mechanisms, in particular at the United Nations level, and through a global technology facilitation mechanism	17.6.1 Fixed Internet broadband subscriptions per 100 inhabitants, by speed

(*continued*)

Table 7.1 *(Cont.)*

Targets	*Indicators*
17.7 Promote the development, transfer, dissemination and diffusion of environmentally sound technologies to developing countries on favourable terms, including on concessional and preferential terms, as mutually agreed	17.7.1 Total amount of funding for developing countries to promote the development, transfer, dissemination and diffusion of environmentally sound technologies
17.8 Fully operationalize the technology bank and science, technology and innovation capacity-building mechanism for least developed countries by 2017 and enhance the use of enabling technology, in particular information and communications technology	17.8.1 Proportion of individuals using the Internet

Capacity-building

17.9 Enhance international support for implementing effective and targeted capacity-building in developing countries to support national plans to implement all the Sustainable Development Goals, including through North-South, South-South and triangular cooperation	17.9.1 Dollar value of financial and technical assistance (including through North-South, South-South and triangular cooperation) committed to developing countries

Trade

17.10 Promote a universal, rules-based, open, non-discriminatory and equitable multilateral trading system under the World Trade Organization, including through the conclusion of negotiations under its Doha Development Agenda	17.10.1 Worldwide weighted tariff-average
17.11 Significantly increase the exports of developing countries, in particular with a view to doubling the least developed countries' share of global exports by 2020	17.11.1 Developing countries' and least developed countries' share of global exports
17.12 Realize timely implementation of duty-free and quota-free market access on a lasting basis for all least developed countries, consistent with World Trade Organization decisions, including by ensuring that preferential rules of origin applicable to imports from least developed countries are transparent and simple, and contribute to facilitating market access	17.12.1 Weighted average tariffs faced by developing countries, least developed countries and small island developing States

Systemic issues

Policy and institutional coherence

17.13 Enhance global macroeconomic stability, including through policy coordination and policy coherence	17.13.1 Macroeconomic Dashboard
17.14 Enhance policy coherence for sustainable development	17.14.1 Number of countries with mechanisms in place to enhance policy coherence of sustainable development
17.15 Respect each country's policy space and leadership to establish and implement policies for poverty eradication and sustainable development	17.15.1 Extent of use of country-owned results frameworks and planning tools by providers of development cooperation

Table 7.1 *(Cont.)*

Targets	Indicators
Multi-stakeholder partnerships	
17.16 Enhance the Global Partnership for Sustainable Development, complemented by multi-stakeholder partnerships that mobilize and share knowledge, expertise, technology and financial resources, to support the achievement of the Sustainable Development Goals in all countries, in particular developing countries	17.16.1 Number of countries reporting progress in multi-stakeholder development effectiveness monitoring frameworks that support the achievement of the Sustainable Development Goals
17.17 Encourage and promote effective public, public- private and civil society partnerships, building on the experience and resourcing strategies of partnerships	17.17.1 Amount in United States dollars committed to public-private partnerships for infrastructure
Data, monitoring and accountability	
17.18 By 2020, enhance capacity building support to developing countries, including for least developed countries and small island developing States, to increase significantly the availability of high-quality, timely and reliable data disaggregated by income, gender, age, race, ethnicity, migratory status, disability, geographic location and other characteristics relevant in national contexts	17.18.1 Statistical capacity indicator for Sustainable Development Goal monitoring
	17.18.2 Number of countries that have national statistical legislation that complies with the Fundamental Principles of Official Statistics
	17.18.3 Number of countries with a national statistical plan that is fully funded and under implementation, by source of funding
17.19 By 2030, build on existing initiatives to develop measurements of progress on sustainable development that complement gross domestic product, and support statistical capacity-building in developing countries	17.19.1 Dollar value of all resources made available to strengthen statistical capacity in developing countries
	17.19.2 Proportion of countries that (*a*) have conducted at least one population and housing census in the last 10 years; and (*b*) have achieved 100 per cent birth

these should be agreed in other fora including the World Trade Organization and, particularly, the Committee of Experts on Sustainable Development Financing that had been established by the Rio+20 Conference in 2012 and would feed into the 2015 Third International Conference on Financing for Development (FfD) at Addis Ababa. The compromise, essentially a delaying tactic pursued by the chairs of the OWG, was that the implementation targets would be agreed but then finalized in Addis Ababa. The meeting took place in July 2015 just ahead of the final Intergovernmental Negotiations on the Post-2015 Development Agenda. While the chairs of both conferences sought to coordinate their preparatory work, decisions on finance took priority and then had to be accommodated in negotiations over the Post-2015 Development Agenda and the SDGs.

The compromise failed to satisfy many participants from low-income countries, placing the SDGs and the entire 2030 Agenda in jeopardy (Kamau *et al.* 2018). They considered the procedures through which decisions were reached to be divisive; the process harking back to the tradition of closed doors negotiation. Moreover, whereas discussion about the SDGs was coordinated by the United Nations, the FfD negotiations involved the World Bank and the IMF as equal partners. This enabled developed countries to argue that the FfD process had "more gravitas" and that the outcome should be prioritized over that of the Open Working Group on the SDGs. The European Union, for example, insisted that a failure to integrate the conclusions of the FfD negotiations into the 2030 Agenda would undermine the latter's credibility. This was certainly not the view of most members of the G77 and China grouping. Rather, they felt that the two processes should be kept separate and, moreover, that consideration of the means of implementation should extend beyond finance. Beneath this disagreement was the fact that developed countries controlled the FfD process through their alignment with the positions of the World Bank and IMF, whereas developing countries had more say in the Open Working Group.

The Addis Ababa agreement included a "new social compact to provide social protection", a "global infrastructure forum", a "LDC [least developed countries] package to support the poorest countries", a Technology Facilitation Mechanism, "enhanced international tax cooperation" and a degree of gender mainstreaming (FAO 2015: n.p.). What disappointed developing countries was the limited contributions offered by richer countries. The social compact emphasized mobilizing domestic public resources with merely a reference to "strong international support". Likewise, cooperation on taxation was primarily a proposal more often to direct ODA to supporting the domestic taxation capacity of developing countries. Even the commitment to the least developed countries did not involve extra funding from donor countries. Instead, developed countries agreed to divert a proportion of ODA equivalent to 0.2 per cent of national income to the least developed countries while recommitting themselves to the longstanding, but mostly neglected, target of increasing total ODA to 0.7 per cent.

Governments of many developing countries participating in the Intergovernmental Negotiations on the Post-2015 Development Agenda did not want to endorse the outcome of the FfD Addis Ababa conference; by merely "welcoming" it, they could ignore it. The International Trade Union Congress (ITUC 2015: 1) described the text as "empty of ambition ... especially in the areas of international cooperation on tax, financial, trade and systemic issues" and the Addis Ababa Civil Society Forum was equally critical calling the failure to commit new financial resources "deplorable" (AACSF 2015: 2). Despite this opposition, the Addis Ababa agreement was declared to be non-negotiable. In fact, negotiations which continued up to the twelfth hour resulted in a paper compromise: the 2030

Agenda document describes the Addis Ababa Agreement as "an integral part of the 2030 Agenda for Sustainable Development" but the text of the agreement is not annexed as many developed countries had initially wanted (UN 2015a: para. 64).

7.2.2 Imprecise targets

The failure of the Addis Ababa Agreement to respond to the World Bank analysis that funding must increase from "millions to trillions" is evident in the paucity of numerical targets in SDG17 (IISD 2015) (Table 6.1). Only the commitment on ODA funding of 0.7 per cent of gross national income and a doubling of the least developed countries' share of global exports have clear metrics but, of course, the former has been in place since 1970, while the latter says nothing about the quality of exports and is subject to the vagaries of economic trade cycles. With the copious use of words such as "enhance", "assist", "promote" and "facilitate" in the framing of the targets, the world community can claim success in all circumstances other than one marked by deterioration. Equally, therefore, there is little pressure on governments to be proactive.

While begrudging the limited commitments in the Addis Ababa agreement from rich countries, negotiators from developing countries also resisted specific targets on the grounds that they had been unfairly judged under the rubric of the MDGs (Kamau *et al.* 2018; Deacon 2016). There was also a deeper resentment in that, in the era of structural adjustment, support for developing countries had been conditional on their governments implementing policies that they considered to be against their best interests. Indeed, with the externally imposed demand for smaller government, the conditionality had often meant dismantling systems that, in accordance with SDG1.3 on social protection, they were now being encouraged to reinstate. Given this context, Target 17.15 ("Respect each country's policy space and leadership to establish and implement policies for poverty eradication and sustainable development"), which could easily be seen as an impediment to external support, attracted much positive comment among developing countries. One manifestation of this sentiment is evident in the Voluntary National Reviews; governments prioritize their own achievements, thus diverting attention from external contributions and the international cooperation necessary to address SDG1 (Adams 2019).

7.2.3 Finance

The SDG17 targets and indicators dealing with finance reinforce the emphasis on national self-sufficiency. They explicitly refer to domestic resource mobilization and increased remittances but demand no new commitments from rich countries. Instead, private sector involvement is encouraged, which has subsequently been promoted under the rubric that "doing good business is doing good". Two targets additionally endorse multistakeholder partnerships aimed at mobilizing and sharing knowledge, expertise, technology and financial resources.

With rich countries loath to commit further ODA and the United Nations and its agencies grossly underfunded, developing countries need to look to the private sector if they are to fulfil their obligations under the SDGs. However, the practical reality is that low-income countries have participated in fewer international partnerships than other countries, possibly because they are seen to offer fewer business opportunities or to lack the infrastructure necessary to set up partnerships (Blicharska *et al.* 2021). Investment agreements and debt obligations can serve to curtail the fiscal space available to recipient countries, thereby reinforcing the systemic imbalance between national states and international commerce (Martens 2019).

The finance targets subsumed under SDG17 are also characterized by a lack of progressive strategies. Many of the ideas initially proposed by the OWG and the G77, such as an international tax body to regulate tax cooperation and measures on debt and technology transfer, were lost entirely or watered down in the Addis Ababa Agreement. The same was true of the initial proposals on technology transfer. For example, a "Food for Thought" paper presented at a preparatory session for the Addis Ababa meeting in May 2015 and intended to compel developed countries to take the technology facilitation mechanism seriously, included detailed suggestions to facilitate technological exchange (UN 2015e; Kamau *et al.* 2018). However, it was decided to defer decisions on the proposal until the main meeting, when the detail was replaced with generic statements of good intent. When a global minimum income guarantee and a global wealth tax, as proposed in Chapter 6, were discussed during the briefing sessions of the Open Working Group, they were dismissed as being too expensive by representatives from high-income countries.

7.2.4 Trade

The SDG17 targets relating to trade are similarly notable for their lack of specificity. There is no indication of how the targets such as an "open, non-discriminatory and equitable multilateral trading system" or "timely implementation of duty-free and quota-free market access" are to be achieved. There is similarly no analysis as to why the targets had not already been met given that they are self-evidently desirable. Of course, this analysis would have needed to acknowledge the asymmetry of the WTO rules and the fact that developed countries often gain more from trade than developing ones (Xu *et al.* 2020).

Even more telling, however, the trade-related targets were premised on a successful conclusion to the Doha Development negotiations which, of course, never happened. One reading of this is that those developed countries opposed to including implementation in the SDGs succeeded in avoiding real negotiation, replacing commitments with platitudes. Indeed, it is arguable that their true positions were exposed during the Doha negotiations. The USA, for example, prevented agreement on agriculture at the 2017 meeting in Buenos Aires and vetoed any commitment "to work towards more effective implementation and enforcement of WTO rules". It did, however, support a "joint statement" promising "to initiate exploratory work together toward future WTO negotiations on trade-related aspects of electronic commerce" (Bissio 2018). This statement was sought by a commercial grouping including the US market leaders Google, Amazon, Facebook (now Meta) and Apple.

In sum, SDG17, which should underpin SDG1 and all other SDGs with a pledge to proactive global partnership, fails to do so. Moreover, collapse of the Doha negotiations additionally lessens the likelihood that either SDG10, to reduce inequality, or SDG2, to end hunger will be successfully attained. It is difficult not to conclude that narrow national self-interest means that righteous and pretentious words substitute for true commitment.

7.3 Conclusion

The SDGs, therefore, both set the objective of eradicating poverty globally while making it virtually impossible to do so. SDG1 is precise: eradicate extreme poverty; halve its other forms. SDG17 is deliberately imprecise, words masking a lack of commitment by the governments of rich nations to act in the interests of anyone but themselves. Support for proactive partnership and effective global governance is notable for its absence.

Outside the text of the SDGs in *Transforming Our World*, the reluctance of rich countries to act in a cosmopolitan fashion is stated more firmly. The United States, under President Trump, withdrew its support for the *Guiding Principles on Extreme Poverty and Human Rights* when the UN Special Rapporteur criticized its policy of funding "financial windfalls to the very wealthy … partly by reducing welfare benefits for the poor" and that of "punishing and imprisoning the poor" (UN 2018: 4, 18; Pilkington 2018). When reaffirming its commitment to the Guiding Principles under President Biden in 2020, Jason Mack, the US Counsellor for Economic and Social Affairs at the UN, made clear his government's red lines:

[The] 2030 Agenda for Sustainable Development and the Addis Ababa Action Agenda, are non-binding documents that do not create rights or obligations under international law ... Regarding the reaffirmation of the Addis Ababa Action Agenda specifically, we note that much of the trade-related language in the Addis outcome document has been overtaken by events since July 2015; therefore, it is immaterial, and our reaffirmation of the outcome document has no standing for ongoing work and negotiations that involve trade. Finally, we note that the "right to development" ... unlike with human rights, is not recognized as a universal right held and enjoyed by individuals and which every individual may demand from his or her own government ... the "right to development" identified within the text protects states instead of individuals. (Mack 2020: n.p.)

Peter Singer (1972) suggests that governments have a moral duty to act if they could prevent something very bad from happening without needing to sacrifice anything else significant. Given that poverty is so bad that SDG1 insists it be eradicated and, as demonstrated in Chapter 4, rich countries could easily afford to do so, their governments would appear to be acting immorally. Setting aside SDG1, rich governments might argue that, while they should not do harm to others abroad, they are not obliged proactively to do good. Indeed, US Counsellor Mack's statement above makes it clear that the US government does not accept this positive duty even for its own citizens, something that might help to explain its willingness to remove the universal national safety net in 1994, the only country yet to do so (Cebulla *et al.* 2005).

Governments, such as that of the US, might also argue, as individuals sometimes do, that poverty is not of their making but the result of ineptitude, corruption, and poor governance (Walker 2014). In so doing, they are ignoring the appropriation of land, the global slave trade and the history of colonial exploitation that led to the concentration of resources that are currently protected by trade regulations, investment controls and legal property rights (Chadwick 2021). Presenting evidence of this, Pogge (2008) argues that, while governments may have cause to reject the proposition that they have positive duties towards the citizens of other countries, they do have a negative duty to avoid harming them and should be prepared to offer reparations for harms previously inflicted. Moreover, Pogge notes that even the self-inflicted harms that might cause poverty – for example, corruption and self-serving leaders – are frequently condoned and facilitated by the governments and financial institutions of rich countries (Pogge 2005). However, while such arguments may be compelling, they seldom result in behavioural change (Brown 2017).

There are, however, dangers both in taking an overly narrow a view of SDG17 as primarily a mechanism for North–South transfers, and in underestimating the potential of the Covid-19 pandemic as an agent of transformative change. The pandemic, its impact on economic growth and the vaccine nationalism exhibited by most Western governments, provided the backcloth to China's October 2021 proposal for a Global Development Initiative (GDI) to speed up implementation of the UN 2030 Agenda (*Economist* 2022). This prioritizes poverty alleviation, food security, vaccination and development. Other details of the GDI have yet to emerge beyond a pledge of US$3 billion to help low-income countries to recover from the pandemic, additional support for the South–South Cooperation Assistance Fund and the China–UN Peace and Development Fund, and an invitation to submit projects for consideration. It is unclear how the GDI will jigsaw into the administrative structures of the UN and whether the 53 countries registering as Friends of the GDI will cohere around an agenda that, beyond "equal and balanced global development partnership", seeks to "improve the global governance system at a faster pace, increase the representation and voice of emerging markets and developing countries, and build an open world economy" (Wang 2022: n.p.).

The GDI aside, the principal structures of global governance are still those that were established by the victors of the Second World War. To date, these have served primarily as agents of those powerful states that now characterize themselves as liberal democracies committed to international trade. Moreover, as explained in Chapter 6, there is more than a suspicion that intergovernmental regulatory institutions have been captured by the interests of big business and by multinational corporations. International business has become so powerful that it can even limit the ability of national governments to regulate their domestic economies. So, when the United States' government rejected "the trade-related language" of SDG17, it was reflecting the interests of American business that has little concern for poverty (Gilens & Page 2014). Given that American business does not care much about global poverty, American leaders are rarely able to do so.

CASE STUDY 7 ALL THE Gs

The G7, a grouping of seven major advanced economies established in 1973–75, is influential but has no formal role in international governance. Not founded by treaty, nor having a permanent secretariat or headquarters, it is exclusive and excluding. Comprising of Canada, France, Germany, Italy, Japan, the United Kingdom, and the United States, with the EU as a non-enumerated member, it accounted for nearly 50 per cent of global net wealth in 2020, but just 10 per cent

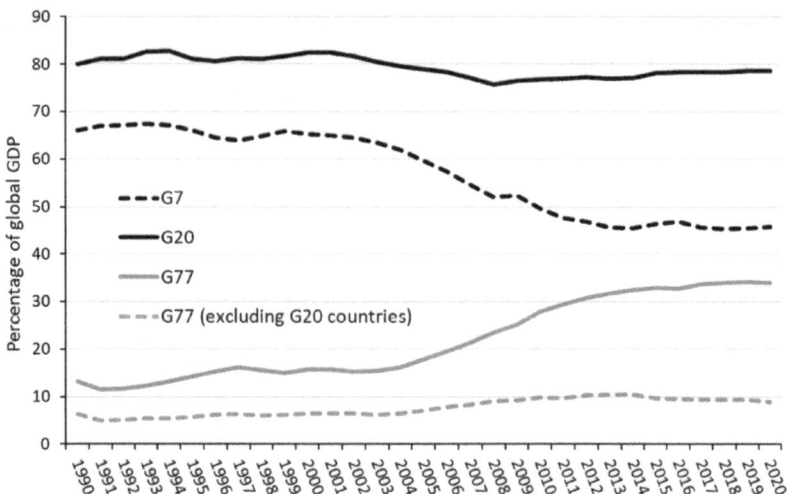

Figure CS7 Relative economic power of the G7, G20 and G77
Source: Calculated from World Bank World Development Indicators.

of the world's population. Under the British presidency in 2021, its membership was self referentially described by the Foreign, Commonwealth & Development Office website as "bound by shared values as open, democratic and outward-looking societies". Summits involving heads of state (the Managing Director of the IMF usually attends) are held annually, and finance ministers usually congregate twice each year.

The G20, a grouping of 19 countries and the EU, materialized from the G7 Summit in Cologne in 1999. At the 2009 summit in Pittsburgh, its leaders declared it to be "the new permanent council for international economic cooperation". Given that 173 member states of the United Nations are excluded, this claim might seem presumptuous. The grouping includes both China and Russia, while Spain attends the annual summit as a permanent guest. It is credited with a quick and effective response to the 2009 global recession but was disrupted by US President Trump's opposing stance on trade tariffs and climate change. President Biden has retained most of the trade tariffs imposed by his predecessor.

The G77, currently embracing 134 countries, was established at the first session of the United Nations Conference on Trade and Development (UNCTAD) in Geneva in 1964. The intention was to promote the collective economic interests of its membership and to strengthen their negotiating capacity within the United Nations system. China, which helps to sponsor the G77 financially, often partners with the G77 but is not formally a member. G77 countries account for an increasing proportion of global GDP but this is largely attributable to the exceptional growth of China and, to a much lesser extent, India.

Additionally, the G10 is a group of affluent countries prepared to support the IMF through the "General Arrangements to Borrow mechanism"; the G15, founded at the Non-Aligned Summit Meeting in Belgrade in 1989 to promote investment, trade, and technology in developing countries, currently comprises 17 countries from Africa, and Asia Latin America; and the G24, originally a chapter of the G77, was established in 1971 to ensure that the interests of developing countries were adequately represented within the Bretton Woods Institutions.

Further reading

IMF 2022. *A Guide to Committees, Groups, and Clubs*. Washington, DC: International Monetary Fund, 11 May. www.imf.org/en/About/Factsheets/A-Guide-to-Committees-Groups-and-Clubs#G15.

McBride, J. & A. Siripurapu 2021. *The Group of Twenty*. Washington, DC: Council on Foreign Relations, 15 November. www.cfr.org/backgrounder/group-twenty.

8

RELYING ON "WE THE PEOPLE"

As explained, achieving SDG1 requires concerted action by national governments and a global partnership that entails the developed world providing financial and other support to less developed countries. However, there is no obligation on national governments to achieve SDG1 nor, as discovered in Chapter 7, much evidence to date that richer countries will actively assist less developed countries in their efforts to eradicate poverty. Aware of this reality, the architects of the SDGs, as noted in Chapter 1, placed their hope in the world's people. The vision was that "*We the people*" would join in a common mission, demanding that governments put an end to all forms of poverty. A lot, therefore, is resting on "we the people".

The dependency on the people reflects both the extreme weakness of global governance and the propensity of intergovernmental organizations, when captured by rich countries, to exacerbate world poverty. As UN Secretary-General António Guterres explained to the General Assembly in January 2022: "The global financial system is morally bankrupt. It favours the rich and punishes the poor."

The United Nations itself, as explained in Chapter 7, although having moral authority as an assembly of nominally equal states, is often riven by divisions and an arena for geopolitical competition with nations vying for the status of "primus inter pares", first among equals. Launching the SDGs, the hope was that "*We the people*" could disrupt this competition, disempower the rich nations that have traditionally shaped policies to further their own interests, and demand policies that benefit the planet's majority.

It is far from clear, however, that the people can be relied upon to demand the eradication of poverty. A simple Google search (28 November 2021), "support for the SDGs", generated some 239 million hits and was headed by paid advertisements by organizations offering support in raising funds or soliciting contributions to support work in relation to the SDGs. Searches have increased over time, which suggests growing interest, but ones relating to specific goals

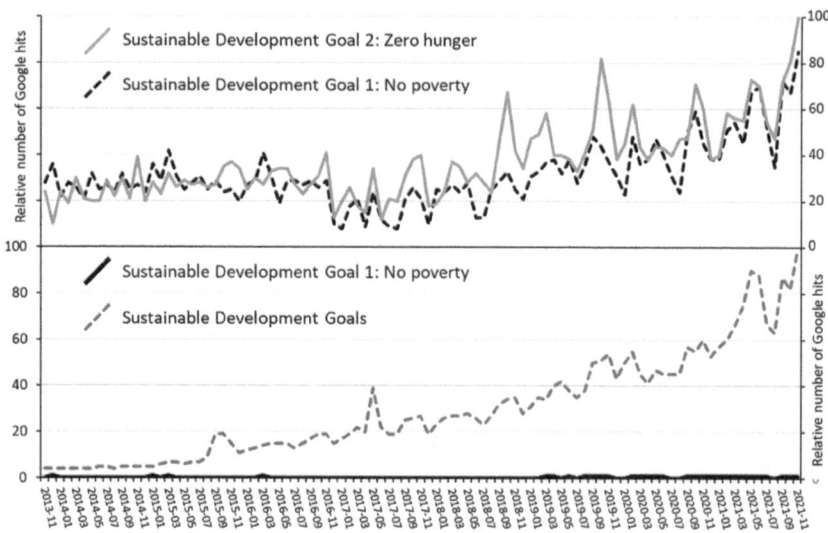

Figure 8.1 Google hits for the topic of "Sustainable Development Goals", November 2013 to November 2021
Source: Google Trends.

were relatively few in number and characterized by high variability, which does not speak to sustained concern (Figure 8.1).

Another way of gauging potential support from "we the people" is to consider charitable contributions to causes embraced by the SDGs and, specifically, by SDG1. Obviously, many factors influence individuals' giving: personality and personal ethics; experience; and structural factors such as religion, local pro-vision and a knowledge of circumstances elsewhere. What is clear, however, is that the proportion of people in developed countries giving money to charitable causes is in steady decline while that in developing countries, although much lower, is increasing only slowly (Figure 8.2).

While charitable contributions to social services, hunger and homelessness benefit people experiencing poverty, there is evidence that poverty, per se, is not attractive to individual donors (Figure 8.3). A common reason for not donating to charity, at least in the United States, is the belief that poverty is unsolvable, and symptomatic of poor motivation and personal failings (TLYCS 2021). Moreover, analysis of the World Values Survey suggests that, while views in the United States might be extreme, they are not unique. The survey poses a question on the causes of poverty that juxtaposes "laziness and lack of will power" against "because society treats them unfairly"; globally, 28 per cent of respondents choose laziness as the cause of poverty, a proportion rising to 50 per cent in

Per cent giving by 10 most generous nations		
	2020	2018
Indonesia	83	78
Myanmar	71	88
Australia	61	71
Thailand	60	
Kosovo	59	
United Kingdom	59	68
Iceland	56	65
Netherlands	56	66
Bahrain	51	
New Zealand	51	68
Norway		65
Ireland		64
Malta		64

Figure 8.2 Charitable giving, 2009–20
Source: Adapted from CAF (2018, 2021).

Australia, 61 per cent in the USA and 72 per cent in Puerto Rico (Barrientos & Neff 2010).

The origin of these attitudes, contradicted by the evidence reviewed earlier on the structural causes of poverty, is complex and linked to personality, ideology and life experience (Xu *et al.* 2022; Walker 2014). Such attitudes reflect, too, the dominant value of the work ethic, necessary to support a capitalist system that so often creates jobs that offer minimal intrinsic satisfaction, and enable people to interpret poverty, not as an injustice, but as the just reward for sloth. Survey evidence also supports the dictum that "charity begins at home"; only about 5 per cent of individuals in the developed world give money to international development and relief (Funraise 2020).

While the United Nations might want to mobilize "we the people", the practical reality is that it is national states that are the principal actors. Therefore, for the people to act collectively to eradicate poverty, they must largely do so through their governments. It might be presumed that people are best able to do this in open democracies that encourage and achieve wide participation (Sen 1981, 1983; de Waal 2000). Equally, there is copious evidence that economic development, and specifically falls in poverty, are precursors to the emergence of democratic principles (Wietzke 2019; Broderstad 2018). No low- or lower-middle-income country is included in the list of full democracies prepared by the Economist Intelligence Unit and only two of the 55 upper-middle-income countries (Costa Rica and Mauritius) make the grade (EIU 2021).

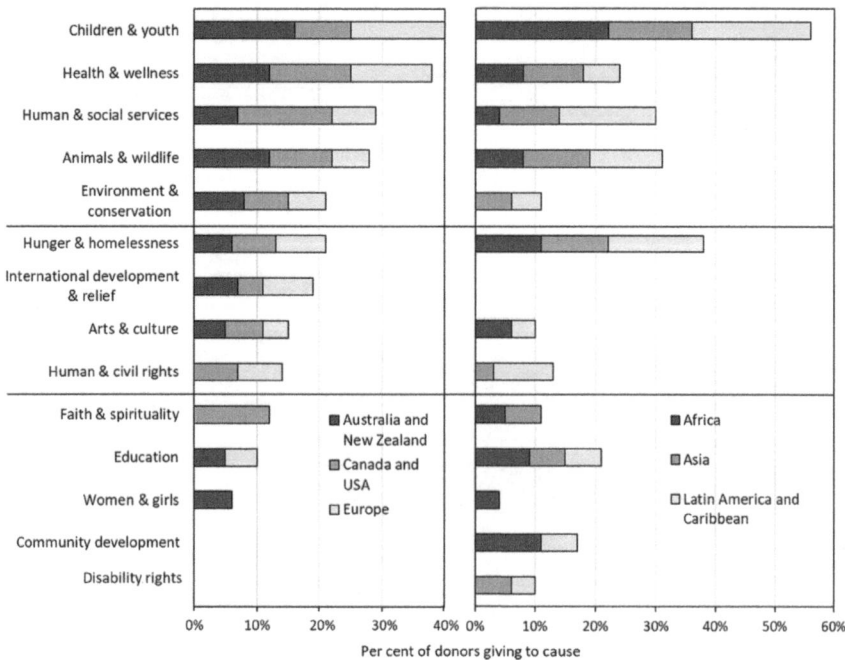

Figure 8.3 Charitable giving, 2020
Source: Adapted from Funraise (2020).

However, the falls in poverty necessary for the emergence of democracy reduce the electoral influence of people experiencing poverty; when poverty rates fall below 50 per cent, those living in poverty become vulnerable to being outvoted by the more prosperous majority. Indeed, the evidence is strong that prosperous elites can capture democratic institutions well before poverty falls below half (Pande 2020). People in poverty are therefore typically reliant on building coalitions with those who are not poor.

By analogy, ending poverty globally requires a coalition of rich and poor nations, "we the nations", supported by "we the people". It is important, therefore, to assess whether "we the people" are likely to support poverty eradication and to consider whether their propensity to do so might be mediated by political systems. Consideration begins with domestic policy before turning to international coalitions.

8.1 Eradicating poverty domestically

The stark fact is that poverty continues to exist in rich countries, many of which are democracies. Therefore, neither democracy nor wealth guarantees an end

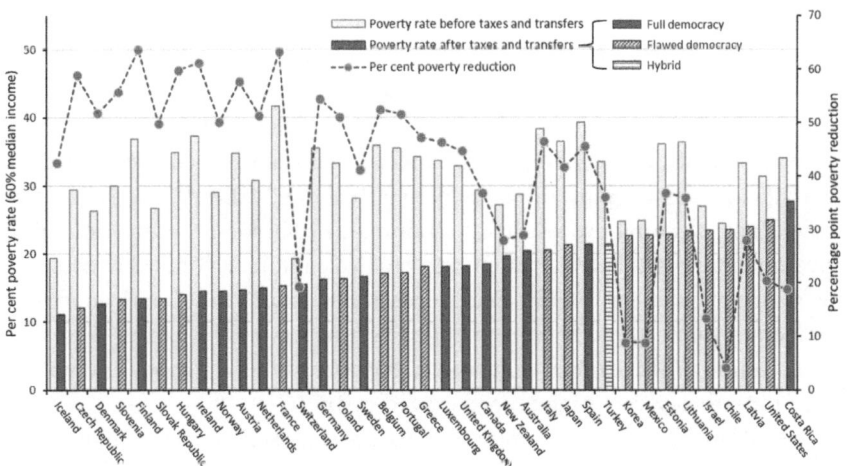

Figure 8.4 Poverty rates and reduction; OECD countries in 2018
Source: OECD database and EIU (2018).

to poverty (Figure 8.4). While it might be argued that this is because poverty measured in relative terms – as it is in many rich countries – is difficult to eradicate, this nevertheless leaves open the question as to why it is still so prevalent. Moreover, there is no aspiration under the rubric of the SDGs to try to eradicate it; governments have merely agreed to halve it and those in Europe have already reneged on that commitment (Chapter 4).

There are three reasons commonly suggested for why democracy should deliver poverty rates lower than other forms of government (Ramos *et al.* 2020). First, people in poverty, enfranchised to vote, constitute a constituency to which politicians must respond (Putman 1993). The second reason rests on median voter theory, which predicts that policies in a democracy are determined by the preferences of the median voter. Given that income is typically distributed unequally, being positively skewed, the median voter's income will be below the mean and so, for reasons of self-interest, they will support progressive redistribution. Third, a free press, as a necessary adjunct to democracy, would be expected to alert governments and public opinion to the individual hardships and social cost of poverty (Wigley & Akkoyunlu-Wigley 2017).

8.1.1 Democracy and poverty in rich countries

Taking the Economist Intelligence Unit (EIU) *Democracy Index* as a guide, all but one of the OECD countries would count as a democracy (Turkey being the exception). However, much depends on what democracy is taken to mean. The

US-based Freedom House organization produces a much-cited index that is the combination of two measures, political freedom (based on ten indicators) and civil liberties (based on 15 indicators). When set against Dahl's (1970) concept of polyarchy, which requires eight dimensions adequately to distinguish between political systems, the Freedom House index is generally considered to be thin. The EIU index is a compromise based on a total of 60 indicators to reflect five dimensions: electoral process and pluralism; civil liberties; the functioning of government; political participation; and political culture. It somewhat counters the strong attachment to individual freedom inherent in the American idea of democracy that considers government to be a necessary evil and is, therefore, better suited to international comparison that accepts the legitimacy of variation while nevertheless requiring a standardized metric.

The EIU index combines composite measures for each of the five dimensions of democracy. Process pluralism seeks to capture free, fair and competitive elections. This is, in turn, dependent on civil liberties that ensure a universal right to vote and the freedoms of speech, expression, assembly and association that are all underpinned by judicial process. The index also assesses the effectiveness of government necessary to deliver the policies voted for, and the existence of a political culture that promotes discussion and engagement and accepts the outcome of elections. Finally, evidence is sought of active and widespread participation to demonstrate that the democracy is in fact working. According to this set of criteria, only a minority of OECD countries counted as fully functioning democracies in 2018 with the United States, Belgium, France, Italy and Japan being counted as "flawed" for a variety of reasons (EIU 2018).

It turns out that differences in the level of poverty observed in OECD countries are not meaningfully correlated with any of the five dimensions of democracy. Nevertheless, when combined and transformed into a simple binary measure of whether a country can be termed a "full democracy" or not, poverty rates in democratic countries are slightly lower than in "flawed" democracies (Figure 8.5). However, poverty rates vary markedly even among fully functioning democracies. In 2018, the poverty rate in Spain (21.7 per cent) was almost twice that in Iceland (11.1 per cent), while that in the USA (25 per cent) – albeit a "flawed democracy" according to the Economist Intelligence Unit – was similarly double that in Demark (12.7 per cent) (Figure 8.4; EIU 2018).

8.1.1a Poverty and politics

Brady (2009: 6; 2019) explains this variation with respect to four elements: "Poverty is lower and equality is more likely to be established where welfare states are generous, Leftist collective political actors are in power, latent coalitions for egalitarianism exert influence, and all of this is institutionalized in the formal political arena."

Welfare states are sets of policies and institutions that help citizens to manage risks to their well-being by providing various benefits in cash or in kind that serve as a form of insurance. Brady links generous state provision to the dominance of left-wing politics finding a strong element of path dependency; that is, policies implemented in one era tend to be retained and to influence the design of later policies. Empirically, he found that coalitions are essential to establish the majority necessary for a sustained attack on poverty. Such coalitions must extend beyond the legislature, embracing people who are not themselves experiencing poverty and, therefore, need to be held together by an ideological commitment to greater equality as well as self-interest. Coalitions can be built around demands for universalistic policies that benefit a majority of the electorate, policies such as education, health provision and retirement pensions. Once created, the socio-political coalitions and the institutions that they instigate become resistant to change, protected by the interest groups that they create.

Many scholars have sought to categorize the various welfare state regimes created by different coalitions, notably Titmuss (1974) and Esping-Andersen (1990) who initially identified three different types. The "social democratic" regime embracing Nordic countries such as Denmark, Finland, Iceland, Norway and Sweden, most closely matches the generous welfare state that Brady characterizes as being based on egalitarian principles with tax-funded universal provision available to all. Conservative regimes, including for example, Austria, France, Germany and Switzerland, frequently trace their origins to the 1880s when, shortly after the first unification of Germany, Bismarck sought to stem the influence of socialist ideas by introducing accident and old-age insurance. Provision, although often universal and nationally cohesive, tends to be differentiated by social and employment status with benefits that, being earnings-related, limit progressive redistribution. A third group of countries, mostly Anglo-Saxon, pursue a market-driven liberal regime that seeks to min-imize the role of the state with minimal, largely selective, provision focused on poverty relief rather than social solidarity.

Prior to the collapse of the Soviet empire in 1991, the countries of the former East Europe typically pursued universalistic welfare regimes, albeit generally offering low-quality provision. Thereafter, some Eastern European countries, fre-quently guided by US advisors, adopted liberal economic policies with low state spending (Fenger 2007; Aidukaite 2009). The Czech Republic, Croatia, Poland, Slovenia, Slovakia and Hungary followed this path. Other formerly communist countries, sometimes referred to as "Central European", have evolved policies similar to those typical of Southern Europe – Greece, Italy, Portugal and Spain (Ferrera 1996). In Lithuania, Latvia, Estonia, Bulgaria and Romania, therefore, rudimentary state services are augmented by voluntary sector provision and access to both is often dependent on clientelism (a reciprocity between provider and recipient that is based on political support and favours) (Lauzadyte-Tutliene *et al.* 2018). Turkey and Israel are sometimes included in the Southern European grouping (Grütjen 2008; Tarshish 2017).

Beyond Europe, there is a long history of welfare provision in many parts of Latin America. Frequently modelled on Bismarckian social security principles, provisions have been much reformed – some might say irrevocably damaged – under the neoliberal agenda promoted as the Washington Consensus (Barrientos 2019; Brearley 2016). In East Asia, the regional economic crisis of the 1990s led to the expansion of income maintenance, modifying earlier systems based on state-encouraged developmentalist policies with, perhaps as a legacy of Confucianism, a strong reliance on the family (Fleckenstein & Lee 2017; Yang 2017).

The logic of Brady's analysis is that the priority given to reducing poverty varies systematically between the different regimes because of distinctive ideologies, political coalitions and priorities. To the extent that policies are successfully implemented, the extent of poverty will vary between different regime types which seems to be the case, as evidenced by Figure 8.5. It should be stressed, however, that the underlying analysis is purely descriptive and not a formal test of Brady's propositions.

While poverty rates in OECD countries reflect differences in national wealth – measured by per capita GDP, this relationship is overshadowed statistically by variations in welfare regime. After taking account of taxation and the provision of benefits, poverty is rank-ordered across the original Esping-Andersen

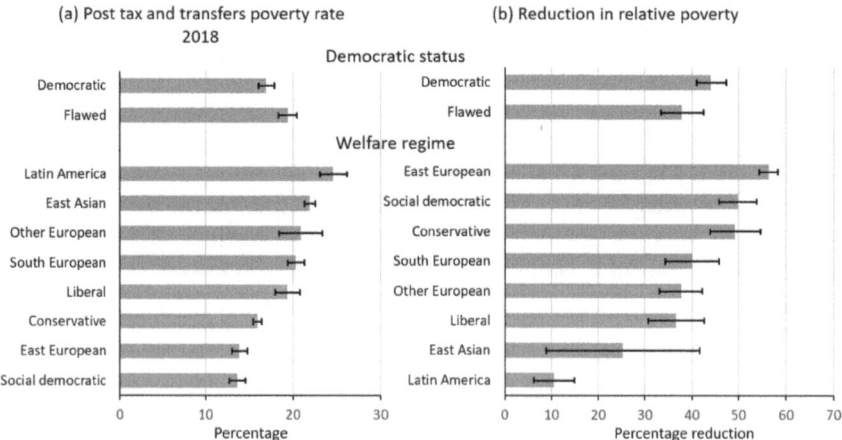

Figure 8.5 Relative poverty and government intervention, 2018
Source: Calculated from OECD database.

regimes, being lowest in social democratic countries and highest in those with liberal regimes. Levels of poverty differ markedly between the two groups of formerly communist countries. In the East European group, poverty is on a par with the relatively low levels achieved by social democratic countries, while poverty rates in the Central European group are much higher and akin to those found in Southern European Countries or in East Asia. Poverty rates are highest in Latin America (averaging 24.6 per cent) although data are only available for three countries – Chile, Costa Rica and Mexico.

Sixty-one per cent of the variation in poverty rates among OECD countries is explicable with reference to regime-type. Social democratic, conservative or Eastern European regimes are all associated with lower poverty while Latin America is notable for correspondingly higher poverty rates. The statistical explanation is increased to 72 per cent by adding the binary measure of democracy; this substitutes for Latin America reflecting the relatively underdeveloped state of democracy – as assessed by the Economic Intelligence Unit – that characterizes the three countries included in the analysis.

There are only minor differences in market income between the different regime types. Moreover, a correlation of –0.76 between the poverty rate and the degree of income redistribution suggests that most of the cross-country differences in poverty rates (57 per cent) are attributable to variations in the degree of income redistribution. Redistributive policies are quite variable even within regime types and especially so among East Asian countries (Figure 8.5). Nevertheless, it is evident that poverty, even when measured relatively, is not a natural occurrence but the outcome of policies shaped by politics. Differences in welfare regimes appear to capture some of the complexity and nuanced processes that Brady describes.

8.1.1b People's views

Having provided evidence consistent with Brady's view that poverty levels in democracies are determined by politics, it becomes important to ascertain if this is because politics reflects the views of "we the people" or vice versa.

Jakobsen (2011), analysing the World Values Survey, claims to have identified a direct influence of welfare regimes on citizens' attitudes towards social expenditure. Electorates in countries with liberal regimes favour low social expenditure and private solutions to risk, those in countries with conservative regimes prioritize social institutions such as the church, family and workplace, while those in social democratic countries seem to be content with existing provision and to demand nothing further. In contrast, Korean respondents typically wish for more assistance and support than the existing very low levels of public expenditure currently deliver, while the citizens of former communist regimes hold very diverse views on welfare. However, given Jakobsen's necessary reliance on a cross-sectional sample, it is difficult to be convinced that the views of his respondents were solely the result of a one-way influence from regime to individual.

Indeed, Roosma *et al.* (2013) report that citizens hold nuanced opinions with respect to different dimensions of welfare provision, while Hills (2002), Taylor-Gooby (1985) and van Oorschot (2006) all demonstrate that citizens' views vary according to the presumed deservedness of the welfare recipients. Wim van Oorschot *et al.* (2017) distil this discriminatory process into a mnemonic, CARIN, differentiating between control, attitude, reciprocity, identity and need, which Jensen (2019: 1106) succinctly restates as: "The most deserving face the least control; the more grateful and compliant, the more deserving. Identity: the closer to us, the more deserving." Gugushvili *et al.* (2021) similarly find in a multinational study that people differentiate between different categories of welfare beneficiary: persons who are elderly, sick or disabled are favoured over single parents and migrants.

This qualified public support for tackling poverty is similarly apparent in Figure 8.6, which shows the proportion of people who, in September 2020, thought that their government should "spend more on income supports (e.g., minimum-income benefits)". While 40 per cent or more people believed that spending should be increased, this proportion fell to 23 per cent when people were required to accept an increase of 2 per cent in their tax or social contributions to cover the cost. Some 43 per cent of the international variation in support for increased spending was explicable in terms of the prevailing poverty rate (the higher the rate, the greater the support), per capita GDP (the wealthier

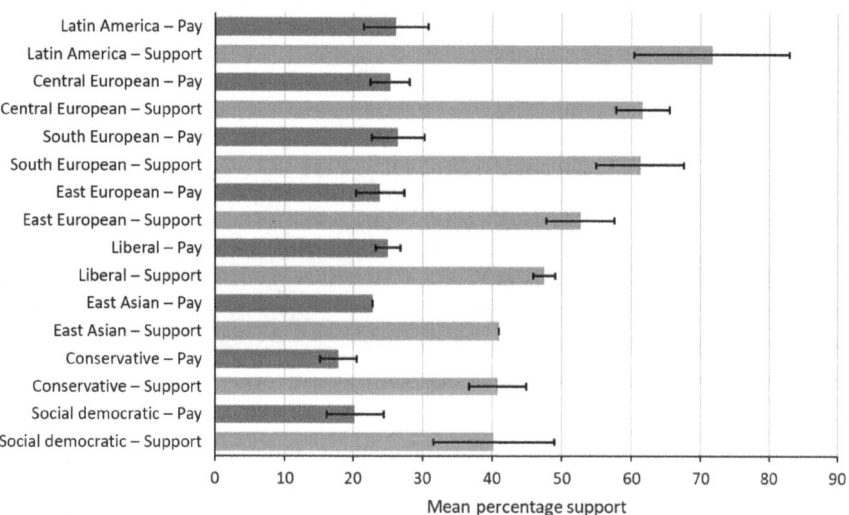

Figure 8.6 Public support for spending on minimum income benefits in 2020
Source: OECD (2021c).

the country, the lower the support) and whether a person lived in East Asia (less support if they did).

The same survey reveals the extent to which support for welfare provisions is driven by individual self-interest and ideological belief. People with above-average incomes were much less likely to support progressive redistribution, despite many of them saying that government should do more to reduce income disparities. Support for progressive reforms was also lower in countries that already had quite progressive systems. It was also low in countries where there was widespread belief that poverty was "due mostly to lack of personal effort" (OECD 2021c). Another study conducted in a similar set of OECD countries reinforces the importance of self-interest in shaping expressed attitudes, concluding that "The average income household is less supportive of greater tax progressivity in countries with pro-poor benefit systems than in countries where programs that insure against middle-class risks make up a relatively larger part of social expenditure" (Berens & Gelepithis 2019: 844). They find similar attitudes among high income households, but small sample sizes restrict confidence in the results.

The evidence overall, therefore, is that self-interest matters a lot in the judgements made by individual voters. Moreover, while publics are concerned by extremely high rates of poverty, once these are thought to have been lowered to "reasonable" levels through growing national propensity and systems of support for the deserving needy, prevailing attitudes may well change. It is possible, therefore, that the process of path dependency, emphasized by Brady, that maintains patterns of provision, no longer truly reflects voter preferences in some countries. Once poverty has been reduced below a certain level, which can vary, the prevailing opinion may well shift towards believing that "enough is enough" or, even, that in future it should be "me first".

8.1.2 Democracy and poverty in developing countries

In 2015, the Economist Intelligence Unit characterized 31 per cent of developing countries as "flawed democracies", 33 per cent as hybrid regimes and 36 per cent as authoritarian. The statistics summarized in Figure 8.7 might be interpreted as prima facie evidence that democracy, albeit flawed, is good for poverty reduction. In 2015, US\$1.90/day poverty rates were much lower in the more democratic states than under either hybrid or authoritarian regimes and the falls in poverty observed after 2000 were much greater. This was despite economic growth rates being highest in authoritarian states.

Of course, the countries are not randomly assigned to their democratic status and the apparent success of the more democratic countries may

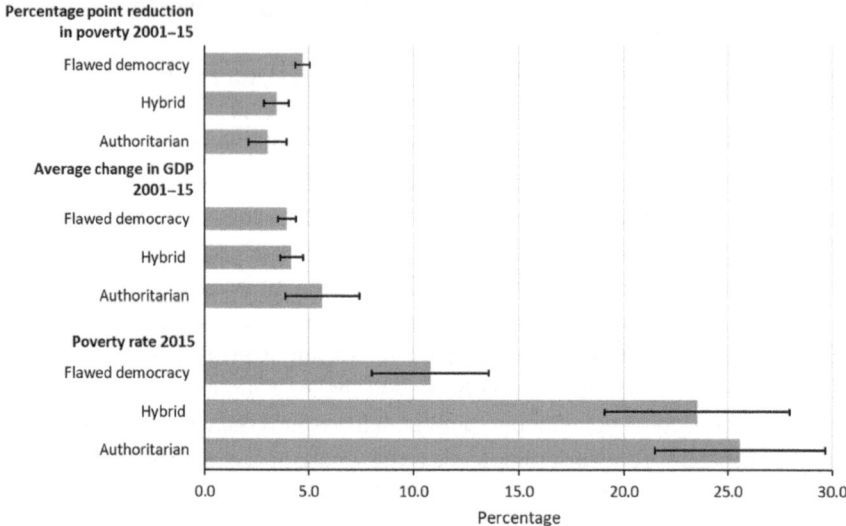

Figure 8.7 Democracy and economic indicators, developing countries
Source: Calculated from the World Bank's *PovcalNet* database and official sources.

reflect predictions from modernization theory that decreases in poverty allow institutions conducive to democracy to emerge (Wietzke 2019; Lipset 1960). Certainly, the empirical evidence supports this thesis. Adding the five dimensions of democracy recognized by the Economist Intelligence Unit did not change the statistical model reported in Chapter 2 that explored factors explaining differential falls in national poverty rates between 2000 and 2015. By forced manipulation of variables, some associations could be found with certain components of the Legatum Prosperity Index that seeks to capture human flourishing but these, investment environment and enterprise conditions, merely reinforce the conclusion that economic growth – not democratic institutions defined by the EIU democracy index – was the major driver of falls in extreme absolute poverty.

A more sophisticated analysis examining 112 countries over a longer period, 1975–2012, similarly found that aspects of democratic governance were much less important in explaining falls in poverty than were economic growth and low income inequality (Doumbia 2019). However, two features of governance did appear to be associated with lower poverty rates; government effectiveness and the rule of law both appeared to have beneficial effects on poverty by increasing the income share of the poorest quintile. Another study, however, this time of 46 new democracies, supported Brady's thesis that social expenditures tend to rise under left-wing governments, but this again was conditional on economic growth (Sirén 2021).

The lack of a discernible impact of democracy per se on reducing poverty might seem surprising given the reasons set out above for why the interests of people in poverty should be better served under a democratic regime. However, other studies have reached similar conclusions (Varshney 2000; de Kadt & Wittels 2019). Ramos *et al.* (2020), for example, were able to study the short- and long-term consequences of 61 transitions to democracy among 175 countries between 1970 and 2009. Taking neonatal, infant and child mortality as indicators of poverty, they found that the average effect of the transition to democracy was close to zero. (The three indicators are all strongly associated with poverty but, unlike income, are typically recorded accurately.) In just over half of the countries, democracy brought no benefits or was associated with an increase in child deaths.

Pande (2020) proposes a series of reasons why democracies appear to be little better than other forms of government in reducing poverty. While middle-income countries may have democratic elections, they may also have weak administrations, limited tax raising ability, clientelist systems and significant corruption. In such circumstances, the interests of people in poverty are easily crowded out and the links between economic and political power remain unbroken. Vote buying can occur, and poor literacy may limit participation and the ability of disadvantaged groups to hold politicians to account.

Varshney, writing from a neoliberal perspective in 2000, blamed the lack of success of democracies in tackling poverty on the pursuit of redistributive policies in the form of cash benefits rather than by stimulating economic growth. Ironically, at the time that he was writing, democracies were growing faster than countries with different systems of government. However, since 2000, the opposite has been true (Narita & Sudo 2021). The mechanisms involved appear to be reduced trade and less capital investment rather than lower employment or reduced productivity. Nevertheless, poor economic growth will certainly make it more difficult for democracies to reduce poverty, not least because necessary redistribution must be taken from the existing resources rather than from enhanced future incomes.

There is, then, little evidence that democracy brings direct benefits to people experiencing poverty and to those at risk of becoming poor. Greater wealth may simultaneously facilitate the emergence of democracy, reduce the incidence of poverty, and increase the possibility of coalitions committed to further reducing poverty. However, there is much evidence that electorates' attitudes towards policy are driven by self-interest and that, once poverty falls below a given level, its salience for the median voter is lost. If this is so at national level, it is pertinent to consider if it is also the case with respect to global poverty reduction.

8.2 Democracies and international aid

It was on 24 October 1970 that the United Nations General Assembly agreed that:

> Each economically advanced country will progressively increase its offi-
> cial development assistance to the developing countries and will exert
> its best efforts to reach a minimum net amount of 0.7 per cent of its
> gross national product at market prices by the middle of the Decade.
>
> (UN 1970: para. 47)

Sweden, Norway, Denmark and the Netherlands had met the target by 1978, Finland achieved it once in 1991 and Luxembourg attained it in 2000 (OECD 2016). The United Kingdom was on target from 2013 until 2020 but then deemed that a cut back to 0.5 per cent was necessary "during the economic hurricane caused by Covid" (Landale 2021). While the 0.7 per cent figure was the result of a complex negotiations, it was not arbitrary but derived from careful analysis of its viability contained in the Pearson Commission, appointed by World Bank in 1968. No other country, except Germany in 2020, has ever lived up to its commitment.

It may not be coincidental that four of the nations that have ever met the 0.7 per cent requirement present as social democratic regimes, the concept of solidarity extending beyond domestic social classes to embrace disadvantaged people globally. Certainly, in 2020, social democratic countries were still devoting a greater proportion of their gross national incomes to development aid than other regime types, with only Iceland lagging the average for all OECD countries (Figure 8.8). On a cursory glance, too, it might appear that more democratic countries give more generously to overseas aid than less democratic ones. However, this merely reflects the statistical reality that richer countries tend to spend proportionately more on development aid than less wealthy ones and are more likely to be full democracies. Taking this into account, a simple descriptive statistical model which explains 65 per cent of the international variation in overseas development aid identifies social democratic and conservative regimes as being more generous than others. Only one dimension of democracy proved to be significant, namely "electoral process and pluralism" which was negatively associated with the level of overseas development assistance.

The failure of governments to fulfil their financial commitments to poorer countries is not limited to ODA. The promises made at the United Nations Climate Change Conference 2009 in Copenhagen, and subsequently in the Paris Agreement in 2015, to help developing countries cope with the costs of climate change have never been met, even under intense global pressure ahead of the Glasgow Climate Pact in November 2021. Likewise, promised funding of

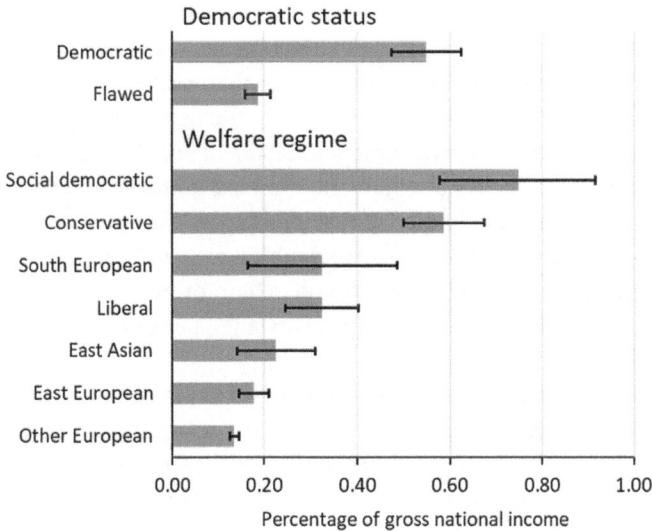

Figure 8.8 Government spending on overseas development assistance, 2020
Source: Calculated from: OECD (2021a).

the COVAX facility to help deliver vaccines against Covid-19 has not yet been forthcoming.

This neglect on the part of rich nations cannot be simply blamed on electorates that believe that charity begins and remains at home. Public opinion is complex and often heterogenous within and between countries. A Eurobarometer study of 27 European Union countries conducted in 2020 while the Covid-19 pandemic was at its height, found that 48 per cent of Europeans were content to retain current levels of spending on overseas development, 41 per cent thought increases were necessary and 7 per cent demanded reductions (EC 2021). However, this high level of support for spending may well reflect the preamble to the question posed: "The EU is a leading humanitarian aid donor worldwide. Every year, the EU spends approximately one to one-and-a-half billion euros on humanitarian aid, which equals around three to four euros per taxpayer in the EU". Respondents could have been confused as to whether "EU" referred to the activities of the European Investment Bank, to the activities of member states, or to both. The self-congratulatory opening sentence might also have influenced responses.

When asked about their emotional response to the level of funding, respondents had to choose one emotion from a short list. Fifty-five per cent chose satisfaction; 17 per cent, pride; 10 per cent, enthusiasm; 7 per cent, disappointment; 3 per cent, anger; and 2 per cent, shame. The inclusion of pride among the list of emotions, and its selection by one in six respondents, hints at the possibility that overseas development assistance is perceived to be a form of charity, provoking the emotion of pride, rather than being viewed as a matter of justice or fairness. On the other hand, framing the question by juxtaposing the fact that EU spending is equivalent to annual tax of just three euros per person against Europe being a "leading humanitarian aid donor worldwide" could be thought to emphasize the limited global effort to address poverty issues. Even so, the proportions wanting cuts rose to double figures in high spending Finland (18 per cent) and Sweden (11 per cent), and in four former communist countries of Central Europe: Estonia (13 per cent), Latvia (12 per cent), Lithuania (10 per cent) and Slovakia (11 per cent).

An earlier study of ten European countries revealed more difference of opinion both within and between countries. Conducted in 2016 by the Pew Research Center, the questions employed made no mention of the scale of spending. Averaged across all the countries, it found 53 per cent of Europeans supporting "increasing aid to developing countries", but also a substantial minority – 41 per cent – opposing any additional expenditure; respondents were not offered the choice of reducing spending. Most people in Greece (69 per cent), Hungary (64 per cent) and the UK (51 per cent) opposed further spending but in Spain, by way of contrast, 85 per cent wanted expenditure increased (Stokes *et al.* 2016).

In the US, according to a survey conducted in 2019, the population is almost evenly split between those wanting to increase "assistance to needy in the world" (35 per cent), those wanting to see it reduced (28 per cent) and those asking to keep it the same (33 per cent) (Doherty *et al.* 2019). The proportion supporting increased expenditure has risen noticeably since 2011, driven by changes in opinion among Democrats and those inclined to support them. By 2019, 49 per cent of Democrats wanted increased spending (up from 29 per cent in 2011) compared with just 15 per cent of Republicans and their supporters. Over the corresponding eight-year period, US spending on ODA had fallen from 0.203 per cent of GNI to 0.154 per cent. It rose slightly to 0.165 in 2020 reflecting a 4.7 per cent increase in spending on aid to multilateral organizations, and a 2.4 per cent fall in GNI due to the Covid-19 pandemic (OECD 2021a).

A study of three European countries and the USA, commissioned by the European Commission in 2018, explored electorates' feelings about global poverty. It found a plurality of people in each country concerned or very concerned about the "levels of poverty in poor countries", ranging from 43 per cent in the USA to 49 per cent in Germany. Equally, however, about a fifth of people were unconcerned about poverty and around a third had no strong feelings one way or another. Pluralities – 46 per cent of Britons and 35 per cent of Germans and

Americans – did not consider their response to government overseas aid as a moral issue and overall, just a third of respondents said that they would feel guilty if they personally "ignored the needs of poor people in poor countries". These somewhat ambivalent attitudes might reflect the fact that most people believed that they individually "could not do anything to make a difference about global poverty".

The electorates' lack of attachment to the idea that international aid is a moral imperative would appear to coincide with the actions of governments. The Overseas Development Institute, a London-based independent thinktank, has, since 2013, compiled a Principled Aid Index based on 15 indicators (Gulrajani & Calleja 2019). While the perfect score would be 30, in 2018 (the most recent year available), the mean score across 30 donor countries was 18.3, 61 per cent of the possible upper limit. Moreover, the score for the poverty related sub-component was just 54 per cent of the maximum.

The scores on the Principled Aid Index reflect the fact that governments use development aid to further their own diplomatic and economic interests (Gulrajani & Calleja 2021; Bindra 2018). It seems that voters, too, may view aid instrumentally. In an experimental study using various scenarios, Australian participants refused to accept that aid should be altruistic, and, in a related experiment, participants were only prepared to countenance any increase in spending after it had been explained that the aid was a matter of enlightened national self-interest (Wood & Hoy 2022). Kiratli (2021) reached similar conclusions from a non-experimental study of 30 European countries. Foreign aid was found to be closely related to the volume of international migration, with public support for aid being conditioned on the premise that it would stem in-migration, a proposition promoted by many European leaders. Similarly, the American public, while overwhelmingly in favour of vaccine nationalism, would be prepared to support vaccinating poor countries provided costs were low, shared or bought economic benefits by vaccines being manufactured in the USA (Nair & Payton 2022).

To summarize, the failure of most rich democracies, full or flawed, to live up to the aspirations of the 1970 United Nations' International Development Strategy becomes more understandable given the lack of popular support for eradicating poverty globally. The issue appears to be below the political radar of most voters. When forced to think about the topic in surveys, the numbers inclined to increase expenditure are more than matched by those against and those content with the status quo. It is likely, however, that few people are aware of the level of spending on overseas development, or the amount needed to bring about meaningful improvements in global living standards. Whether knowledge would change people's response is a moot point, but it appears clear that any attempt to build support for increased spending will need to emphasize self-interest as well as morality.

8.3 Conclusion

It had been hoped that "*We the people*" would enthusiastically join in a common mission, demanding that their governments put an end to all forms of poverty. Having reviewed the evidence, this seems unlikely. The sustained failure by governments, both individually or in concert, to eradicate or reduce global poverty will probably continue to be met by public passivity; voices urging action will be matched by others effectively saying "me first", and both will be muffled by the complacency of the plurality. There is, after all, only qualified support for tackling domestic poverty once it falls below "unacceptable" levels; even while it remains high, only about a quarter of voters in most countries are prepared to forgo personal income so that the problem can be addressed. Global poverty is a minority concern, low on most people's priority list.

In the absence of spontaneous support from "we the people", there is a need for political leadership. Brady (2009) argues that, domestically, this is possible only when leftist governments coexist with active coalitions working within supportive institutions to defend positive gains for those in poverty and to resist demands from others. Social democratic governments may further seek to pursue solidarity with people in poverty in other countries – although evidence reported above suggests that voters may be less inclined to identify with international solidarity than their leaders.

If Brady is right, and the evidence is indeed supportive, the immediate outlook is bleak since this is not the age of social democracy. Governments are still moving to the political right, with nationalism and populism emerging as manifestations of individual selfishness that neoliberal policies have supported if not fostered.

If there is to be hope, it must be for political leaders to argue that what is morally right is also socially beneficial. No one, aestheticism aside, would choose to be poor. Therefore, it is right – and a human right – that those who are poor should be aided out of poverty. Moreover, there are plentiful resources more than sufficient to end poverty globally (Chapters 4 and 6). Despite the supposed benefits of democracy, a national leader who does not need to stand for re-election might find it easier to take the potentially unpopular but moral stance of supporting global redistribution. Indeed, the Chinese leadership presents China as a developing country prepared to assist other developing countries in eradicating poverty. For democratic leaders in high-income countries, it may be necessary to recast the socially beneficial as blatant self-interest. Ending poverty is likely to mean less disease, lower migration and greater global security. It also offers the prospect of more sustainable development, higher productivity and greater wealth more equitably shared.

CASE STUDY 8 VACCINATING AGAINST COVID-19

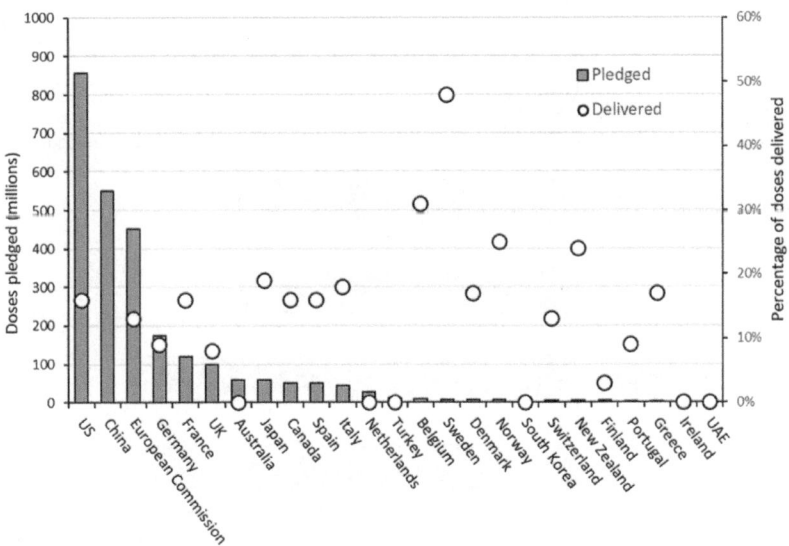

Figure CS8.1 Covid-19 vaccine doses donated to COVAX (29 November 2021)
Source: Adapted from Loft (2021).

The rapid development of vaccines against Covid-19 was a triumph for public–private partnerships, with private companies and universities providing knowhow and national governments supplying resources and taking on the financial risk.

Both morality and science demanded a uniform global roll-out of vaccine as the World Health Organization proposed in August 2020 to reduce the chance of virus mutation. However, as Kennan (1954: 48) long ago observed, "international politics is a practical exercise and not a moral one".

The COVAX facility, a joint venture between the World Health Organization (WHO), the Coalition for Epidemic Preparedness Innovations (CEPI) and Gavi (the Vaccine Alliance) was established to build a global coalition through a multilateral purchasing agreement. However, to attract rich nations, COVAX allowed nations to retain bilateral purchasing agreements. This reduced the collective resources and purchasing power of COVAX, while inadvertently creating competition with individual governments as to which should receive vaccine from manufacturers first. The main countries developing vaccines – the USA, China, and Russia – initially refused to join COVAX, with the USA eventually joining only after China had done so.

Rich countries over-ordered vaccines while under-resourcing COVAX. Canada purchased 5.7 times more vaccine than needed; Australia, the European Union, the UK and the USA did likewise, although to a slightly lesser extent (respectively 4.6, 3.3, 3.2 and 2.8 times too much). Even in June 2022, 18 months after vaccines became available at scale, 84 per cent of people in low-income countries remained unvaccinated.

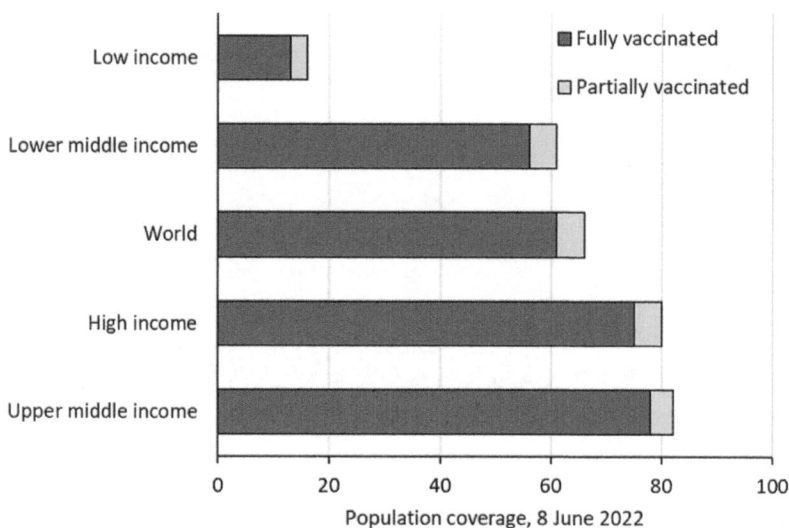

Figure CS8.2 Vaccination rates against Covid-19, 2022
Source: Calculated from https://ourworldindata.org/covid-vaccinations.

Further reading

Kennan, G. 1954. *Realities of American Foreign Policy*. Princeton, NJ: Princeton University Press.

Loft, P. 2021. *COVAX and Global Access to Covid-19 Vaccines*. London: House of Commons Library, 10 December.

9

TOWARDS A MORAL WORLD ORDER

The SDGs are a quest for human progress. They symbolize the call that all recognize a shared humanity, acknowledge human failure and accept responsibility for together building a better world. They are equally products – some would say tools – of global politics and the gulf between the aspiration for a better world and the political reality is enormous. The intention in this chapter is to identify means of bridging this gulf.

In the 2000s, the Millennium Development Goals (MDGs) served to protect the United Nations (UN) when under attack by powerful nation states that view intergovernmental organizations as threats to their sovereignty (Chapter 2). The SDGs continue to give the UN credibility: no politician will be elected on a mandate to increase poverty; hence, it is difficult to criticize the UN for seeking to reduce it.

However, each SDG is a compromise in which the influence of powerful nations is writ large. SDG Targets 1.1 and 1.2 were intended to engage the rich world in obligations that they avoided during the time of the MDGs (Chapters 2 and 3). However, the targets are inherently divisive, referring to different conceptions of poverty: absolute and multidimensional. The former target is internationally prescribed for the developing world and the poverty must be eradicated; in the latter case, the target is nationally determined by developed countries and poverty needs only to be halved (Chapters 1 and 3). While both targets are affordable when set against global wealth, that applying to the poorest countries is considerably more ambitious (Chapters 4 and 5).

Successful fulfilment of the SDGs is also contingent on global politics and especially on the willingness of countries to collaborate and to make sacrifices for the global good. However, as the poorly coordinated response to the Covid-19 pandemic illustrates, political commitments to global solidarity and to multilateralism are typically more rhetorical than real (Chapters 6 and 7). The Covid-19 pandemic worsened the relative position of the least developed countries, further increasing global inequalities and poverty (Chapter 5).

The limited commitment to collective working is further evidenced by the lack of quantifiable targets for SDG17 – the all-important partnership goal – which, as a result, is almost purely aspirational. There is a very real risk, therefore, that the SDGs will prove to be mirages, tantalizingly beyond reach with millions of people unnecessarily condemned to continuing poverty.

Sadly, this is nothing new: "To those who have, more will be given. From those who have little, even that will be taken" (Matthew 25:29). When St Matthew's Gospel was written, poverty was endemic and reduction almost impossible. Now, extreme poverty can be eradicated and other forms of poverty much reduced. However, to achieve this requires political will as well as words, determined political leadership and, most difficult of all, institutional reform to curb national self-interest and the power of international business and finance.

Therefore, the importance of global partnership is first reiterated, before subsequently specifying the institutional reforms required. However, it is accepted that institutional reform is unlikely since it would require fundamental change to the neorealist world order in which powerful nations seek ultimate control. It would also demand reform of the neoliberal economic order that has concentrated great power in the hands of very few influential individuals living mostly in the Global North. Necessarily, therefore, thought is given to the prospect of a new world order in which the hegemony of the United States and its rich allies is challenged. Finally, seeking to salvage SDG1, support is offered to the proposal for a global social protection fund, very small to begin with but with the possibility of expansion. One can only hope that human progress will win over human selfishness.

9.1 SDGs and the importance of global partnership

Attaining SDG1 is beyond the competence of many governments if left to their own devices. Relying purely on global economic growth to eradicate poverty – leaving aside concerns about the sustainability of continuous growth policies – would condemn many more generations to poverty. Modelling suggests that, assuming a global growth rate of 2.35 per cent (as achieved between 1993–2008, before the Great Recession), extreme poverty (defined as per capita income of less than US$1.25/day) would not be eradicated until 2115 (Woodward 2015).

It is for this reason that the partnership goal SDG17 is so important together with the SDG implementation Targets 1.a and 1.b. However, as explained in

Chapters 3 and 7, the refusal of developed countries to agree to measurable targets demonstrates the limits to multilateralism imposed by the persistence of national self-interest. National leaders see it as their first responsibility to ensure the material well-being of their own populations, a commitment strengthened by the imperative to remain in power. Populations tend to prioritize their own needs and those of fellow citizens above those of foreigners (Chapter 8). The designation "We the peoples" used in the UN Charter is a more accurate reflection of global public opinion than "we the people" called upon by the UN to promote the SDGs. International development is a low public priority as, probably, are the SDGs.

The reality, one still underpinned by the hegemony of economic neoliberalism, is that nation states must engineer their own growth under the SDGs and eradicate poverty by engaging openly in the global marketplace. Therefore, the intergovernmental organizations that have the economic power to incentivize and coerce, the IMF and World Bank in particular, continue to interpret their role as being to enforce market-orientated reforms (Chapters 6 and 7). It might be cynical to assert that the rich nations, which largely fund and control these institutions, deliberately pursue policies that disproportionately benefit their own economies and enterprises. But this has hitherto proved to be the outcome, further increasing global economic inequalities (Chapter 6). International development assistance and other support under the MDGs, and now the SDGs, is akin to charitable giving, based on the whims of governmental or philanthropic donors.

A true global partnership necessitates replacing charity with deliberate governance. This could be the model of global public investment discussed in Chapter 6 or some other approach yet to be specified. Regardless of approach, it is important to recognize that this is not just an investment in people directly experiencing poverty, adding to their incomes and capabilities. Rather it is an investment to sustain the globalized market economy that governments generally support, and which has delivered technological advances and benefited millions of people, albeit to date largely those living in the Global North. Inequality and poverty are inevitable by-products of a market economy that cannot be prevented without concerted intervention.

The substance of SDG 17 must be realized with practical and measurable reform involving multinational partnerships in the areas of technological transfer, capacity building, trade reform and development-orientated financing; without this, failure is guaranteed. Borrowing the model of the ideal welfare state, transplanted into the global arena, reveals several strategies for attaining SDG1 (Chapter 6). The development of national policies in low- and middle-income countries could be facilitated by providing access to global finance on terms comparable to those available to rich countries. There is scope for implementing various forms of global taxation, for example on wealth, financial transactions, and carbon. Revenues raised through taxation could then be allocated in proportion to national needs so as to finance the implementation of social protection floors as envisaged in SDG Target 1.3 or, perhaps, to provide a global minimum income.

A global partnership to address the SDGs would benefit the peoples of all countries, both rich and poor (Figure 9.1). SDG Target 1.b, for example, focuses attention on improving policy frameworks. These currently vary markedly even among OECD countries in terms of the coverage of social protection, poverty rates and, as revealed by the Covid-19 pandemic, resilience (Chapters 4 and 5). SDG Target 1.4 concerns equal treatment and human rights and reports by UN special rapporteurs demonstrate the global need for improvement. The governments of the European Union were admonished in 2021 for the gendered nature of poverty and for reducing expenditures on poverty relief and social protection after 2009, even though the International Covenant on Economic, Social and Cultural Rights includes "the obligation to progressively realize human rights and not take retrogressive measures that could hinder that progress" (OHCHR 2021). In 2018, the USA was criticized for "the distinctively American response to poverty" of "punishing

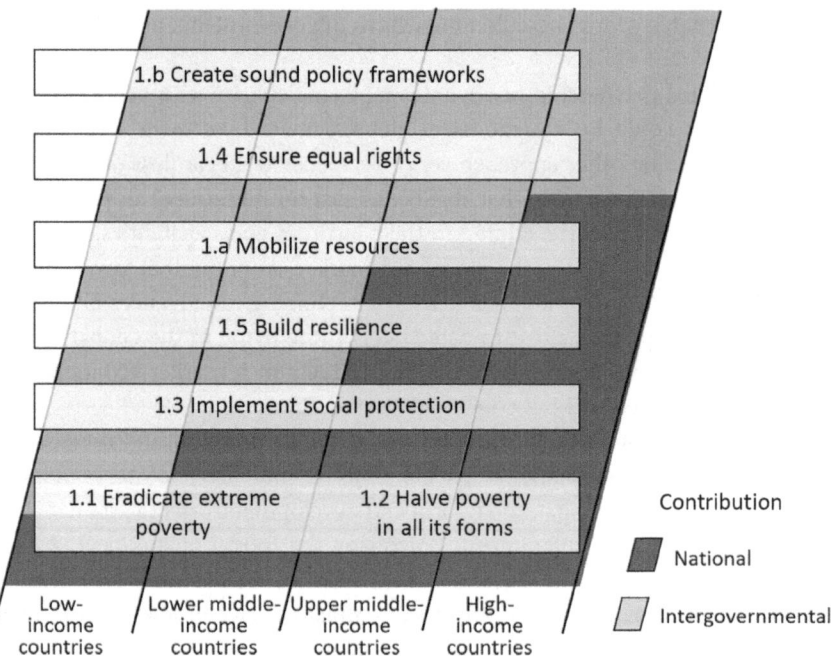

Figure 9.1 SDG1 targets: allocating responsibility

and imprisoning the poor" (HRC 2018: 18), for "shameful statistics" revealing "long-standing structural discrimination on the basis of race" (2018: 14–15) and for its failure to "recognize a right to health care" (2018: 20). China, although praised for reducing poverty, was rebuked for not "giving special attention to gender in its anti-poverty policies" (HRC 2017: 10) while also running the "real risk" that "the root causes of poverty" would "be insufficiently addressed" in the pursuit of official targets (HRC 2017: 9).

While there is much consensus about the need for global partnership and about reforms necessary to enable the SDGs to be met, there is equally agreement that they cannot be realized within the existing system of global governance. It will be recalled from Chapter 8 that the UN Secretary-General, António Guterres, when outlining his priorities for 2022 to the UN General Assembly, opined that: "the global financial system is morally bankrupt. It favours the rich and punishes the poor." He went on to say that: "One of the main functions of the global financial system is to ensure stability, by supporting economies through financial shocks. Yet faced with precisely such a shock – a global pandemic – it has failed the Global South." And that: "All these challenges are, at heart, failures of global governance. From global health to digital technology, many of today's multilateral frameworks are outdated and no longer fit for purpose" (21 January 2022).

In the belief that the SDGs are unattainable given the current structures of international governance, it is imperative to consider the reforms needed and how they might be achieved.

9.2 Pathways to reforming global governance

The United Nations is the nearest the world has to legitimate global governance, while the Bretton Woods organizations provide financial tools necessary to deliver global policies. However, this complementarity between the Bretton Woods organizations and the United Nations, envisaged by at least some the architects of the postwar reforms, has never materialized (Clark & Sohn 1962). Instead, the IMF and World Bank have come to dominate development policy emboldened by belief in the efficacy of economic theory and supported by resources and powers of coercion beyond the control of the United Nations. Often equating development with economic growth, a conception that simultaneously supports the interests of rich countries that principally fund both organizations, they have been able to condition policy change on poor countries while relying on exhortation to persuade others of the merits of their actions (Lopez-Claros *et al.* 2020).

In marked contrast, the United Nations family of organizations is chronically underfunded and has needed to rely on persuasion, seed corn funding and example to propagate the view of development as the manifestation of rights and individual freedoms. With a General Assembly, whose strongest power is that of recommendation, the United Nations has often been paralysed by differences emanating from the powerful Security Council. Such differences are largely geopolitical, manifestations of the anarchy that neorealist theorists contend epitomizes international relations with powerful nations competing for global dominance. The differences are, of course, also ideological.

Different conceptions of the nature of rights and freedoms affect beliefs about the causes of poverty and the most appropriate remedies (Chapter 1). When freedom is interpreted as freeing up markets and freedom from big government (both neoliberal imperatives), it curtails the freedom of governments to act on behalf of citizens, limits the scope for democracy and undermines public accountability. Hence, structural adjustment policies weakened democracy around the world by curtailing the space for government action (Brown 2009; Olukoshi 1998). Emphasizing community rights can leave the weak unprotected and elders – or the state – too strong (Seekings 2019). Prioritizing individual rights over collective ones can arguably undermine the family and community, and direct attention away from the structural causes of poverty to focus on individualistic ones. With the UN and Bretton Woods organizations dominating the US and its "like-minded" – mostly rich – allies, alternatives to a neoliberal economic agenda are often suppressed, and the interests of the developing world ignored.

Recognizing these realities, with economic governance being "driven disproportionately by a small number of States and financial actors ... siloed from other areas of international agenda-setting and decision-making", the UN Secretary-General was at the time of writing proposing a Biennial Summit involving the leadership of ECOSOC, the World Bank and IMF, and the G20 (UN 2021d, para. 73). He was also seeking to establish a High-Level Advisory Board on Global Public Goods to suggest improvements in governance, including that of the global economy. This is in preparation for a "Summit of the Future" to be held in conjunction with the UN General Assembly meeting in September 2023.

These are important developments and testimony to the UN Secretary-General's recognition that fundamental changes are required to rebalance the global political power that has ensured the perpetuation of economic inequality, and looks sure to prevent poverty from being eradicated by 2030. It is also understandable that the UN Secretary-General is seeking to work within existing international institutions since he is seeking to initiate change from a position of comparative weakness. He argues that good governance "does not require new institutions. Rather, we need new resolve and ways of working" (UN 2021e: 48), "a form of multilateralism that is more networked, more inclusive and more effective" (2021e: 66), "anchored within the United Nations" (2021e: 4).

Announcing his idea for a Biennial Summit he did so "in the spirit of previous proposals for an Economic Security Council" (UN 2021e: 54). In so doing, he draws attention to the fact that earlier attempts to create an executive body on a par with the Security Council have all been rejected in favour of the status quo. Powerful nations have insisted on remaining powerful.

As the UN Secretary-General inches towards reform, others have detailed the changes that are necessary if the SDGs are to be achieved and the world is to be capable of adequately responding to threats to global well-being (Falk & Strauss 2001; Schwartzberg 2013; Lopez-Claros et al. 2018). Necessary though these reforms are, they are unlikely to be accepted while the world order is fuelled by a neorealist philosophy of geopolitics based on Darwinian competition to achieve global domination (Chapter 6). This approach to international relations must change if poverty is be eliminated and the world's peoples are to live as envisaged by the UN Charter. Alternative philosophies exist and may become more accepted as the United States' economic domination slips, even if history over the past 70 years suggests otherwise.

Lopez-Claros et al. (2018, 2020) provide an unusually detailed and comprehensive programme of reform that is at once ambitious and reasonable, being broadly representative of informed opinion that rejects the status quo. The proposal won the 2018 New Shape award sponsored by Stockholm's Global Challenges Foundation.

9.2.1 Empowering the United Nations

A core objective is to rebalance global governance in favour of the United Nations and away from the Bretton Woods organizations. This entails strengthening the UN General Assembly by changing its composition, altering its voting procedures, and increasing its powers to include the ability to legislate. A second chamber is proposed, initially advisory, that would derive its authority directly from the global citizenry. The Security Council would be replaced by an Executive Council of 24 members, chaired by a Director General, and elected by the General Assembly to operate under its direction. Its responsibilities would be the implementation, management, and effective operation of the UN. A bill of rights is proposed, new funding sources and responsibilities extended beyond security explicitly to embrace climate change and inequality, the SDGs being a precursor to the role of a reformed United Nations.

The logic of the reform is to disrupt the institutional architecture that prioritizes national perspectives over global ones and that permits the interests of the most powerful nations to dominate all others. A global vision requires global participation. Ironically, however, Lopez-Claros et al. (2020) argue persuasively that the influence of the General Assembly has been undermined by the principle of one member, one vote; nominally the opinions of Monaco with a population of 39,000 carry the same weight as those of China or India with populations of 1.4 billion. The solution proposed, therefore, is a weighted voting system balancing population, economic size and an invariant factor capturing the sovereign equality of nations. This, Lopez-Claros *et al.* (2020) believe, would provide sufficient legitimacy to enable the General Assembly to issue resolutions binding on its members.

However, their aspiration is to realize the United Nation's commitment to democracy as a universal value: "We reaffirm that democracy is a universal value based on the freely expressed will of people to determine their own political, economic, social and cultural systems and their full participation in all aspects of their lives" (UN 2005b: para. 135).

They recommend transitioning to a General Assembly elected by popular vote in three stages. Representatives would first be selected by national legislatures for four-year terms, the number per country reflecting population size with predetermined minima and maxima. After two four-year sessions, half of representatives would be elected by popular vote and then, after a further eight years, all representatives would be elected. This would fundamentally change the personnel engaged in global governance from government appointees and diplomats to statespeople, as Albert Einstein opined as long ago as 1947.

The representational legitimacy thus accorded to the General Assembly would mean that its subservient role with respect to the Security Council could justifiably be reversed. Indeed, as already noted, Lopez-Claros *et al.* propose replacing the Security Council with an Executive Committee. This would have a membership of 24. The three most populous states (currently China, India and the USA) would be permanent members; eight of the next 16 largest nations would participate in rotation with four-year terms, leaving 13 places to be chosen by the Assembly from the other member nations, again with terms of four years. Vetoes would be abolished but votes of substance would require 60 per cent agreement including majorities among both the largest eight and smallest 16 members.

These changes would require alteration of the UN Charter which is unlikely to receive immediate approval given that the intention is to reduce the power exerted by the permanent members of the Security Council. Lopez-Claros *et al.*, therefore, suggest an elected advisory World Parliamentary Assembly as an interim measure since this could be established by a simple vote of the General Assembly and might, in time, evolve into a formal second chamber. In different places they suggest varying membership criteria including a repeat of the composition of the reformed General Assembly (Lopez-Claros *et al.* 2018, 2020). Some influential commentators have already opposed the idea of a parliamentary assembly that included representatives from countries that were not liberal democracies (Laurenti 2003). However, faced with the fact that, in 2021, 54.3 per cent of the world's population did not live in "liberal" democracies and the mounting evidence of discontent with, and a retreat from, democracy, this position would itself seem undemocratic (EIU 2022).

A World Parliamentary Assembly has the potential to counter the nationalistic policymaking that has hitherto undermined the SDGs and much else, prioritizing – instead – the communal global interest. Lopez-Claros *et al.* (2020) speculate that, in time, representatives would form ideological groups, as has happened in the European Parliament, and thereby "see ... problems through the lens of humanity's better interests rather than narrow national considerations". Elsewhere, however, they suggest a membership comprising persons from accredited NGOs bringing relevant expertise and global advocacy into international decision-making (Lopez-Claros *et al.* 2018). The tripartite model of the ILO involving workers, employers and national governments, perhaps with the addition of representatives from civil society, might be an alternative way of moving towards a cosmopolitan style of governance. In the short-term, however, an elected body directly representing the people of the world would perhaps do most to strengthen the authority of the UN vis-à-vis nation states.

It is also necessary to break the financial leverage of the richest states which has created uncertainty and been used to hold the United Nations to ransom (Chapter 7). Various proposals have been advocated for providing an independent, or at least an automatic, income stream that is less vulnerable to political influences (Schwartzberg 2013; Clark & Sohn 1962). These include imposing a fixed percentage of gross national income as a membership fee, applying a levy on national income but with progressive adjustments reflecting the ability to pay, and tapping into additional systems of global taxation such as those discussed in Chapter 6. Lopez-Claros *et al.* (2020) suggest following the model of the European Union and levying a contribution linked to national indirect taxes on goods and services – although they do not rule out other forms of global taxation.

These reforms are needed to ensure that priority is given to the ethical principles underlying the SDGs and to counter the self-interest of the world's richest nations. They might further enhance the legitimacy of the Office of the High Commissioner on Human Rights and the status of national visits and appraisals by special rapporteurs. This might, in turn, discourage countries from striking defensive postures when attention is drawn to the limitations of their policies; the UK, for example, in 2019 filed a complaint to the United Nations while the US in 2018 withdrew from the Human Rights Council (Ashmore 2019; Pilkington 2018). Lopez-Claros *et al.* (2018: 10), however, suggest the need for an International Human Rights Tribunal, modelled on the European Court of Human Rights, "with a 'margin of appreciation' doctrine appropriate to existing international cultural and social diversity" to adjudicate on UN human rights treaties.

More immediately, there is the need to update the UN Guiding Principles on Extreme Poverty and Human Rights and the narrow remit afforded to its special rapporteur. Drawn up under the rubric of the MDGs, the Principles embrace only extreme poverty and not poverty in all its dimensions, SDG Target 1.1 not Target 1.2. While rapporteurs have interpreted their mandate to embrace different forms of poverty, they have been reluctant to seek reform fearing the consequences of opposition from high-income countries. Consequently, they are open to the challenge that criticisms of economically advanced countries are misplaced because extreme poverty is exceedingly rare. Poverty, as recognized in the SDGs, takes many forms and exists in all countries. Moreover, its negative effects on the individuals concerned and on the societies in which it occurs are severe, comparable with, if not precisely the same as for, extreme poverty (Bray *et al.* 2020; Walker 2014).

9.2.2 Managing the global economy

Corresponding reform of the Bretton Woods organizations is required since they currently perpetuate historic power imbalances. Lopez-Claros *et al.* (2020) suggest lowering the voting thresholds used by Bretton Woods organizations to remove the US veto, and updating voting weights better to reflect the status of emerging economies. China, for example, with a GDP two-thirds as large as that of the USA, has an IMF quota just one-third as great. With more national voices involved, the hope is that the policy focus will shift from that of "liberalizing, deregulating, privatizing" towards a broader concept of development more in keeping with that advocated by Amartya Sen and which underpins the SDGs (Chapter 1).

They also anticipate an expanded role for the IMF in managing global financial risks by taking on regulatory, surveillance and intervention responsibilities that parallel those performed by central banks at national level. For example, they propose that the IMF could adopt norms with respect to current account deficits, real exchange rates, budget deficits and debt levels that, if breached by governments, would trigger consultations and various remedial actions. This, they believe, would also go some way to removing the insidious asymmetry in which the IMF can direct the economic behaviour of the mostly low-income countries receiving support, but not that of large rich countries the actions of which could put the entire global economy at risk. They also foresee the IMF becoming a lender of last resort and thereby supplementing the role of the US Federal Reserve which, as an overt example of US power politics, currently restricts access to "like-minded nations". This reform echoes the suggestion, in Chapter 6, that IMF Special Drawing Rights should be extended as a means of increasing the fiscal space available to individual developing countries.

Whether the rebalancing of voting powers would succeed in shifting the underlying neoliberal ideology of the Bretton Woods organizations is debateable. The title of the World Bank's 2015 response to the SDGs, *"From Billions to Trillions"*, certainly recognized the scale of the challenge posed by the SDGs, but the policy content amounted to another "iteration of neoliberal development" strategy (Mawdsley 2018: 193; World Bank 2015). It heavily promoted "blending", the use of ODA funding to lever flows of private finance for development by reducing the risks involved for international capital. Development defined as an investment opportunity for multinationals seems likely to add to global inequality not to reduce it (Akyuz 2017).

Indeed, Lopez-Claros *et al.* (2018: 10) call for "a new multilateral organization with the primary mandate to help redress global income inequalities, in a way that existing international economic institutions for poverty alleviation, financial system surveillance and trade regulation have not been able to do". Elsewhere (2020: 330), they propose a "UN Organization for the Economy" noting that "the economy is still an area where the raw exercise of power is dominant, rather than considerations of fundamental justice, equity or the rule of law in service to shared and sustainable prosperity" (2020: 332).

Undeniably, the globalization of the economy has reduced the control that national governments once exerted over business in terms of regulation to prevent monopolies and excess profits, to insist on good practice and to encourage strategic investment. Business has thrived, free to maximize profits and returns on investment unfettered by constraints on their ability to exploit tax regimes and human and environmental resources. Benefits have been privatized and costs – pollution, resource degradation, climate change, migration, inequality – socialized. Governments of less well-endowed countries have become subservient to business, desperate to avoid losing investment and employment to other nations. Other governments, notably the United States, have worked in tandem with business towards a hegemony of economic, military and diplomatic power in which public accountability is minimized, and even the concept of national interest is blurred by the influence of economic elites.

Viewed both from the broad perspective of the interests of humanity and from the narrow focus on SDG1 and the eradication of poverty, the remit of a strengthened United Nations must embrace regulation and, indeed, management of the global economy. It should include a focus on the primary and secondary distribution of incomes. Minimum standards in relation to work, social protection, progressive taxation, environmental protection and social and human rights should not only be established but ensured and, as necessary and appropriate, harmonized. Recognition must be given to the death and suffering caused by economic exploitation which much exceeds that caused by warfare (Pogge 2007). Limits need to be placed on nations – and international corporations – that now act with impunity in the economic and social sphere.

9.3 Challenging neorealist geopolitics

There is considerable agreement about the structural reforms necessary to initiate inclusive global governance and to disrupt the cabal of governments and business interests that have largely ruled the world since 1945. Equally, as noted above, few expect substantive reform to be accomplished soon. After all, the purpose of the reform is to reduce the influence of the world's most powerful countries that have framed, and most benefited from, global governance for at least 75 years.

Intergovernmental organizations and the concept of global governance fit uneasily into the neorealist framework of international relations. As explained in Chapter 7, neorealism portrays nations as being locked in competition, intent on pursuing their own self-interests with the most powerful seeking primacy and ultimately dominance. Although neorealism is primarily an idealized description of intergovernmental relations, reflecting a school of thought rather than a single deterministic theory, it often forms the core of what advisors advise and national leaders practice. International governance seeks to impose order on the anarchy that favours the already powerful and the diplomatically ruthless.

Since 1945, the Bretton Woods organizations, and to a lesser extent the United Nations, have served the interests of the West and of the United States in particular (Chapters 6 and 7). Indeed, some scholars argue that the United States has used these institutions to perpetuate its hegemony, accepting and obeying rules and supporting the institutions only when it was convenient to do so (Wade 2020). Others suggest that its influence has proved more enduring because of the restraint shown in constructing these institutions and largely abiding by their rules (Ikenberry 2001). Either way, to the extent that these organizations require reform, it is to readdress the imbalance of power which favours the United States and its allies. Moreover, the reforms discussed above, necessary to deliver the SDGs, are also likely to impact on what the United States considers to be its core security, defence and strategic interests.

Reform of the UN and Bretton Woods organizations that has occurred has been incremental and rarely transformative to the degree that is needed. This is not due to an absence of ideas or the lack of attempts at reform. Instead, it is again explicable in terms of neorealist theory. Powerful nations have used their control of the institutions to prevent change that would negatively affect their interests, be it through the legitimate use of disproportionate voting, vetoes and threat of vetoes, or through the illicit retention of funds or the abuse of systems (Chapters 6 and 7). Within a system driven by neorealist principles, institutional change is unlikely unless provoked by seismic shifts in the macro geopolitical plates. It remains to be seen whether the 2022 invasion of Ukraine might present such a shift. It has again revealed the impotence of the Security Council because of the veto held by Russia as one of the protagonists and, while reform has not followed occasions when the United States has defied the popular will, this was most likely to have been because of its hegemonic position.

There are other traditions in international relations which have had much less impact outside academe. Liberalism takes a more optimistic, less cynical view of human nature and the drivers of state actions (von Mises 2005). Liberal institutionalists emphasize the importance of global governance, suggesting that intergovernmental organizations are not merely epiphenomenon solely controlled by nation states (Stein 2008). Instead, they independently structure the collective behaviour of national governments and successfully promote or limit the influence of various interests to benefit the common good. The so-called English School goes further to conceptualize a society of states with shared norms and behaviour and, to a degree, common interests that might accommodate initiatives such as global public investment (Dunne 1998). However, in the age of neorealism, liberalism has seemed utopian.

A global development that might make liberalism more relevant is the rise of China and its challenge to Western hegemony. Neorealists see China's growing influence raising the prospect of cold or hot wars with some offering strategies to avoid them (Rudd 2022). However, taken at face value, something neorealists would never do, Chinese statements on development and global governance chime with English School values and the changes necessary for the SDGs to be attained by 2030. President Xi Jinping's speech to the 26th Session of the General Assembly of the United Nations on 25 October 2021 is illustrative (*China Daily* 2021):

> On development, China joins many in recognizing that "it is important to resolve the problem of unbalanced and inadequate development, and make development more balanced, coordinated and inclusive". It acknowledges the need to "strengthen people's capacity for development" and "to create a development paradigm where its outcome benefits every person in every country more directly and fairly".
>
> Turning to global governance, China prioritizes "peaceful development and the welfare of all humanity" and speaks "to solidarity and cooperation with people around the world" and to the need to "uphold international equity and justice". It argues that "we should vigorously

advocate peace, development, equity, justice, democracy and freedom, which are the common values of humanity, and work together to provide the right guiding philosophy for building a better world". It is "resolutely opposed to hegemony and power politics" and calls for "more inclusive global governance, more effective multilateral mechanisms, and more active regional cooperation". It opines that "to build a community with a shared future for mankind is not to replace one system or civilization with another". Instead, "it is about countries with different social systems, ideologies, histories, cultures and levels of development coming together for shared interests, shared rights and shared responsibilities in global affairs, and creating the greatest synergy for building a better world".

Neorealists might challenge China's words, claiming them to be a ruse designed to build an anti-Western alliance to oppose Western hegemony. If neorealists are correct, they will also realize that it is a strategy that could well prove successful given the past failures of rich nations to respond to the needs of poorer ones while, instead, actively promoting policies that exploit and further impoverish them. This is precisely the threat that leads *The Economist* (2022) to urge Western governments to be "wary" of China's Global Development Initiative. Returning, however, to the aspirations expressed by President Xi's speech to the United Nations General Assembly, taken to be sincere, rather than mere platitudes or neorealist deceit, they match exactly the principles necessary to deliver the SDGs. Much less, and the SDGs are doomed.

9.4 Mobilizing global resources

With the dismal prospect that neorealism will continue accurately to describe international relations for some years to come and that, therefore, the major engines of poverty generation will remain in place, it becomes a challenge to identify credible means of achieving any of the SDG targets.

The commitment to mobilize resources (SDG Target 1.a) necessary to implement social protection and to reach the other targets is currently unfulfilled (Chapter 7). If the first of the biennial financial summits proposed by the UN Secretary-General were to take place, and an Economic Security Council were to result, then making this commitment real should be its first responsibility. In the meantime, a proposal to establish a Global Social Protection Fund has attracted the support of the International Trade Union Confederation (ITUC) and the Global Coalition for Social Protection. The fund, proposed by Olivier De Schutter, UN Special Rapporteur on extreme poverty and human rights, would provide international financial support to bridge the gap between national resources and the cost of implementing a basic social protection floor. It would also include a facility to insure against national crises that might cause caseloads and expenditure unexpectedly to increase (De Schutter 2021).

Framed explicitly within the rubric of the SDGs, the intention is to aid developing countries simultaneously to attain Targets 1.1 (end extreme poverty), 1.3 (implement social protection) and 3.8 (achieve universal health coverage) by 2030. In terms of breadth, therefore, the Global Social Protection Fund appears more ambitious than the Global Citizen's Income discussed in Chapter 6, but, because coverage is restricted to low-income countries, the cost – and the likely achievements – are much more modest.

Preferring to work within existing structures, De Schutter suggests that strategic direction could be provided by a high-level political alliance that might be developed from USP2030, the Global Partnership for Universal Social Protection to Achieve the Sustainable Development Goals, a multistakeholder grouping founded in 2016 to promote SDG3.8 and social protection more generally. Administrative responsibilities would be integrated within the ILO Global Flagship Programme on Building Social Protection Floors for All (Chapter 4). The ILO clearly has the necessary infrastructure and expertise. Indeed, it currently undertakes several of the functions envisaged for the Fund within its Flagship Programme, albeit with very insecure funding.

The economic rationale for the Fund is essentially Keynesian: social protection provides demand-driven growth, stabilizes the economy, has multiplier effects for local economies and increases income equality with associated falls in poverty (Chapter 2). At an individual level, the fund would enhance human capital and savings that, combined with the macroeconomic benefits, would increase national resilience.

The projected cost is just US$53.9 billion for 2022, with the international contribution predicted to fall from US$48.5 in 2022 to US$10.1 billion in 2030. As De Schutter is at pains to demonstrate, the Fund is affordable within OECD-DAC budgets even in its most expensive year – "less than half" of the total (Figure 9.2). Extending implementation of a social protection floor across all developing countries – SDG Target 1.3 – would cost much more: US$683 billion in 2022 rising to US$1.3 trillion in 2030 (Figure 9.3).

De Schutter rightly emphasizes national ownership of social protection policies and the importance of national dialogues with local stakeholders in accordance with ILO Recommendation 202. It is here important to recognize that the merits of a social protection floor are not universally recognized. For example, Seekings (2019) explains how political elites across Africa, especially those with a rural heritage, have resisted the idea, believing that welfare benefits are an imposition of the Global North and exacerbate the "problem of laziness".

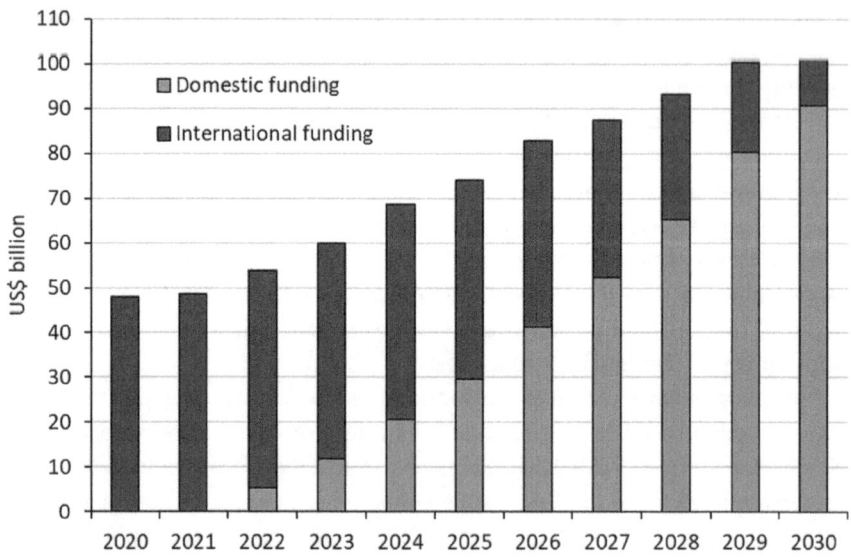

Figure 9.2 Cost of the Global Social Protection Fund, 2020–30
Source: Adapted from Bierbaum and Schmitt (2022).

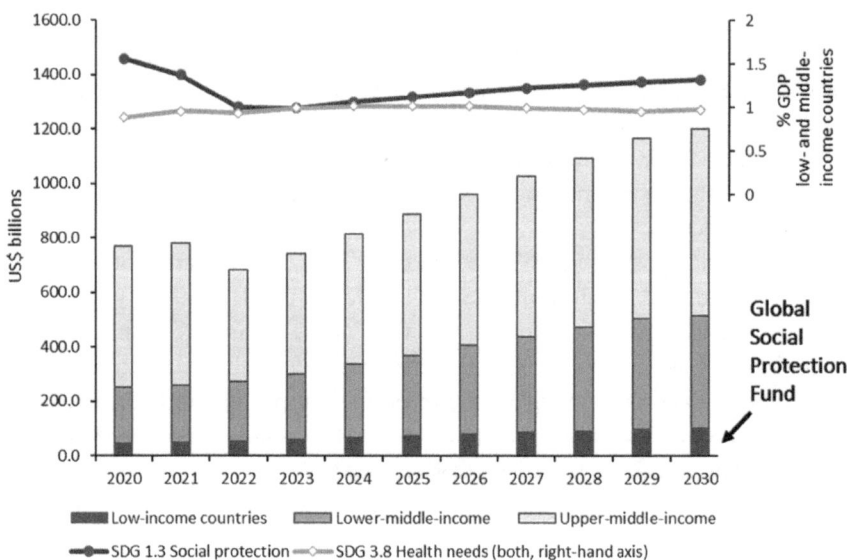

Figure 9.3 Cost of providing a social protection floor
Source: Adapted from Durán-Valverde *et al.* (2020).

The UN *Guiding Principles on Human Rights and Extreme Poverty* requires the elimination of all forms of official discrimination and insists that governments "must take all appropriate measures to modify sociocultural patterns with a view to eliminating prejudices and stereotypes" (OHCHR 2012: 6). However, discrimination against people in poverty is a daily occurrence globally and, therefore, the Global Social Protection Fund may encounter resistance from unexpected sources (Bray *et al.* 2020; Walker 2014).

Given the demonstrable unwillingness of rich countries and populations to address global poverty (Chapters 7 and 8), De Schutter's focus on cost restraint is understandable. He is somewhat circumspect about sources of funding suggesting that "funding sources other than ODA could be explored" (De Schutter 2021: 8) and mentions special drawing rights and, in the context of domestic funding, increased personal taxation, borrowing and debt restructuring, use of foreign exchange reserves and clamping down on illicit financial flows.

In limiting the coverage of the fund to eradicating US\$1.90 poverty, De Schutter is working within his human rights remit to focus on extreme poverty. However, in so doing, SDG Target 1.2 is ignored, and the Global Social Protection Fund pays homage to the limited ambition of the MDGs. As noted above, Paragraph 13 of ILO Recommendation 202 on social protection floors anticipates that nations "progressively build and maintain comprehensive and adequate social security systems" and "provide higher levels of protection to as many people as possible". While it is generally true that only low-income countries would find it impossible to end extreme poverty, over 20 lower-middle-income countries would have difficulty implementing a protection floor that would eradicate poverty set at US\$3.20; they would need to divert 6 per cent or more of their GDP with some required to devote over 16 per cent (Figure 9.4).

The case for extending the Global Social Protection Fund to all developing countries with coverage of health care and child, maternity, disability and old-age is extremely strong. The estimated cost, US\$1.04 trillion or 1.2 per cent of global GDP in 2020 (during the peak of the Covid-19 pandemic) would have been fully covered by a global tax on either wealth or carbon (Table 6.2). In comparison, the cost of the fund proposed by De Schutter, US\$48 billion, is trivial and, as noted above, the cost to the supporting global community falls over time. How depressing, therefore, that at the time of writing (June 2022) there is no commitment to fund even this basic safety net.

9.5 Conclusion

A book about the eradication of poverty globally should end on an optimistic note. Taking the long view, the proportion of the world's population suffering

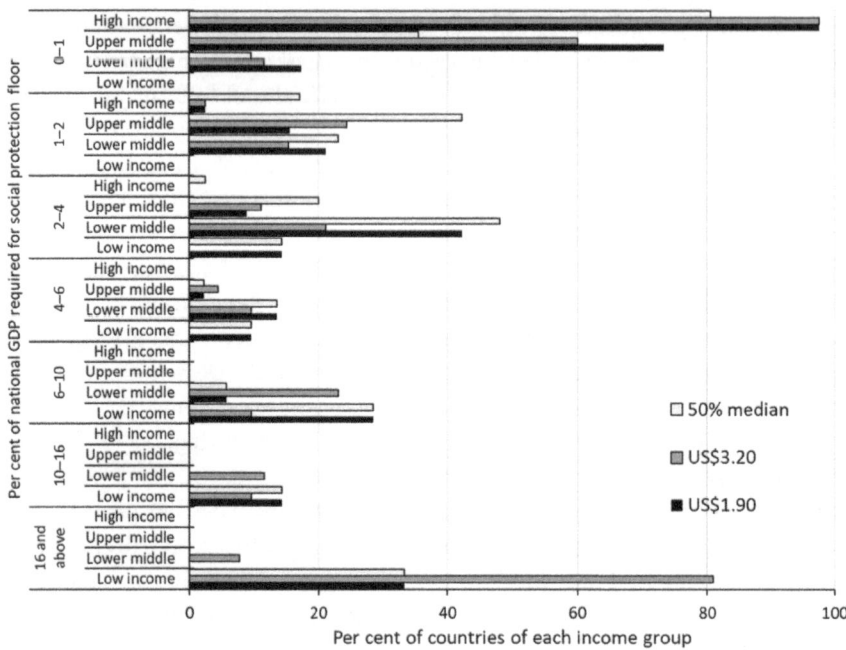

Figure 9.4 National cost of implementing a social protection floor
Source: Adapted from FES (2022).

poverty of all kinds has fallen at an unprecedented rate over the past 200 years. The decline in income poverty has been particularly dramatic during the past 25 years – even accounting for the marked upturn associated with the Covid-19 pandemic. While numbers have dropped more slowly than percentages, this is because populations have tended to rise more quickly in countries where poverty rates are high.

Today, in contrast with much of human history, poverty is not a problem without a solution. Thanks to technological development, global trade and greater productivity, resources are sufficient to guarantee that poverty is eradicated. Administrative systems nominally exist intended to ensure that everyone enjoys a dignified life and that no one is left behind. There are legal and quasi-legal instruments that seek to guarantee the equal enjoyment of all human rights even by persons living in poverty. Guidance exists to ensure decent employment and protect persons against the many risks that accompany life. All this is backed up by at least 100 years of practical administrative experience on every inhabited continent.

There are challenges, yes. The economy tends to concentrate wealth and takes time to accommodate to change. There are arguably even fundamental contradictions arising from the way that the economy functions: informal and insecure employment are increasing; and global warming is real, but decarbonization is slow. Natural resources are not evenly distributed geographically, and it takes time to rectify past injustices. Not everyone is born equal. Each person does not have the same opportunities, abilities or equal potential. But again, there are well worked out solutions to all these difficulties, many tried and tested.

Poverty need be no more. And yet over 650 million children, women and men – including possibly two million in the United States – still live in extreme poverty without the basic necessities of life, 3.25 billion people cannot afford the lifestyle of an upper-middle-income developing country, and 22 per cent of Europeans experience relative poverty. In every city in the world, people live in districts that others would not want to be seen in. In most villages, some families survive in material conditions that others seek to avoid. Each person living in poverty risks abuse and humiliation. They are castigated by officials and despised by their in-laws. When asked, they say that they "suffer poverty in body, mind and heart" (Bray *et al.* 2020).

That poverty continues when the resources and administrative technology exist to eliminate it is explicable with respect to human selfishness and greed, laced with hypocrisy and deceit. Whether such selfishness is an innate human characteristic or a by-product of an economic system exclusively geared toward self-interest and utility maximization is a moot point. Either way, companies maximize their income by minimizing that of their employees and suppliers. Individuals legitimate their selfishness with the belief that their prosperity and the poverty of others are both deserved. Opportunists and idealists become successful politicians by pandering to the selfishness of their supporters, and national leaders retain power by grabbing as much of the world's resources as possible for their citizens and/or for themselves.

The solution to poverty, therefore, is not simply a matter of economics or politics. As evidenced in Chapter 8, it is also to be found in individual morality – "we the people" are not much interested in poverty relief – and is manifest in a lack of moral political leadership, placing national interests above global ones.

As previously revealed, the causes of poverty are complex but very largely structural: unequal natural resources; historic exploitation; and a global economic and trading system that delivers its greatest rewards to the powerful companies and nations that largely control it. The institutional reforms proposed above to help ensure that SDG1 is achieved by 2030 seek to modify, moderate and ultimately to reverse the structural forces that perpetuate poverty. While building a fairer economic system is likely to prove extremely difficult, the decision to start rests on a simple moral choice between two principles: 1. Me and my country first, or 2. Shared prosperity for all.

It takes courage to make the right choice and enough people to choose to do so. Insufficient numbers have yet done so – conceivably due to choosing

expediency when faced with perceived constraints imposed, directly and indirectly, by the global economic system. While poverty denies people the freedom
to live with dignity, the current world order may additionally deny others the
freedom to act with humanity and call for an end to poverty.

**CASE STUDY 9 LOW INCOME AND A GLOBAL FUND FOR SOCIAL
PROTECTION**

Figure CS9 Olivier De Schutter advocating a Global Fund for Social Protection

Charles Lwanga-Ntale has collated early reactions to the proposal for Global
Fund for Social Protection from civil society, bilateral donors and agencies, government representatives, academia and multilateral agencies in Uganda, Kenya
and Zambia. He reports cautious optimism tinged with doubt and scepticism
seeping into cynicism. Both governments and citizens attach importance to
social protection and welcome the possibility of a "global facility to inspire and
drive progress" (Lwanga-Ntale 2022: 20). There are, however, conflicting views
about the scope and level of social protection sought and confusion about the

nature and terms of the fund proposed. The experience of Covid-19 has drawn attention to the need for enhanced social protection and provoked government commitments, although these have often not been matched by budgetary allocations. The scale of poverty that must be addressed can seem daunting.

Much scepticism arises from the lack of guarantees yet as to the adequacy and sustainability of financing of any fund. There is concern, too, about creating further indebtedness, especially among countries already having difficulty in servicing debt, and a fear that donors will impose conditionality. Apart from rec-reating dependencies, the worry is that conditionality could result in the imposition of models of provision that are culturally insensitive and might obliterate innovation.

Underlying these concerns is the view that the programme design may be too North-centric, not least because low-income countries feel that they are not party to the ongoing discussions. The notion that social protection should be available as a right sits uneasily alongside severe resource constraints. The inclination, then, is to restrict provision to those who are most deprived, especially vulnerable informal workers, although this can erode support among the more politically vocal middle class.

Politics, however, will determine the acceptability of the Global Fund for Social Protection. In African countries, the presidential lead is often critical and sometimes framed by patterns of patronage. However, parliaments are increasingly taking the view that all who are vulnerable should be equally entitled to a share of welfare.

Lwanga-Ntale advocates further clarification of the goals, strategy and outcomes and then working with a small group of five to seven low-income countries, using a safe space to explore and resolve outstanding issues.

Further reading

Lwanga-Ntale, C. 2022. *A Global Fund for Social Protection: Views from Selected Low-income Countries*. Bonn: Friedrich Ebert Stiftung

10
A POSTSCRIPT

While books may end, history does not. Stories need to be continuously retold and often revised.

It was clear, even before the start of the Covid-19 pandemic, that the chances of the world being able to eradicate poverty by 2030 were reducing by the minute. The pandemic added substantially to the challenge and underlined the difficulties that national governments confront in working together for the common good (Chapter 5; Case Study 8). Politicians feel compelled to serve their own populations first, others second if at all.

Then, in February 2022, Russia invaded Ukraine with yet incalculable consequences that include a possible tenfold increase in US5.50/day poverty in Ukraine during 2022, together with a 75 million increase in extreme (below US$1.90/day) poverty globally (World Bank 2022b). Although unexpected, the invasion is explicable in terms of a failure in statecraft and the impotence of the United Nations discussed in Chapter 7.

The origins of the war are traceable to euphoria in the 1990s concerning the ascendancy of Western liberal democracy that encouraged the American political scientist Francis Fukuyama to author *The End of History and the Last Man* (1992). In the aftermath of the collapse of the Soviet Union, Russia's pleas to join the European Union were rebuffed and the United States sought to contain the growth of a potential economic rival, financially supporting its former satellite countries at the expense of Russia (Walker 2022). With the eastwards expansion of NATO and with US bases in countries to its east, the Russian president, Vladimir Putin, under pressure from failures in domestic policy, found reason to ignore international law and attempt a full takeover of Ukraine, having annexed Crimea in 2014.

While the invasion of Ukraine is understandable in terms of neorealist theories of international relations, they say little about how the world can lessen the consequences of the war for the world's most disadvantaged citizens. At the time of writing, it seems likely that global economic growth will collapse due to surging inflation, with rising energy and food prices directly attributable to the war compounding increases arising from economic dislocations following the pandemic. Interest rates are expected to continue to rise with stagflation – high inflation and low growth – likely to persist risking, according to the World Bank (2022b: xv), "potentially destabilizing consequences for low- and middle-income economies". Developing countries are now predicted to grow, on average, by 3.4 per cent in 2022, half the rate witnessed over the past decade, while the Ukraine war is likely to lower the growth rate of middle-income countries by 1.3 percentage points (Figure 10.1).

Low-income countries are expected to be hardest hit by the consequences of the war in Ukraine. Being food deficient and reliant on imports, they are particularly exposed to the effects of rising food costs. Furthermore, food consumption already accounts for 45 per cent of total household expenditure in low-income countries, with rising prices likely to push tens of millions into acute food insecurity and deepening poverty. Fourteen per cent of the total caloric intake of the median low-income country can be traced to wheat imports from either the Ukraine or Russia (OECD/FAO 2021).

Not all developing countries will be equally affected by the war. Some lower- and middle-income countries will benefit from rising oil and commodity prices

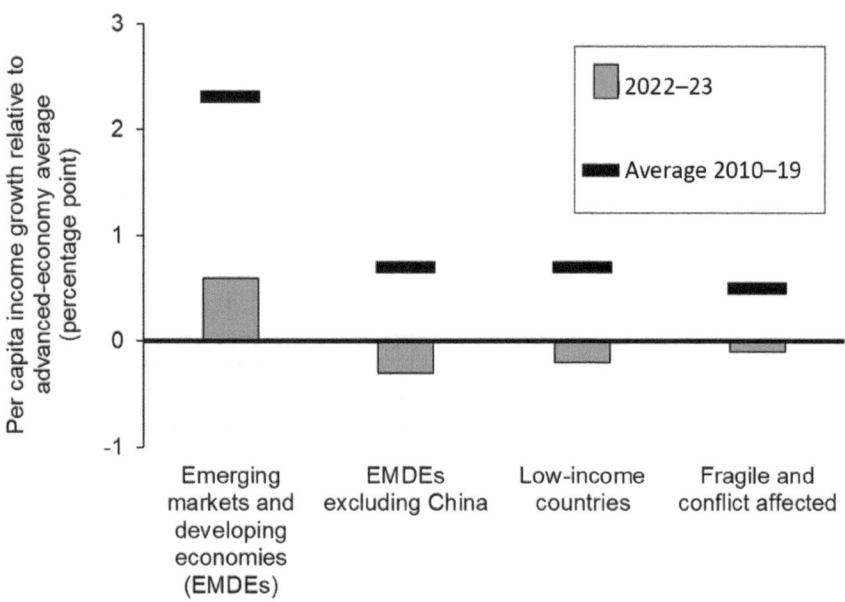

Figure 10.1 Predicted per capita income, 2022–23
Source: Adapted from World Bank (2022b).

increasing their fiscal space although, with social protection policies still typically underdeveloped, there is little assurance that the poorest sections of the community will benefit equally. Moreover, further increases in the price of seeds, fuel and fertilizers essential for farming could have marked negative consequences. There is also real concern that remittances, which held up well during the pandemic, may decline as inflation rises and special Covid-19-related schemes in advanced economies are withdrawn.

The impact of the war on high-income countries is likely to be indirect, except for those European countries that are highly dependent on Russian energy exports. However, much depends on developments on the battlefield and the risk of geographical expansion cannot be overlooked. Even on the presumption that the theatre of war does not expand and that hostilities end, higher energy prices will reduce disposable income and profit margins, slowing growth and possibly triggering a price-wage spiral. The corporatist and social democratic regimes may well be able to limit the regressive distributive effects of inflation by protecting the incomes of the poorest. However, low-income families are likely to be more exposed in liberal regimes such as Britain where fuel poverty is reported to be rising sharply along with the use of food banks

While rich countries can ameliorate the worst effects of inflationary pressures induced by the Ukraine war through subsidies and special assistance schemes, governments of low-income countries typically have very limited room for manoeuvre. This is especially true of those countries where public safety nets are predominantly donor-financed. Consequently, the World Bank predicts incomes in low-income countries to increase more slowly in 2022/23 than those in high-income countries, reversing the pattern of the past decade that has marginally reduced global income inequality. This pattern of slower growth applies to virtually the entire developing world.

With the invasion of Ukraine, the image of the world successfully attaining SDG1 seems even more likely to be a mirage.

CASE STUDY 10 INCOME POVERTY AND THE MPI, 2021

SDG Target 1.2 refers to halving poverty in all its dimensions according to national definitions. Since very few countries have incorporated a measure of multidimensional poverty into their national policy strategies, the UN Sustainable Development Solutions Network has advocated use of the global Multidimensional Poverty Index (MPI) developed by Oxford University's Poverty and Human Development Initiative (OPHI) in collaboration with the UNDP.

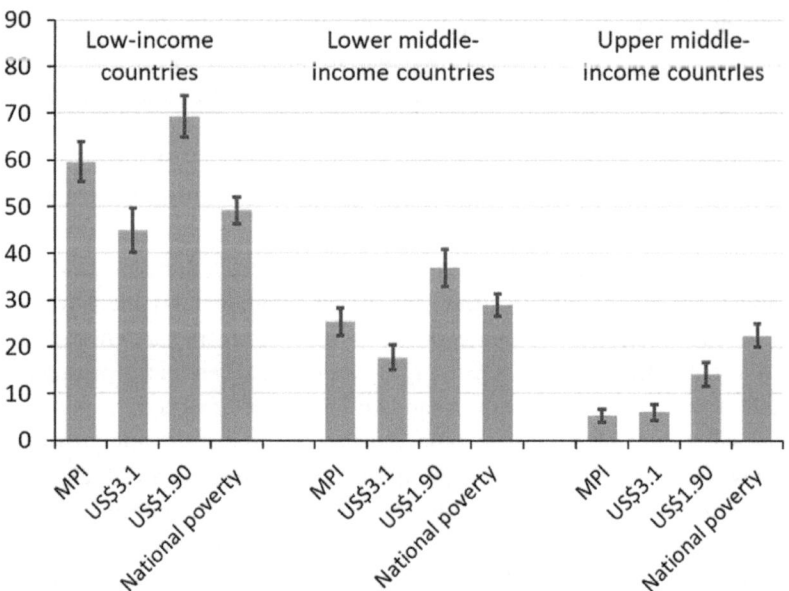

Figure CS10 Incidence of different forms of poverty 2021 (or nearest year)
Source: Calculated from Alkire *et al.* (2021).

The MPI combines ten indicators reflecting three dimensions: health; education; and living standards, the last indexed by five measures of material deprivation. Depending on perspective and timescale, the first two dimensions might be considered as either causes or consequences of poverty. The OPHI presents the MPI as a complement to measures of income poverty. This is appropriate since the three dimensions are measured independently of income with the MPI being a gauge of low well-being.

The MPI measure is generally considered inappropriate for high-income countries; it is available for just three of them. Averaged across low-income and lower-middle-income countries, the incidence of MPI poverty falls between that of US$1.90/day and US$3.10/day poverty; among upper-middle-income countries it is similar to US$3.10/day poverty.

The MPI is more closely associated with the Human Development Index (HDI) (from which it was developed) than with either of the measures of income poverty. It predicts 85 per cent of the variation in national HDI scores compared with, for example, just 60 per cent of the variation in US$1.90/day poverty. This means that, for some countries, the incidence of MPI "poverty" may be very different from income poverty with significant consequences for the rank order of countries. For example, whereas South Sudan ranked highest and Niger second highest on the 2021 MPI, having 92 per cent and 91 per cent of their respective populations being counted as poor, the corresponding rates of US$1.90/day and US$3.10/day poverty were 76 per cent and 92 per cent for South Sudan, and 45 percent and 77 per cent for Niger. Niger ranked 17th and 11th highest for US$1.90/day and US$3.10/day poverty respectively.

The MPI is highly correlated with gross national income, as is US$3.10/day poverty, but this is noticeably less true of US$1.90/day poverty which is, in turn, associated with income inequality, whereas the MPI is not. While extreme poverty is a direct product of income inequality, the MPI would appear to be determined by other factors.

Further reading

Alkire, S., U. Kanagaratnum & N. Suppa 2021. *The Global Multidimensional Poverty Index 2021*. Oxford: Oxford Poverty and Human Development Initiative, Methodological Note 51. https://ophi.org.uk/multidimensional-poverty-Index/global-mpi-databank/.

GLOSSARY

2030 Agenda: the 2030 Agenda for Sustainable Development is the United Nations' globally shared development programme launched in 2015; it includes the Sustainable Development Goals.

Absolute poverty: poverty that does not vary with context is termed absolute. More generally absolute poverty often equates with extreme or subsistence poverty where resources are insufficient to ensure survival.

Activation policies: labour market activation policies seek to reduce the numbers receiving welfare benefits by increasing the employment rate through job search assistance, vocational training, wage subsidies, public works, etc.

ATD Fourth World: a French-based international non-governmental organization (NGO) with consultation rights at the UN. It pursues a human-rights based approach to the eradication of chronic poverty.

Basic income schemes: periodic cash payments paid to all citizens in a jurisdiction irrespective of income, demographic, or other characteristics. Also referred to as "Universal Basic Income" or "citizens' income".

Bismarckian social security: provision of insurance organized by the state (and hence often termed "social insurance") to cover such contingencies as accident, sickness, invalidity, old age and unemployment. This form of provision was first introduced in Germany in the 1880s under Chancellor Otto von Bismarck.

Bretton Woods Institutions: these include the World Bank and the International Monetary Fund (IMF) that were established at a meeting involving 43 countries held at Bretton Woods in New Hampshire in July 1944. An International Trade Organization (ITO) was planned but not established; the World Trade Organization (WTO) fulfils a similar function.

Capabilities: this term, coined by Amartya Sen, refers to the freedom – that is the substantive opportunity – to achieve the functionings that people desire. (See below for "functionings".)

Conditional cash transfer (CCT): as opposed to an unconditional cash transfer – is a payment made conditional on behavioural change by the recipient.

Committee of Experts on Sustainable Development Financing: an international committee established by Rio+20 Conference, comprising 30 experts nominated by regional groups of nations. It reported in 2014.

Copenhagen: the World Summit on Social Development held in Copenhagen in 1995 that introduced poverty as a multidimensional concept incorporating employment and social integration.

Counterfactual: an estimate of what would have happened in the absence of action that was taken.

Democracy: a system of government in which political power is vested in the people and exercised by them, directly or indirectly, through a system of representation usually involving periodic elections.

DESA: the Department of Economic and Social Affairs, a part of the UN Secretariat responsible for follow-up to major UN summits and conferences. It also services the UN Economic and Social Council and acts as the Secretariat for the SDGs.

Development Assistance Committee (DAC): a committee of the OECD comprising 30 countries that sets standards for overseas development assistance and monitors and reviews progress. Separate meetings are held involving, respectively, development ministers, official heads of aid agencies and Paris-based delegates of DAC members.

Doha Agenda: 15 years of unsuccessful negotiations conducted by the WTO to reduce unfairness in the global trade system.

EIU Democracy Index: an index of democracy that has been complied annually since 2006 by the Economist Intelligence Unit, the research division of the Economist Group. It assesses democracy on the basis of five dimensions: electoral process and pluralism; civil liberties; the functioning of government; political participation; and political culture.

English School: a school of international relations theory which maintains that ideas can shape international politics and that the operation of international law makes a degree of order possible within the otherwise anarchic world of international relations.

FfD 2015: the Third International Conference on Financing for Development held at Addis Ababa in 2015. It prepared the global framework for financing development post-2015.

Fiscal space: the scope that a government has for additional spending without risking destabilizing the national economy.

Functionings: the "doings and beings" that people might be expected or aspire to undertake or become. The term was coined by Amartya Sen.

Furlough schemes: policies to assist people temporarily laid-off from work (for example, due to a pandemic) without requiring the cessation of their employment contract.

G77 + China: a grouping of countries within the UN involved in negotiating the SDGs. The G77 was founded in 1964 by 77 developing countries. China has provided continuing financial and political support but does not regard itself as a member.

GATT: the General Agreement on Tariffs and Trade (GATT) was signed by the US and 22 other countries in 1947. It became the WTO in 1995.

GDI: the Global Development Initiative was announced by China's President Xi Jinping at the UN General Assembly in September 2021 as "an open and inclusive partnership" to serve as an accelerator of the 2030 Agenda.

GDP: gross domestic product, the market value of all the final goods and services produced by a country in a given period.

Gini coefficient: a measure of statistical dispersion which, when used to measure national income inequality, takes the value of 1 (or 100) when all income is held by one person and the value of 0 when everyone's income is the same.

Global North: refers to developed countries in the West, embracing Australia and New Zealand but excluding Japan, South Korea and Singapore unless stated otherwise.

Global public investment: a vision of international fiscal allocation to which all nations contribute and benefit, international aid being viewed as an investment for the common good.

Global Social Protection Fund: the proposal for a global fund to increase the financial support for low-income countries establishing social protection schemes.

Global South: refers collectively to regions of Africa, Asia, Latin America and Oceania, where poverty rates in many countries are high.

GNI: gross national income is the total earned by a nation's people and businesses. It is the sum of the GDP and net income flows from abroad. See GDP.

HIC: High-income country as defined by the World Bank (GNI per capita of $12,696 or more in 2020).

High-Level Panel: the High-Level Panel of Eminent Persons on the Post-2015 Development Agenda, comprised of 17 persons appointed by the UN Secretary-General in 2012.

HLPF: the UN High-Level Political Forum on Sustainable Development, the UN's main platform/meeting on sustainable development with a central role to follow-up and review of the 2030 Agenda.

IAEG: the Inter-Agency and Expert Group on SDGs, comprising 27 representatives of national statistical offices charged to develop the indicator framework for the SDGs and to provide ongoing technical support towards 2030.

ILO: the International Labour Organization is a tripartite United Nations agency involving governments and both employers' and workers' organizations. It was established in 1919 to advance social and economic justice by setting and monitoring international labour standards.

ILO Global Flagship Programme: a programme focused on "building social protection floors for all" by offering in-country and thematic support combined with strategic partnerships.

IMF: the International Monetary Fund is an international financial institution based in Washington, DC, working to foster global monetary cooperation, financial stability, international trade, sustainable economic growth, and to reduce poverty.

Income poverty: a lack of income – money and money-like resources – in relation to a person's needs.

International Development Targets (IDTs): seven quantifiable development targets introduced by DAC in 1996. They influenced the form of the MDGs, especially MDG1.

IPL: the international poverty line, in 2015, defined poverty as per capita income of less than US$1.25/day; this was used as the basis for Target 1.1. The IPL was increased to US$1.90 in 2017 and to US$2.15 in September 2022. The IPL originated as the average of the official poverty lines for the world's 15 poorest countries.

ITUC: the International Trade Union Confederation has 332 national affiliated trade unions and workers' organizations in 163 countries and territories.

Liberalism: a theoretical approach to international relations that rejects power politics, emphasizing the mutual benefit of cooperation and the positive role of international organizations.

LIC: a low-income country as defined by the World Bank (GNI per capita of $1,045 or less in 2020).

LMIC: a lower-middle-income country as defined by the World Bank (GNI per capita between $1,046 and $4,095 in 2020).

Millennium Assembly, Summit and Declaration: United Nations activities held in September 2000 to commemorate the second millennium CE; the Declaration included a draft of the MDGs that was subsequently refined.

MDGs: the eight Millennium Development Goals included in the United Nations Millennium Declaration in 2000 relating to poverty, hunger, disease, illiteracy, environmental degradation and discrimination against women. They were to have been achieved by 2015.

MLD: mean log deviation is a measure of dispersion that uses all values in the sample. It takes the value 0 when all incomes are equal with large values indicating high inequality.

Multidimensional poverty: refers to the multiple and immediate consequences of lacking money or money-like resources in relation to needs that tend to be experienced simultaneously.

MPI: the global Multidimensional Poverty Index measures acute deprivations in health, education and living standards that persons may experience simultaneously. Published annually by the UNDP for more than 100 developing countries, it complements measures of monetary poverty.

Neorealism: a theory of international relations that considers competition and conflict between states to be necessary and inevitable.

Needs: a need is something necessary for a person to live and function. Needs may be absolute, matters of life or death, or relative, necessary to live appropriately in a particular culture or context. Needs are often contrasted with wants, which are desires for things that can further improve a person's quality of life.

New International Economic Order (NIEO): a vision of reform prevalent in the 1970s, especially among non-aligned governments, that would have given developing countries more influence.

NVR: National Voluntary Reviews are prepared by national governments as a basis for monitoring progress towards fulfilling the SDGs.

ODA: Official development assistance is government aid that specifically targets and promotes the economic development and welfare of developing countries.

OECD: the Organisation for Economic Development and Co-operation is a grouping of 38 developed countries founded in 1948 as the Organisation for European Economic Co-operation (OEEC).

OHCHR: Office of the United Nations' High Commissioner for Human Rights.

OWG: the Open Working Group on Sustainable Development Goals was a 30-member group of the UN General Assembly tasked with preparing a proposal on the SDGs as recommended by Rio+20.

PovcalNet: an interactive computational tool and database enabling replication of poverty calculations made by World Bank.

Poverty: the experience of a lack of resources in relation to needs.

Poverty gap: the amount by which the income of persons living in poverty falls short of the poverty threshold.

Poverty rate: the proportion of the population with resources less than the poverty threshold.

Poverty threshold (or line): an income-to-needs ratio dividing people experiencing poverty from those not.

Poverty Reduction Strategy Papers (PRSPs): documents required by the World Bank, IMF and most major donors and lenders before low-income countries can receive aid or be considered for debt relief.

Purchasing power parities (PPPs): rates of currency conversion that try to equalize the purchasing power of different currencies by comparing the cost of a single basket of goods.

Progressive policies: policies that benefit persons with limited resources more than people with greater resources. The effect is a "Robin Hood" redistribution, taking from richer persons to give to poorer ones.

Relative poverty: poverty, the definition/level of which varies according to the socioeconomic context. The poverty threshold is often fixed as a proportion of median disposable income.

Rio+20: the United Nations Conference on Sustainable Development held in Rio de Janeiro in June 2012.

SDG "Good Practice" case-studies: 997 examples of innovation published by DESA.

SDSN: the Sustainable Development Solutions Network is a non-profit organization established by the United Nations in 2012 to advance the SDGs.

Skewness: is a measure of the asymmetry of a distribution. Income is usually positively skewed meaning the median (the middle) income is less than the mean (mean).

Social Catholicism: a movement, originating in France in the 1870s, that seeks progressive social change and blends the teaching of the Catholic Church with socialism.

Social exclusion: the state and process of being denied access to the rights and privileges offered by society – often due to a person's poverty.

Social Watch: an international network of citizens' organizations in the struggle to eradicate poverty and the causes of poverty. Its secretariat is based in Montevideo, Uruguay.

Special Drawing Rights: supplementary foreign exchange reserve assets maintained by the IMF. They are claims to currency held by IMF member countries for which they may be exchanged.

Structural adjustment: a policy framework applied by the Bretton Woods organizations that made support conditional on the privatization of state-owned enterprises, deregulation of the economy, trade liberalization, "competitive" exchange rates and the elimination of barriers to foreign direct investment.

Sustainable Development Goals (SDGs): 17 global development goals (usually including the associated targets and indicators) that form part of the United Nations 2030 Agenda and are to be met by 2030.

UMIC: a upper middle-income country as defined by the World Bank (GNI per capita between $4,096 and $12,695 in 2020).

UN: the United Nations was founded in 1945 to maintain international peace and security, and to develop friendly relations among nations based on respect for the principle of equal rights and self-determination of people. Based in New York, it has 193 UN member states and numerous agencies.

UN System Task Team: the UN System Task Team on the Post-2015 UN Development Agenda that was established by the UN Secretary-General to support system-wide preparations for the 2030 Agenda.

UNDP: the United Nations Development Programme is a United Nations' organization focused on poverty reduction and human development.

UNICEF: originally called the United Nations International Children's Emergency Fund, UNICEF is the United Nations' agency responsible for providing humanitarian and developmental aid to children.

Welfare regime: the organizing principles and structures by means of which a society distributes and redistributes resources in the form of cash and services to enhance the social and individual well-being (welfare) of its members.

World Bank: the International Bank for Reconstruction and Development is a development bank established in 1944 and based in Washington, DC, which focuses on support to the Global South.

World Parliamentary Assembly: the proposal for an elected body in the United System to complement or replace the General Assembly.

WTO: the World Trade Organization replaced GATT in 1995 and seeks to facilitate and regulate international trade.

WVS: the World Values Survey is a global research project originating in 1981. It is based on representative national surveys conducted in almost 100 countries by an international network of social scientists.

REFERENCES

AACSF 2015. *Declaration from the Addis Ababa Civil Society Forum on Financing for Development Addis Ababa Civil Society Forum*, 12 July. https://csoforffd.files.wordpress. com/2015/07/addis-ababa-cso-ffd-forum-declaration-12-july-2015.pdf.

Abe, A. 2010. "Social exclusion and earlier disadvantages". *Social Science Japan Journal* 13(1): 5–30.

Acemoglu, D. & J. Robinson 2012. *Why Nations Fail*. New York: Crown.

Acemoglu, D. & J. Robinson 2017. "The economic impact of colonialism". In S. Michalopoulos & E. Papaioannou (eds), *The Long Economic and Political Shadow of History Vol. I*, 81–8. London: CEPR Press.

Adams, B. 2019. "Democratic global governance: if it doesn't challenge power it isn't democratic". Spotlight on Sustainable Development 2019. www.2030spotlight.org/sites/default/ files/spot2019/Spotlight_Innenteil_2019_web_chapter_I_Adams.pdf.

Advani, A., H. Miller & A. Summer 2021. "Taxes on wealth". *Fiscal Studies* 42(3/4): 389–95.

Aidukaite, J. 2009. "Old welfare state theories and new welfare regimes in Eastern Europe". *Communist and Post-Communist Studies* 42: 23–39.

Akanbi, O. *et al.* 2021. *A Post-Pandemic Assessment of the Sustainable Development Goals*. Washington, DC: IMF Staff Discussion Note, SDN/2021/003 BN.

Akyuz, Y. 2017. *Playing with Fire*. Oxford: Oxford University Press.

Alawattage, C. & M. Elshihry 2017. "The managerialism in neoliberal global governance". In A. Littoz-Monnet (ed.), *The Politics of Expertise in International Organizations: How International Bureaucracies Produce and Mobilize Knowledge*, 167–86. Abingdon: Routledge.

Alfani, G. 2020. "Pandemics and inequality". *VoxEu/CEPR*, 15 October. https://voxeu.org/ article/pandemics-and-inequality-historical-overview.

Ali, S. *et al.* 2018. "Rationalizing poverty in New York". *Journal of Poverty* 22(4): 310–33.

Alkire, S., U. Kanagaratnum & N. Suppa 2021. *The Global Multidimensional Poverty Index 2021*. Oxford: Oxford Poverty and Human Development Initiative, Methodological Note 51. https://ophi.org.uk/multidimensional-poverty-index/global-mpi-databank/.

Anker, R. 2011. "Engel's law around the world 150 years later". University of Massachusetts, Amherst, Political Economy Research Institute, Working Paper 247. https://peri.umass. edu/fileadmin/pdf/working_papers/working_papers_201-250/WP247.pdf.

Annan, K. 2000. *We the Peoples*. New York: United Nations.

Archibong, B., B. Coulibaly & N. Okonjo-Iweala 2021. *Washington Consensus Reforms and Economic Performance in Sub-Saharan Africa*. Washington, DC: Brookings Institution AGI Working Paper 27.

Ashmore, J. 2019. "Amber Rudd is right to complain about the UN's shrill, partisan report". *CAPX*, 23 May. https://capx.co/amber-rudd-is-right-to-complain-about-the-uns-shrill-partisan-report/.

ATD4W 2014. *Challenge 2015: Towards Sustainable Development that Leaves No One Behind*. Pierrelaye: ATD Fourth World.

Atkinson, R. & S. Davoudi 2000. "The concept of social exclusion in the European Union". *Journal of Common Market Studies* 38(3): 427–48.

Barrientos, A. 2019. "Social protection in Latin America". In G. Cruz-Martínez (ed.), *Welfare and Social Protection in Contemporary Latin America*, 59–71. London: Routledge.

Barrientos, A. & D. Neff 2010. "Attitudes to chronic poverty in the 'Global Village'". Hamburg: GIGA German Institute of Global and Area Studies, Working Paper 134.

Batana, Y. & J. Cockburn 2018. *Do Demographics Matter for African Child Poverty?* Washington, DC: World Bank, Policy Research Working Paper 8426.

BdF 2022. *IMF Members, Quotas, Voting Right*. Paris: Banque de France. www.banque-france.fr/en/economics/international-relations/international-monetary-fund/members-quotas-voting-rights.

Bello, W. 2013. "Post-2015 development assessment". *Development* 56(1): 93–102.

Benedek, D. *et al.* 2021. *A Post-Pandemic Assessment of the Sustainable Development Goals*. Washington, DC: IMF Staff Discussion Note, SDN/2021/003.

Berens, S. & M. Gelepithis 2019. "Welfare state structure, inequality, and public attitudes towards progressive taxation". *Socio-Economic Review* 17(4): 823–50.

Berglund, N. 2018. "Poverty grabs the political spotlight". *News in English*, 10 October. www.newsinenglish.no/2018/10/10/poverty-grabs-the-political-spotlight/.

Bertin, G., M. Ellison & G. Moro 2021. *Repairing the Social Fabric of European Societies*. Cheltenham: Edward Elgar.

Besharov, D. & D. Call 2009. "Income transfers alone won't eradicate poverty". *Policy Studies Journal* 37(4): 599–621.

Bhattacharyya, S. 2016. "The historical origins of poverty in developing countries". In D. Brady & L. Burton (eds), *The Oxford Handbook of the Social Science of Poverty*, 270–92. Oxford: Oxford University Press.

Bhouraskar, D. 2013. *United Nations Development Aid*. New Delhi: Academic Foundation.

Bierbaum, M. & V. Schmitt 2022. *Investing Better in Universal Social Protection*. Geneva: International Labour Organization, Working Paper 43.

Bindra, S. 2018. "Foreign aid and foreign policy". *World Affairs* 22(3): 126–41.

Bissio, R. 2018. *SDG17 Trading Away the SDGs? Spotlight on Sustainable Development 2018*. www.2030spotlight.org/en/book/1730/chapter/sdg-17-trading-away-sdgs.

Blatchford, A. 2022. "Morneau unleashes on Trudeau's economic policies". *Politico*, 1 June. www.politico.com/news/2022/06/01/morneau-critiques-trudeau-government-policies-00036606.

Blicharska, M., C. Teutschbein & R. Smithers 2021. "SDG partnerships may perpetuate the global North–South divide". *Nature Scientific Reports* 11, 22092. https://doi.org/10.1038/s41598-021-01534-6.

Bond, P. 2015. "UN Development Goals replaced by new 'Distraction Gimmicks'". *CounterPunch*, 25 September. www.counterpunch.org/2015/09/25/un-millennium-development-goals-replaced-by-new-distraction-gimmicks/.

Booth, C. 1892. *Life and Labour of the People in London 1889–1903*. London: Macmillan.

Bown, C. & S. Keynes 2020. "Why Trump shot the sheriffs". *Journal of Policy Modeling* 42: 799–819.

Bradford, C. 2002. *Towards 2015*. Washington, DC: Brookings Institute. Mimeo.

Brady, D. 2009. *Rich Democracies, Poor People*. New York: Oxford University Press.

Brady, D. 2019. "Theories of the causes of poverty". *Annual Review of Sociology* 45: 155–75.

Bramley, G. & N. Bailey (eds) 2018. *Poverty and Social Exclusion in the UK: Volume 1*. Bristol: Policy Press.

Bray, R. *et al.* 2020. "Realising poverty in all its dimensions". *World Development* 13(4). https://doi.org/10.1016/j.worlddev.2020.105025.

Brearley, E. 2016. "A history of social protection in Latin America". *Revue Interventions économiques [En ligne]* 56.

Broderstad, T. 2018. "A meta-analysis of income and democracy". *Democratization* 25(2): 293–311.

Broom, D. 2021. "Ending hunger and poverty are the top priorities for global public". Forum, Ipsos poll, 9 June, Davos: World Economic Forum. www.weforum.org/agenda/2021/06/hunger-poverty-improve-health-survey/.

Brown, C. 2009. "Democracy's friend or foe?" *International Political Science Review* 30(4): 431–57.

Brown, C. 2017. "Poverty alleviation, global justice, and the real world". *Ethics & International Affairs* 31(3): 357–65.

Brundtland, G. 1987. *Our Common Future: Report of the World Commission on Environment and Development.* Geneva: United Nations.

Brumby, J. 2021. "A wealth tax to address five global disruptions". World Bank blog, 6 January. https://blogs.worldbank.org/governance/wealth-tax-address-five-global-disruptions.

Bundervoet, T., M. Dávalos & N. Garcia 2021. *The Short-Term Impacts of Covid-19 on Households in Developing Countries.* Washington, DC: World Bank, Policy Research Working Paper 9582.

Burki, T. 2021. "Undetected COVID-19 cases in Africa". *The Lancet Respiratory Medicine.* https://doi.org/10.1016/S2213-2600(21)00504-X.

Byrne, D. 1999. *Social Exclusion.* Buckingham: Open University Press.

CAF 2018. *World Giving Index 2018.* London: Charities Aid Foundation, October.

CAF 2021. *World Giving Index 2021.* London: Charities Aid Foundation, June.

Cai, Y. & T. Smeeding 2020. "Deep and extreme child poverty in rich and poor nations". *Italian Economic Journal* 6(1): 109–28.

Catalán, N., V. Fifita & W. Faingaanuku 2020. "Small-area multidimensional poverty estimates for Tonga 2016". *Applied Spatial Analysis* 13: 305–28.

Cebulla, A. *et al.* 2005. *Welfare to Work.* Aldershot: Ashgate.

Chadwick, A. 2021. "Human rights, poverty and capitalism". In S. Egan & A. Chadwick (eds), *Poverty and Human Rights*, 68–90. Cheltenham: Edward Elgar.

Chancel, L. & T. Piketty 2021. *Global Income Inequality, 1820–2020.* https://halshs.archives-ouvertes.fr/halshs-033218870938-8249.

Chancel, L. *et al.* 2021. *World Inequality Report 2022.* Paris: World Inequality Lab.

Charlton, A. 2006. "The collapse of the Doha trade round". *CentrePiece* 11(2): 26.

Chase, E. & G. Bantebya-Kyomuhendo (eds) 2015. *Poverty and Shame.* Oxford: Oxford University Press.

Chase, E. & R. Walker 2013. "The co-construction of shame in the context of poverty". *Sociology* 47(4): 739–54.

Chasek, P. & L. Wagner 2016. "Breaking the mold". *International Environment Agreements* 16: 397–413.

Chimhowu, A., D. Hulme & L. Munro 2019. "The 'new' national development planning and global development goals". *World Development* 120: 76–89.

China Daily 2021. "Xi's speech at the conference marking the 50th Anniversary of the Restoration of the Lawful Seat of the People's Republic of China in the United Nations". *China Daily*, 26 October. www.chinadaily.com.cn/a/202110/25/WS61762387a310cdd39bc710f5.html.

China Power 2021. "Is China succeeding at eradicating poverty?" *China Power*, 23 October. Updated 12 May 2021. https://chinapower.csis.org/poverty/.

Cianci, R. & P. Gambrel 2003. "Maslow's hierarchy of needs". *Journal of Applied Management and Entrepreneurship* 8(2): 143–61.

CIKD 2021. *China's Progress Report on Implementation of the 2030 Agenda for Sustainable Development.* Beijing: Center for International Knowledge on Development.

Cimadamore, A. 2016. "Global justice, international relations and the Sustainable Development Goals". *Journal of International and Comparative Social Policy* 32(2): 131–48.

City University 2018. "Economist calls for creation of global tax authority to tackle inequality". City University London. www.city.ac.uk/news-and-events/news/2018/11/economist-calls-for-creation-of-global-tax-authority-to-tackle-inequality.

Clark, A., C. D'Ambrosio & A. Lepinteur 2021. "The fall in income inequality during Covid-19 in four European countries". https://halshs.archives-ouvertes.fr/halshs-03230629.

Clark, G. & L. Sohn 1962. *World Peace through World Law*, 2nd edn. Cambridge, MA: Harvard University Press.

Cowen, T. 2014. "Capital punishment". *Foreign Affairs* 93(3): 158–64.

Crabtree, A. & D. Gasper 2020. "The Sustainable Development Goals and capability and human security analysis". In A. Crabtree (ed.), *Sustainability, Capabilities and Human Security*, 169–82. London: Palgrave Macmillan.

Cribb, J. *et al.* 2021. *Living Standards, Poverty and Inequality in the UK*. London: Institute for Fiscal Studies, IFS Report R194.

Crocker, G. 2020. *Basic Income and Sovereign Money Policy*. London: Palgrave Macmillan.

Crossley, T. *et al.* 2021. *A Year of COVID*. Colchester: ESRC Understanding Society, Working Paper Series 21-8.

D'Ambrosio, C. *et al.* 2021. "The fall in income inequality during COVID-19 in 4 European countries". Paris School of Economics, Pandemic Research News. www.parisschoolofec onomics.eu/IMG/pdf/pandemic-policy-brief-fall-income-inequality-june-2021.pdf.

Dahl, R. 1970. *Polyarchy*. New Haven, CT: Yale University Press.

Daruich, D. & R. Fernández 2021. *Universal Basic Income*. Cambridge, MA: National Bureau of Economic Research, Working Paper 27351.

Davies, R. *et al.* 2021. *An Overview of Workers Who Were Furloughed in the UK: October 2021*. London: Office of National Statistics. www.ons.gov.uk/employmentandlabourmar ket/peopleinwork/employmentandemployeetypes/articles/anoverviewofworkerswhowe refurloughedintheuk/october2021#data-sources-and-quality.

Davis, A. *et al.* 2021. *A Minimum Income Standard for the United Kingdom in 2021*. York: Joseph Rowntree Foundation.

de Kadt, D. & S. Wittels 2019. "Democratization and economic output in sub-Saharan Africa". *Political Science Research and Methods* 7(1): 63–84.

de Melo, J. & A. Nicita 2018. "Non-tariff measures". In UNCTAD (ed.), *Non-Tariff Measures: Economic Assessment and Policy Options for Development*, 1-12. Geneva: UNCTD.

De Neve, J.-E. & J. Sachs 2020. "Sustainable development and human well-being". In J. Helliwell *et al.* (eds), *Happiness Report 2020*. New York: Sustainable Development Solutions Network.

De Schutter, O. 2021. *Global Fund for Social Protection*. New York: United Nations General Assembly, A/HRC/47/36.

De Schutter, O. & M. Sepúlveda 2012. *Underwriting the Poor*. New York: United Nations Human Rights Council, Briefing note 7, October.

de Waal, A. 2000. *The Democratic Process and the Fight Against Famine*. Brighton: IDS, Working Paper 107.

Deacon, B. 2016. "Assessing the SDGs from the point of view of global social governance". *Journal of International and Comparative Social Policy* 32(2): 116–30.

Deaton, A. 2021. "Covid-19 and global income inequality". *Milken Institute Review.* www.milke nreview.org/articles/covid-19-and-global-income-inequality.

Deeming, C. 2017. "Defining minimum income and living standards in Europe". *Social Policy & Society* 16(1): 33–48.

Deeming, C. 2020. *Minimum Income Standards and Reference Budgets*. Bristol: Policy Press.

Demombynes, G. *et al.* 2021. *Covid-19 Age-Mortality Curves for 2020 Are Flatter in Developing Countries Using Both Official Death Counts and Excess Deaths*. Washington, DC: World Bank, Policy Research Working Paper 9807.

Dodds, F., D. Donoghue & J. Roesch 2017. *Negotiating the Sustainable Development Goals*. Abingdon: Routledge.

Doherty, C., J. Kiley & B. Johnson 2019. *Little Public Support for Reductions in Federal Spending*. Washington, DC: Pew Research Center.

Dorn, F., C. Fuest & N. Potrafke 2021. *Trade Openness and Income Inequality*. Munich: CESifo, Working Papers 9203.

Doumbia, D. 2019. "The quest for pro-poor and inclusive growth". *Applied Economics* 51(16): 1762–83.

Du Bois, W. 1996 [1899]. *The Philadelphia Negro*. Philadelphia. PA: University of Pennsylvania Press.

Dudel, C., J. Garbuszus & J. Schmied 2021. "Assessing differences in household needs". *Empirical Economics* 60: 1629–59.

Dunn, R. 2017. "Relative poverty, British social policy writing and public experience". *Social Policy & Society* 16(3): 377–90.

Dunne, T. 1998. *Inventing International Society*. London: Macmillan.

Durán-Valverde, F. *et al.* 2020. *Financing Gaps in Social Protection*. Geneva: International Labour Organization, Working Paper 14.

Durokifa, A. & E. Ijeoma 2018. "Neo-colonialism and Millennium Development Goals (MDGs) in Africa". *African Journal of Science, Technology, Innovation and Development* 10(3): 355–66.

Easterly, W. 2001. "The lost decades". *Journal of Economic Growth* 6: 135–57.

Easterly, W. 2009. "How the Millennium Development Goals are unfair to Africa 2008". *World Development* 37(1): 26–35.

Economist 2015. "Development". *The Economist*, editorial, 28 March.

Economist 2022. "A new challenge to the West". *The Economist*, 11 June.

Economist Intelligence Unit (EIU) 2018. *Me Too?* London: Economist Intelligence Unit.

Economist Intelligence Unit (EIU) 2021. *Democracy Index 2020*. London: Economist Intelligence Unit.

Economist Intelligence Unit (EIU) 2022. *Democracy Index 2021*. London: Economist Intelligence Unit.

ECOSOC 2012. *Summary of the Special Ministerial Meeting of the Economic and Social Council*. New York: UN Economic and Social Council, 24 September.

Edward, P. 2006. "The ethical poverty line". *Third World Quarterly* 27(2): 377–93.

Eilstrup-Sangiovanni, M. 2020. "Death of international organizations". *Review of International Organisations* 15: 339–70.

Einstein, A. 1947. "To the General Assembly of the United Nations". http://lotoisdumonde.fr/initiatives/FSMAN/Einstein-UN-letter-1947-oct.pdf.

Engel, J. *et al.* 2021. *The Distributional Impacts of Trade*. Washington, DC: World Bank.

ESD 2018. *Opportunity for All: Canada's First Poverty Reduction Strategy*. Ottawa: Employment and Social Development Canada.

Esping-Andersen, G. 1990. *The Three Worlds of Welfare Capitalism*. Princeton, NJ: Princeton University Press.

European Commission (EC) 2011. *Impact Assessment*. Brussels: European Commission, Tax and Amending Directive 2008/7/EC, Working Paper 1102.

European Commission (EC) 2021. *EU Humanitarian Aid*. Brussels: European Commission, Special Eurobarometer 511a – Wave EB94.2 – Kantar. https://ec.europa.eu/commfrontoffice/publicopinion/index.cfm.

EWG 2022. "Global Public Investment: a transformation in international cooperation". https://globalpublicinvestment.org/.

Falk, R. & A. Strauss 2001. "Toward global parliament". *Foreign Affairs* 80(1): 212–20.

Falkingham, J. & C. Namazie 2002. *Measuring Health and Poverty*. London: DFID Health Systems Resource Centre.

FAO 2015. "Third International Conference on Financing for Development". www.fao.org/sustainable-development-goals/overview/means-of-implementation-and-the-third-international-conference-on-financing-for-development/ffd3/en/.

FCDO 2022. *The UK Government's Strategy for International Development*. London: Foreign, Commonwealth & Development Office.

Feng, J. & M. Nguyen 2014. "Relative versus absolute poverty headcount ratios". World Bank blog, 24 November.

Fenger, H. 2007. "Welfare regimes in Central and Eastern Europe". *Contemporary Issues and Ideas in Social Sciences* 3(2): 1–30.

Ferreira, F. *et al.* 2016. "A global count of the extreme poor in 2012". *Journal of Economic Inequality* 14(2): 141–72.

Ferrera, M. 1996. "The southern model of welfare in social Europe". *Journal of European Social Policy* 6: 17–37.

FES 2022. *Social Protection Floor: Social Security for All*. Geneva: Friedrich-Ebert-Stiftung. www.fes.de/en/shaping-a-just-world/international-community-and-civil-society/transl ate-to-english-social-protection-floor-index-2020.

Fialová, K. & M. Mysíková 2021. "Intra-household distribution of resources and income poverty and inequality in Visegrád countries". *International Journal of Social Economics* 48(6): 914–30.

Fisher, G. 1992. "The development and history of the poverty thresholds". *Social Security Bulletin* 554. www.ssa.gov/history/fisheronpoverty.html.

Fisher, G. 1995. *Is There Such a Thing as an Absolute Poverty Line Over Time?* Washington, DC: US Department of Health and Human Services.

Fleckenstein, T. & S. Lee 2017. "Democratization, post-industrialization, and East Asian welfare capitalism". *Journal of International and Comparative Social Policy* 33(1): 36–54.

Foster, J. 1998. "Absolute versus relative poverty". *American Economic Review* 88(2): 335–41.

Frank, A. 1967. *Capitalism and Underdevelopment in Latin America*. New York: Monthly Review Press.

Freije, S., B. Hofman & L. Johnston 2020. "China's economic reforms, poverty reduction and the role of the World Bank". Social Science Research Network. https://papers.ssrn.com/sol3/papers.cfm?abstract_id=3501983.

Fry, P. 2021. "Why the Doha Rounds failed". *End Poverty*, 9 November. www.endpoverty. org/blog/why-the-doha-rounds-failed?gclid=Cj0KCQiAi9mPBhCJARIsAHchl1zvF NqY_Odp-7eHe_BPtahNtJ2kMp5qp6DU3DKUceZFDqOOMjg3JT0aAkPCEALw_wcB.

Fukuda-Parr, S. 2013. "MDG strengths as weaknesses 2013" *Great Insights* 2(3): 1–3.

Fukuda-Parr, S. & D. Hulme 2011. "International norm dynamics and the 'end of poverty': understanding the Millennium Development Goals". *Global Governance* 17(1): 17–36.

Fukuda-Parr, S. & B. Muchhala 2020. "The Southern origins of Sustainable Development Goals". *World Development* 126: 104706.

Fukuyama, F. 1992. *The End of History and the Last Man*. New York: The Free Press.

Funraise 2020. *Global Trends in Giving Report*. www.funraise.org/giving-report/thank-you?sub missionGuid=d28b963c-b4a4-430f-8b08-96bbccaf2a48.

Furceri, D. *et al.* 2020. "Covid-19 will raise inequality if past pandemics are a guide". VoxEu/ CEPR, 8 May. https://voxeu.org/article/covid-19-will-raise-inequality-if-past-pandem ics-are-guide.

Gaspar, V. *et al.* 2019. *Fiscal Policy and Development*. Washington, DC: IMF Staff Discussion Note, SDN/19/03.

Gasper, D. 2019. "The road to the Sustainable Development Goals". *Journal of Global Ethics* 15(2): 118–37.

Gilbert, N. 2017. *Never Enough*. New York: Oxford University Press.

Gilens, M. & B. Page 2014. "Testing theories of American politics". *Perspectives on Politics* 12(3): 564–81.

Gilman, N. 2015. "The new international economic order". *Humanity* 6: 1–16.

Glaister, K., N. Driffield & Y. Lin 2020. "Foreign direct investment to Africa". *Management International Review* 3.

Glennie, J. 2021. *The Future of Aid*. Abingdon: Routledge.

Godinot, X. 2019. "Unveiling the hidden dimensions of poverty". Spotlight on Sustainable Development. Special Contribution 1. www.2030spotlight.org/en/book/1883/chapter/unveiling-hidden-dimensions-poverty

Gold, D. & S. McGlinchey 2017. "International relations theory". In S. McGlinchey (ed.), *International Relations*, 46–56. Bristol: E-International Relations.

Gong, J. 2018. "An arithmocratic agenda". CGTN, 1 January. https://news.cgtn.com/news/77496a4d35637a6333566d54/index.html.

Gornick, J. & N. Johnson 2020. "Income inequality in rich countries". *Items*, 5 May. https://items.ssrc.org/what-is-inequality/income-inequality-in-rich-countries-examining-changes-in-economic-disparities/.

Görtz, C., D. McGowan & M. Yeromonahos 2021. *Furlough and Household Financial Distress during the Covid-19 Pandemic*. Munich: Munich Society for the Promotion of Economic Research, CESifo Working Papers 9285.

Grimalda, G. *et al.* 2020. "Building global citizenship through global basic income and progressive global taxation". T20 Task Force 4, Social Cohesion and the State Policy Brief. www.t20 saudiarabia.org.sa/en/briefs/Pages/Policy-Brief.aspx?pb=TF4_PB6.

Grimalda, G. *et al.* 2021. *Building Global Citizenship through a Global Citizen Income and Progressive Global Taxation*. Task Force 6 Social Cohesion and the Future of Welfare Systems, Working Paper. September.

Grütjen, D. 2008. "The Turkish welfare regime". *Turkish Policy Quarterly* 7(1): 111–29.

Gugushvili, D., M. Lukac & W. van Oorschot 2021. "Perceived welfare deservingness of needy people in transition countries". *Global Social Policy* 21(2): 234–57.

Gulrajani, N. & R. Calleja 2019. *Understanding Donor Motivations Developing the Principled Aid Index*. London: Overseas Development Institute, Working Paper 548, March.

Gulrajani, N. & R. Calleja 2021. "Interest-based development cooperation". In S. Chaturvedi *et al.* (eds), *The Palgrave Handbook of Development Cooperation for Achieving the 2030 Agenda*, 271–88. Cham: Springer.

Harris, J. 2000. *Basic Principles of Sustainable Development*. Medford, MA: Tufts University Global Development and Environment Institute, Working Paper 00-04.

HCHR 2006. *Principles and Guidelines for a Human Rights Approach to Poverty Reduction Strategies*. Geneva: Office of the United Nations High Commissioner for Human Rights.

HCHR 2012. *Guiding Principles on Extreme Poverty and Human Rights*. Geneva: Office of the United Nations High Commissioner for Human Rights.

Helleiner, E. 2014. *The Status Quo Crisis*. Oxford: Oxford University Press.

Heron, T. 2006. "The ending of the multifibre arrangement". *European Journal of Development Research* 18(1): 1–21.

Hickel, J. 2021. *Less is More*. London: Windmill Books.

Hicks, M. & Devaraj, S. 2015. *The Myth and the Reality of Manufacturing in America*. Muncle: Ball State University, Center for Business and Economic Research.

Hill, R. *et al.* 2021. *Poverty, Median Incomes, and Inequality in 2021*. Washington, DC: World Bank. https://documents1.worldbank.org/curated/en/936001635880885713/pdf/Poverty-Median-Incomes-and-Inequality-in-2021-A-Diverging-Recovery.pdf.

Hillis, S. *et al.* 2021. "Global minimum estimates of children affected by Covid-19-associated orphanhood and deaths of caregivers". *The Lancet* 398: 391–402.

Hills, J. 2002. "Following or leading public opinion?" *Fiscal Studies* 23(4): 539–58.

Hirschman, A. 1961. *The Strategy of Economic Development*. New Haven, CT: Yale University Press.

Houthakker, H. 1957. "An international comparison of household expenditure patterns, commemorating the centenary of Engel's law". *Econometrica* 25(4): 532–51.

Howard, M. & F. Bennett 2021. "Distribution of money within the household and current social security issues for couples in the UK". Women's Budget Group, research briefing. https://wbg.org.uk/wp-content/uploads/2021/01/Money-in-the-household-FINAL-with-cover-2.pdf.

HRC 2017. *Report of the Special Rapporteur on Extreme Poverty and Human Rights on His Mission to China*. New York: Human Rights Council, 35th session, 6–23 June, A/HRC/35/26/Add.2.

HRC 2018. *Report of the Special Rapporteur on Extreme Poverty and Human Rights on His Mission to the United States of America*. New York: Human Rights Council, 38th session, 18 June–6 July, A/HRC/38/33/Add.1.

Hudson, J. *et al.* 2020. "Not one, but many 'publics'". *Development in Practice* 30(6): 795–808.

Hulme, D. 2009. *The Millennium Development Goals (MDGs)*. Manchester: Brooks World Poverty Institute, Working Paper Series, 100.

Hunter, R. 1904. *Poverty*. New York: Macmillan.

Hynes, W. & S. Scott 2013. *The Evolution of Official Development Assistance*. Paris: OECD, Development Co-operation Working Papers, 12.

IISD 2015. "Summary of the Fourth Session of the Intergovernmental Negotiation Process on the Post-2015 Development Agenda: 21–24 April 2015". *Earth Negotiations Bulletin*, 27 April. http://enb.iisd.org/download/pdf/enb3217e.pdf.

Ikenberry, G. 2001. *After Victory: Institutions, Strategic Restraint, and the Rebuilding of Order After Major Wars*. Princeton, NJ: Princeton University Press.

ILO 2012. *The ILO Social Protection Floors Recommendation, 2012 (No. 202)*. Geneva: ILO. www.ilo.org/secsoc/areas-of-work/legal-advice/WCMS_205341/lang--en/index.htm.

ILO 2021a. *World Social Protection Report: 2020–22*. Geneva: ILO.

ILO 2021b. *Social Protection Floor*. Geneva: ILO. www.ilo.org/secsoc/areas-of-work/policy-development-and-applied-research/social-protection-floor/lang--en/index.htm.

ILO 2021c. *Building Social Protection Floors For All: ILO Global Flagship Programme Report of the First Phase 2016–2020*. Geneva: ILO.

ILO 2021d. *Building Social Protection Floors For All: ILO Global Flagship Strategy for the First Phase 2021–2025*. Geneva: ILO.

ILO 2021e. *World Social Protection Report 2020–22*. Geneva: ILO.

IMF 2010. *A Fair and Substantial Contribution by the Financial Sector*. Washington, DC: International Monetary Fund.

IMF 2017. "Tackling inequality". *Fiscal Monitor*, October. Washington, DC: International Monetary Fund.

IMF 2022. *A Guide to Committees, Groups, and Clubs*. Washington, DC: International Monetary Fund, 11 May. www.imf.org/en/About/Factsheets/A-Guide-to-Committees-Groups-and-Clubs#G15.

Irwin, D. 2019. *Does Trade Reform Promote Economic Growth?* Cambridge, MA: National Bureau of Economic Research, Working Paper 25927.

ITUC 2015. "Trade union reaction to the Addis Ababa Action Agenda (AAAA) on Financing for Development (FFD3)". Trade Union Development Cooperation Network, 16 July. www.ituc-csi.org/IMG/pdf/trade_unions_reaction_to_ffd3_action_agenda_final.pdf.

Ivanova, M. & N. Escobar-Pemberthy 2016. "The quest for sustainable development". In A. Cimadamore, G. Koehler & T. Pogge (eds), *Poverty and the Millennium Development*, 83–111. London: Zed Books.

Jacob, M. *et al.* 2016. "Carbon pricing revenues could close infrastructure access gaps". *World Development* 84: 254–65.

Jakobsen, T. 2011. "Welfare attitudes and social expenditure". *Social Indicators Research* 101: 323–40.

Jakovleski, V., S. Jerbi & T. Biersteker 2019. "The ILO's role in global governance: limits and potential". *International Development Policy/Revue internationale de politique de développement* 11: 82–108.

Jensen, N. 2019. "The social legitimacy of targeted welfare". *European Journal of Social Work* 22(6): 1105–7.

Jerusalem Post 2021. "About two million Israelis live below the poverty line". *Jerusalem Post*, 22 January. www.jpost.com/israel-news/israel-report-about-two-million-people-live-below-the-poverty-line-656317

Jolliffe, D. & E. Prydz 2021. "Societal poverty". *World Bank Economic Review* 35(1): 180–206.

Jolly, R. 2004. "Global Development Goals". *Journal of Human Development* 5(1): 69–95.

Joulaei, H. *et al.* 2016. "The Millennium Development Goals". *Shiraz E-Medical Journal* 17(1): e35479. DOI:10.17795/semj35479.

Kamau, M., P. Chasek & D. O'Connor 2018. *Transforming Multilateral Diplomacy.* Abingdon: Routledge.

Kangas, O. *et al.* 2020. *Suomen Perustulokokeilun Arviointi.* Helsinki: Sosiaali-ja terveysministeriö.

Kela 2020. "Results of Finland's basic income experiment". www.kela.fi/web/en/news-archive/-/asset_publisher/lN08GY2nIrZo/content/results-of-the-basic-income-experiment-small-employment-effects-better-perceived-economic-security-and-mental-wellbeing.

Kennan, G. 1954. *Realities of American Foreign Policy.* Princeton, NJ: Princeton University Press.

Khanna, R. 2022. *Dignity in a Digital Age.* New York: Simon & Schuster.

Kiratli, O. 2021. "Politicization of aiding others". *Journal of Common Market Studies* 59(1): 53–71.

Kochhar, R. & J. Bennett 2021. *Despite the Pandemic, Wage Growth Held Firm for Most US Workers, with Little Effect on Inequality.* Washington, DC: Pew Research Center. www.pewresearch.org/fact-tank/2021/09/07/despite-the-pandemic-wage-growth-held-firm-for-most-u-s-workers-with-little-effect-on-inequality/.

Koltko-Rivera, M. 2006. "Rediscovering the later version of Maslow's hierarchy of needs". *Review of General Psychology* 10(4): 302–17.

Koopman, R. *et al.* 2020. "The value of the WTO". *Journal of Policy Modeling* 42: 829–49.

Kroll, C., A. Warchold & P. Pradhan 2019. "Sustainable Development Goals: are we successful in turning trade-offs into synergies?" *Palgrave Communications* 5: 140. https://doi.org/10.1057/s41599-019-0335-5.

Kuwait, State of 2019. *Kuwait Voluntary National Review 2019.* Report on the Implementation of the 2030 Agenda to the UN High-Level Political Forum on Sustainable Development. https://sdgs.un.org/sites/default/files/documents/23384Kuwait_VNR_FINAL.PDF.

La Hovary, C. 2015. "A challenging ménage à trois?" *International Organizations Law Review* 12: 204–36.

Lakner, C. *et al.* 2020. *How Much Does Reducing Inequality Matter for Global Poverty?* Washington, DC: World Bank, Global Poverty Monitoring Technical Note 13.

Landale, J. 2021. "Foreign aid: Covid costs mean we have to cut payments, says PM". BBC News, 13 July. www.bbc.co.uk/news/uk-57815034.

Landale, J. 2022. "Foreign aid: UK cuts funding to UN in change of strategy". *BBC News*, 17 May. www.bbc.co.uk/news/uk-61466163.

Lara, J. & F. Mendez-Ramos 2021 "Poverty vulnerability: the role of poverty lines in the post pandemic era". *Economics Bulletin* 41(4): 2690–6.

Laudage, S. & C. von Haldenwang 2021. "Historic restructuring?" *The Current Column*, 8 November.

Laurenti, J. 2003. "An idea whose time has not come". In S. Medlovitz & B. Walker (eds), *A Reader on Second Assembly & Parliamentary Proposals*, 119–29. New Jersey: Center for UN Reform Education.

Lauzadyte-Tutliene, A., T. Balezentis & E. Goculenko 2018. "Welfare state in Central and Eastern Europe". *Economics and Sociology* 11(1): 100–23.

Li, M. & J. Yue 2020. "Relative poverty and long-term mechanisms". *Sociological Studies* 6 [in Chinese].

Lipset, S. 1960. *Political Man.* New York: Doubleday.

Lødemel, I. & A. Moreira 2014. *Activation or Workfare?* New York: Oxford University Press.

Lødemel, I. & H. Trickey (eds) 2001. *An Offer You Can't Refuse.* Bristol: Policy Press.

Loft P. 2021. *COVAX and Global Access to Covid-19 Vaccines.* London: House of Commons Library, 10 December.

Lopez-Claros, A., A. Dahl & M. Groff 2018. *Global Governance and the Emergence of Global Institutions for the 21st Century.* Stockholm: Global Challenges Foundation.

Lopez-Claros, A., A. Dahl & M. Groff 2020. *Global Governance and the Emergence of Global Institutions for the 21st Century.* Cambridge: Cambridge University Press.

Lwanga-Ntale, C. 2022. *A Global Fund for Social Protection: Views from Selected Low-Income Countries.* Bonn: Friedrich Ebert Stiftung.

Lyons, J. 2014. "Foreign aid is hurting, not helping Sub-Saharan Africa". *Le Journal International*, 13 October. www.lejournalinternational.fr/Foreign-aid-is-hurting-not-helping-Sub-Saha ran-Africa_a2085.html.

Lysandrou, P. 2019. *Commodity.* Abingdon: Routledge.

Macdonald, K. 2018. "Of shame and poverty". In F. Forman (ed.), *The Adam Smith Review 11*, 111–262. Abingdon: Routledge.

Machin, R. *et al.* 2021. *Investigation of Data Irregularities in* Doing Business 2018 *and* Doing Business 2020. Washington, DC: WilmerHale. https://thedocs.worldbank.org/en/doc/ 84a922cc9273b7b120d49ad3b9e9d3f9-0090012021/original/DB-Investigation-Findings-and-Report-to-the-Board-of-Executive-Directors-September-15-2021.pdf.

Mack, J. 2020. "Explanation of vote on a resolution on human rights and extreme poverty". US Mission to the United Nations. https://usun.usmission.gov/explanation-of-vote-on-a-res olution-on-human-rights-and-extreme-poverty/.

Mackinder, H. 1904 "Geographical pivot of history". *Geographical Journal* 22: 421–37.

Mackinder, H. 1910. *Distant Lands.* London: Philip.

Mahler, D. *et al.* 2021. "Updated estimates of the impact of Covid-19 on global poverty". World Bank Data Blog, 24 June. https://blogs.worldbank.org/opendata/updated-estimates-imp act-covid-19-global-poverty-turning-corner-pandemic-2021.

Martens, J. 2019. "Revisiting the hardware of sustainable development". In GCS (ed.), *Spotlight on Sustainable Development 2019*, 11–19. New York: Global Civil Society.

Martin, A. & B. Mercurio 2017. "Doha dead and buried in Nairobi". *Journal of International Trade Law and Policy* 16(1): 49–66.

Maslow, A. 1954. *Motivation and Personality.* New York: Harper.

Mattson, C., R. Bushardt & A. Artino 2021. "When a measure becomes a target, it ceases to be a good measure". *Journal of Graduate Medical Education* 13(1): 2–5.

Mawdsley, E. 2018. "From billions to trillions". *Dialogues in Human Geography* 8(2): 191–5.

McBride, J. & A. Siripurapu 2021. *The Group of Twenty.* Washington, DC: Council on Foreign Relations, 15 November. www.cfr.org/backgrounder/group-twenty.

McCloskey, S. 2015. "From MDGS to SDGS". *Policy & Practice* 20(1): 186–94.

McQuillan, L. 2021. *International Monetary Fund.* Chicago, IL: Encyclopaedia Britannica, Inc.

Meadows, D. *et al.* 1972. *The Limits to Growth.* New York: Universe Books.

Mees, H. 2012. "How China's boom caused the financial crisis and why it matters today". *FPNews*, 17 January.

Meibauer, G. 2021. "Neorealism, neoclassical realism and the problem(s) of history". International Relations. DOI:10.1177/00471178211033943.

Mensah, J. 2019. "Sustainable". *Cogent Social Sciences* 5(1): DOI:10.1080/23311886.2019.1653531.

Mesarovic, M. 1974. *Mankind at the Turning Point.* New York: New American Library.

Michalopoulos, S. & E. Papaioannou 2017. "Series introduction". In S. Michalopoulos & E. Papaioannou (eds), *The Long Economic and Political Shadow of History, Volume I*, viii–xxxi. London: CEPR Press.

Millán, T. *et al.* 2019. "Long-term impacts of conditional cash transfers". *World Bank Research Observer* 34(1): 119–59.

Missoni, E. 2014. "The twists and turns of the history of the United Nations Development Programme". *Public Administration Review* 74(5): 679–81.

Mizuno, T, S Doi & S Kurizaki 2020. The power of corporate control in the global ownership network. *PLoS ONE* 15(8): e0237862.

Moatsos, M. 2016. "Global absolute poverty". *Journal of Globalization and Development* 7(2): 1–28.

Moreno, R. 1998. "What caused East Asia's financial crisis?" *FRBSF Economic Letter* 1998-24. www.frbsf.org/economic-research/publications/economic-letter/1998/august/what-caused-east-asia-financial-crisis/.

Moss, T. 2010. "What next for the Millennium Development Goals?" *Global Policy* 1(2): 218–20.

Muñoz, J., E. Álvarez-Verdejo & R. García-Fernández 2018. "On estimating the poverty gap and the poverty severity indices with auxiliary information". *Sociological Methods & Research* 47(3): 598–625.

Nair, G. & K. Peyton 2022. *Building Mass Support for Global Pandemic Recovery Efforts in the United States*. Cambridge, MA: Harvard Kennedy School, Faculty Research Working Paper Series, RWP22-002.

Nandy, S. & M. Pomati 2015. "Applying the consensual method of estimating poverty in a low income African setting". *Social Indicators Research* 12(4): 693–726.

Narita, Y. & A. Sudo 2021. *The Curse of Democracy*. New Haven, CT: Yale University Press.

Nègre, F. 2021. *The Doha Round and Agriculture*. Brussels: European Parliament Fact Sheets on the European Union.

Nepomuceno, M. *et al.* 2020. "Besides population age structure, health and other demographic factors can contribute to understanding the Covid-19 burden". *Proceedings of the National Academy of Science* 117: 13881–3.

Nordhaus, W. 2006. "After Kyoto". *American Economic Review* 96(2): 31–4.

Norrie, R. 2018. "How the UN gets poverty wrong". Institute of Economic Affairs, 22 November. https://iea.org.uk/how-the-un-gets-poverty-wrong-part-1/.

OECD 2016. "History of the 0.7% ODA Target". OECD. www.oecd.org/development/stats/ODA-history-of-the-0-7-target.pdf.

OECD 2021a. "Covid-19 spending helped to lift foreign aid to an all-time high in 2020". OECD, 13 April. www.oecd.org/dac/financing-sustainable-development/development-finance-data/ODA-2020-detailed-summary.pdf.

OECD 2021b. "The 0.7% ODA/GNI target – a history". OECD. www.oecd.org/dac/financing-sustainable-development/development-finance-standards/the07odagnitarget-ahistory.htm.

OECD 2021c. *Does Inequality Matter?* Paris: OECD.

OECD/FAO 2021. *Agricultural Outlook 2021–2030*. Paris: OECD/FAO.

OHCHR 2004. *Human Rights and Poverty Reduction*. New York: United Nations Office of the High Commissioner for Human Rights.

OHCHR 2012. *The UN Guiding Principles on Human Rights and Extreme Poverty*. Geneva: United Nations Office of the High Commissioner for Human Rights.

OHCHR 2021. Statement by Professor Olivier De Schutter, United Nations Special Rapporteur on extreme poverty and human rights, on his visit to the European Union, 29 January. www.ohchr.org/en/statements-and-speeches/2021/01/statement-professor-olivier-de-schutter-united-nations-special.

Olarreaga, M., R. Piermartini & G. Porto 2020. "Industry wages and the tariffs of the rest of the world". In M. Bacchetta & M. Helble (eds), *Trade Adjustments in Asia*, 67–80. Tokyo: ADBI/WTO.

Olukoshi, A. 1998. *The Elusive Prince of Denmark*. Uppsala: Nordic Africa Institute.

Orshansky, M. 1969. "How poverty is measured". *Monthly Labor Review* 92(2): 37–41.

Ortiz, I. *et al.* 2018. *Universal Basic Income Proposals in light of ILO Standards*. Geneva: International Labour Organization, ESS Working Paper No. 62.

Ortiz-Ospina, E. 2017. "Extreme poverty in rich countries". Our World in Data. https://ourworldindata.org/extreme-poverty-in-rich-countries-what-we-know-and-what-we-dont-know.

Oxfam 2022. "Taxing extreme wealth". Factsheet Report. Oxford: Oxfam/Institute for Policy Studies. https://patrioticmillionaires.org/wp-content/uploads/Annual-Wealth-Tax-Factsheet.pdf.

Palacio, F. 2013. *Understanding Poverty*. New York: ATD Fourth World.

Pande, R. 2020. "Can democracy work for the poor?" *Science* 369: 1188–92.

Papadopoulos, T. & R. Velázquez Leyer 2016. "Two decades of social investment in Latin America". *Social Policy and Society* 15(3): 435–49.

Pastor, R. 1974. "The platonic acorn". *International Organization* 28(3): 375–97.

Pavcnik, N. 2017. "The impact of trade on inequality in developing countries". The Jackson Hole Economic Policy Symposium Proceedings, Fostering a Dynamic Global Economy, 61–114.

Pearson, L. 1969. *Partners in Development*. New York: Praeger.

Pekanov, A. & M. Schratzenstaller 2019. *A Global Financial Transaction Tax Theory, Practice and Potential Revenues*. Vienna: Austrian Institute of Economic Research, WIFO Working Paper 582.

PHE 2020. *Disparities in the Risk and Outcomes of Covid-19*. London: Public Health England.

Phillips, N. 2020. "The political economy of development". In J. Ravenhill (ed.), *Global Political Economy*, 6th edn, 354–83. Oxford: Oxford University Press.

PHM 2017. *Global Health Watch 5*. London: Zed Books.

Piketty, T. 2014. *Capital in the 21st Century*. Cambridge, MA: Harvard University Press.

Piketty, T. 2022. *A Brief History of Inequality*. Cambridge, MA: Harvard University Press.

Pilkington, E. 2018. "Nikki Haley attacks damning UN report on US poverty under Trump". *The Guardian*, 21 June. www.theguardian.com/world/2018/jun/21/nikki-haley-un-pove rty-report-misleading-politically-motivated.

Pirlot, A. 2021. "How and why a global carbon tax could revolutionize international climate change law?" Oxford University Centre for Business Taxation. https://oxfordtax.sbs.ox.ac. uk/article/how-and-why-a-global-carbon-tax-could-revolutionize-international-climate-change-law.

Pogge, T. 2005. "World poverty and human rights". *Ethics and International Affairs* 19(1): 1–7.

Pogge, T. 2007. "Severe poverty as a human rights violation". In T. Pogge (ed.), *Freedom from Poverty as a Human Right*, 11–53. Oxford: Oxford University Press.

Pogge, T. 2008. "How should human rights be conceived?" In T. Pogge (ed.), *World Poverty and Human Rights*, 58–76. Cambridge: Polity.

PRC 2016. *China's National Plan on Implementation of the Foreign Ministry*. Beijing: Foreign Ministry. www.fmprc.gov.cn/mfa_eng/zxxx_662805/W020161014332600482185.pdf.

PRC 2021. *China's VNR Report on Implementation of the 2030 Agenda for Sustainable Development*. Beijing: Ministry of Foreign Affairs.

Putman, R. 1993. *Making Democracy Work*. Princeton, NJ: Princeton University Press.

Ramos, A. *et al.* 2020. "Where has democracy helped the poor?" *Social Science & Medicine* 265: 113442.

Ravallion, M. 2016. "Are the world's poorest being left behind?" *Journal of Economic Growth* 21(1): 139–64.

Raworth, K. 2017. *Doughnut Economics*. Hartford: Chelsea Green Publishing.

Reddy, S. & R. Lahoti 2015. *$1.90 Per Day*. New York: New School for Social Research, Department of Economics, Working Paper 25/2015.

Ringen, S. 1988. "Direct and indirect measures of poverty". *Journal of Social Policy* 17(3): 351–65.

Ritchie, H. & Roser, M. 2018. Now it is possible to take stock – did the world achieve the Millennium Development Goals? *Our World in Data*, 20 September. https://ourworldind ata.org/millennium-development-goals.

Robeyns, I. & M. Fibieger Byskov 2021. "The capability approach". In E. Zalta (ed.), *The Stanford Encyclopedia of Philosophy*, Fall 2021 edn. https://plato.stanford.edu/archives/fall2021/ entries/capability-approach/.

Rodrik, D. 2020. *Why Does Globalization Fuel Populism?* Cambridge, MA: National Bureau of Economic Research, Working Paper 27526.

Rönkkö, R., S. Rutherford & K. Sen 2022. "The impact of the Covid-19 pandemic on the poor: insights from the Hrishipara diaries". *World Development* 149: 105689.

Roosma, F., J. Gelissen & W. van Oorschot 2013. "The multidimensionality of welfare state attitudes". *Social Indicators Research* 113: 235–55.

Rosenthal, G. 2018. "Economic and social council". In T. Weiss & S. Daws (eds), *The Oxford Handbook on the United Nations*, 2nd edn, 165–77. Oxford: Oxford University Press.

Roth, A. *et al.* 2018. "Trump calls European Union a 'foe' – ahead of Russia and China". *The Guardian*, 15 July.

Rowntree, B. 1901. *Poverty*. London: Macmillan.

Rudd, K. 2022. *The Avoidable War*. New York: Public Affairs.

Sachs, J. *et al.* 2021. *Sustainable Development Report 2021*. Cambridge: Cambridge University Press.

Sainsbury, D. & A. Morissens 2002. "Poverty in Europe in the mid-1990s". *Journal of European Social Policy* 12(4): 307–27.

Schuyler, M. 2014. *The Impact of Piketty's Wealth Tax on the Poor, the Rich, and the Middle Class*. Washington, DC: Tax Foundation, Special Report, 225.

Schwartzberg, J. 2013. *Transforming the United Nations System: Designs for a Workable World*. Washington, DC: Brookings Institution.

SDGF 2022. *Millennium Development Goals*. New York: Sustainable Development Goals Fund, United Nations Development Programme. www.sdgfund.org/mdgs-sdgs.

SDG Zone 2021. *What Are Sustainable Development Goals (SDGs)?* New York: UN Sustainable Development Solutions Network. https://sdgzone.com/learn/what-are-the-sdgs/.

SDSN n.d. About us. www.unsdsn.org/about-us.

SDSN 2015. *Indicators and a Monitoring Framework for Sustainable Development Goals*. New York: Sustainable Development Solutions Network. https://resources.unsdsn.org/indicators-and-a-monitoring-framework-for-sustainable-development-goals-launching-a-data-revolution-for-the-sdgs.

Seekings, J. 2019. "The limits to 'global' social policy". *Global Social Policy* 19(1/2): 139–58.

Sen, A. 1981. *Poverty and Famines*. Oxford: Clarendon Press.

Sen, A. 1983. Poor, relatively speaking. *Oxford Economic Papers, New Series* 35(2): 153–69.

Sen, A. 1987. The standard of living. In G. Hawthorn (ed.), *The Standard of Living*, 1–38. Cambridge: Cambridge University Press.

Sen, A. 1992. *Inequality Re-examined*. Oxford: Clarendon Press.

Shildrick, T. *et al.* 2012. *Are "Cultures of Worklessness" Passed Down the Generations?* York: Joseph Rowntree Foundation.

Singer, P. 1972. "Famine, affluence, and morality". *Philosophy and Public Affairs* 1(3): 229–43.

Sirén, S. 2021. "Is there anything left?" *Governance* 34: 67–86.

Smaniotto, C. *et al.* 2020. "Sustainable Development Goals and 2030 Agenda". *International Journal of Environmental Research and Public Health* 17(23).

Standing, G. 2017. *Basic Income*. New Haven, CT: Yale University Press.

Stanton, E. 2007. *The Human Development Index*. Amherst, MA: University of Massachusetts, Political Economy Research Institute, Working Paper 127. https://scholarworks.umass.edu/cgi/viewcontent.cgi?article=1101&context=peri_workingpapers.

Stein, A. 2008. "Neoliberal institutionalism". In C. Reus-Smit & D. Snida (eds), *The Oxford Handbook of International Relations*, 201–21. Oxford: Oxford University Press.

Stern, A. & L. Kravitz 2016. *Raising the Floor*. New York: Public Affairs.

Stewart, T. 2021. "Global agricultural trade: US efforts at the WTO to expand agricultural trade". https://currentthoughtsontrade.com/2021/04/11/global-agricultural-trade-u-s-effo rts-at-the-wto-to-expand-agricultural-trade/

Stokes, B., R. Wike & J. Poushter 2016. *Europeans Face the World Divided*. Washington, DC: Pew Research Center.

Stokke, O. 2009. *The UN and Development*. Bloomington, IN: Indiana University Press.

Sundaram, J. 2016. "The MDGs and poverty reduction". In A. Cimadamore, G. Koehler & T. Pogge (eds), *Poverty and the Millennium Development Goals*, 26–44. London: Zed Books.

Surender, R. 2013. "The role of historical contexts in shaping social policy in the global south". In R. Surender & R. Walker (eds), *Social Policy in a Developing World*, 14–34. Cheltenham: Edward Elgar.

Szmigiera, M. 2022. *Forecasted Global Real GDP Growth Due to Covid-19, 2019–2023*. New York: Statista.

Tarshish, N. 2017. "Israel as a welfare state: a visual essay". Taub Center for Social Policy Studies in Israel. www.taubcenter.org.il/wp-content/uploads/2020/12/welfarestatesvisu alessay.pdf.

Tasioulas, J. & A. Sen 2018. *Capabilities, Development and Human Rights*. Sydney: ABC. www. abc.net.au/religion/conversation-with-amartya-sen/10599038.

Taylor-Gooby, P. 1985. *Public Opinion, Ideology and State Welfare*. London: Routledge & Kegan Paul.

Tedeneke, A. 2019. "Global survey shows 74% are aware of the Sustainable Development Goals". World Economic Forum, 23 September. www.weforum.org/press/2019/09/global-survey-shows-74-are-aware-of-the-sustainable-development-goals/.

Thornton, R. & H. Boylan 2021. *Examining the Accuracy of Inflation Adjustment and Quantifying the Impact of Basket Changes*. Dublin: Minimum Essential Budget Standards Research Centre, MESL Working Paper, February.

Tippet, B. 2020. *Paying for the Pandemic and a Just Transition*. Amsterdam: Transnational Institute.

Titmuss, R. 1974. *Social Policy*. London: Allen & Unwin.

TLYCS 2021. "Ten reasons why people don't donate to charity". The Life You Can Save. www. thelifeyoucansave.org/common-objections-to-giving/.

Toussaint, E. 2020. *Domination of the United States on the World Bank*. Liège: Committee for the Abolition of Illegitimate Debt. www.cadtm.org/Domination-of-the-United-Sta tes-on-the-World-Bank.

Townsend, P. 1979. *Poverty in the United Kingdom*. Harmondsworth: Penguin.

Troesken, W. 2015. *The Pox of Liberty*. Chicago, IL: University of Chicago Press.

Truman, E. 2018. *IMF Quota and Governance Reform Once Again*. Washington, DC: Peterson Institute for International Economics, Policy Brief 18-9.

UN 1970. *International Development Strategy for the Second United Nations Development Decade*, New York: UN General Assembly, Resolution 2626 (XXV), 24 October, paragraph 43.

UN 1973. *Report of the United Nations Conference on the Human Environment Stockholm, 5–16 June 1972*. New York: United Nations.

UN 1992a. *Rio Declaration on Environment and Development*. New York: United Nations Conference on Environment and Development, Annex I, A/CONF.151/26 (Vol. I).

UN 1992b. *Earth Summit*. New York: United Nations Conference on Environment & Development, Rio de Janeiro, Brazil, 3–14 June.

UN 2000. *United Nations Millennium Declaration*. New York: United Nations General Assembly, Resolution 55/2, 8 September.

UN 2001. *Road Map Towards the Implementation of the United Nations Millennium Declaration, Report of the Secretary-General*. New York: United Nations, A/56/326, September.

UN 2005a. *Handbook on Poverty Statistics*. New York: United Nations Statistics Division.

UN 2005b. *World Summit Outcome*. New York: United Nations, Resolution A/RES/60/1 adopted by General Assembly September 16. www.un.org/ga/search/view_doc.asp?sym bol=A/RES/60/1.

UN 2012a. *The Future We Want*. New York: United Nations, Outcome document of the United Nations Conference on Sustainable Development Rio de Janeiro, Brazil, 20–22 June.

UN 2012b. *Initial Input of the Secretary-General to the Open Working Group on Sustainable Development Goals*. New York, UN General Assembly, 67th session, Agenda item 20 (a) A/ 67/634.

UN 2012c. *Guiding Principles on Extreme Poverty and Human Rights*. New York: United Nations, Human Rights Council Twenty-first session, A/HRC/RES/21/11 Agenda item 3.

UN 2012d. *Realizing the Future We Want for All*. New York: UN System Task Team.

UN 2013. *A New Global Partnership*. New York: United Nations.

UN 2015a. *Transforming Our World: The 2030 Agenda for Sustainable Development.* New York: United Nations.

UN 2015b. *The Millennium Development Goals Report 2015.* New York: United Nations.

UN 2015c. *Millennium Development Goals, 2015 Progress Chart.* New York: United Nations. www.un.org/millenniumgoals/2015_MDG_Report/pdf/MDG%202015%20PC%20final.pdf.

UN 2015d. *Millennium Development Goals, Targets and Indicators, 2015: Statistical Tables.* New York: United Nations. http://mdgs.un.org/unsd/mdg/Resources/Static/Products/Progress2015/Statannex.pdf.

UN 2015e. *Food for Thought Paper on a Possible Technology Facilitation Mechanism.* New York: United Nations. https://sustainabledevelopment.un.org/content/documents/7167TFM%20Food%20for%20Thought%20Paper.pdf.

UN 2018. Report of the Special Rapporteur on Extreme Poverty and Human Rights on His Mission to the United States of America, UN, General Assembly Human Rights Council Thirty-eighth session 18 June–6 July.

UN 2020a. *The Sustainable Development Goals Report 2020.* New York: United Nations.

UN 2020b. *National Voluntary Reviews Synthesis Report.* New York: United Nations with the DESA's Office of Intergovernmental Support and Coordination for Sustainable Development.

UN 2020c. *Financing for Sustainable Development Report 2020.* New York: Inter-agency Task Force on Financing for Development.

UN 2020d. *Contributions Received for 2020 for the United Nations Regular Budget.* New York: United Nations Committee on Contributions. www.un.org/en/ga/contributions/honourroll_2020.shtml.

UN 2021a. *Decade of Action.* New York: United Nations. www.un.org/sustainabledevelopment/decade-of-action/

UN 2021b. "'Tremendously off track' to meet 2030 SDGs". *UN News*, 12 July. https://news.un.org/en/story/2021/07/1095722.

UN 2021c. *Progress Towards the Sustainable Development Goals. Report of the Secretary-General.* New York: High-Level Political Forum on Sustainable Development, convened under the auspices of the Economic and Social Council.

UN 2021d. *International Financial System and Development.* New York: United Nations.

UN 2021e. *Our Common Agenda.* New York: United Nations.

UNDP 1990. *Human Development Report 1990.* New York: United Nations Development Programme.

UNDP 1997. *Human Development Report 1997.* Oxford: Oxford University Press.

UNDP 2010. *Evaluation of UNDP Contribution to Strengthening Local Governance.* New York: United Nations Development Programme.

UNDP 2013. *The Global Conversation Begins.* New York: United Nations Development Programme.

UNDP n.d. *How Does the MPI Fit the 2030 Agenda?* New York: United Nations Development Programme. http://hdr.undp.org/en/content/how-does-mpi-fit-2030-agenda.

UNEP 2012. *Global Environmental Outlook 5.* Nairobi: United Nations.

van Oorschot, W. 2006. "Making the difference in social Europe". *Journal of European Social Policy* 16(1): 23–42.

van Oorschot, W. *et al.* (eds) 2017. *The Social Legitimacy of Targeted Welfare.* Cheltenham: Edward Elgar.

van Parijs, P. & Y. Vanderborght 2017. *Basic Income.* Cambridge, MA: Harvard University Press.

von Mises, J. 2005. *Liberalism.* Indianapolis: Liberty Fund.

Varshney, A. 2000. "Why have poor democracies not eliminated poverty?" *Asian Survey* 40(5): 718–36.

Wade, R. 2002. "US hegemony and the World Bank". *Review of Political International Economy* 9(2): 201–21.

Wade, R. 2017a. "Global growth, inequality, and poverty". In J. Ravenhill (ed.), *Global Political Economy*, 319–55. Oxford: Oxford University Press.

Wade, R. 2017b. "The American paradox". *Cambridge Journal of Economics* 41: 859–80.

Wade, R. 2018. *Escaping the Periphery*. Helsinki: United Nations University World Institute for Development Economics Research, Working Paper 2018/101. www.wider.unu.edu/sites/default/files/Publications/Working-paper/PDF/wp2018-101.pdf.

Wade, R. 2020. "Global growth, inequality, and poverty". In J. Ravenhill (ed.), *Global Political Economy*, 313–53. Oxford: Oxford University Press.

Walker, R. 2005. *Social Security and Welfare*. Milton Keynes: Open University Press.

Walker, R. 2010. "The potential of Eurotarget". In E. Marlier, D. Natali & R. Van Dam (eds), *Europe 2020: Towards a More Social EU?*, 201–23. Brussels: Peter Lang.

Walker, R. 2014. *The Shame of Poverty*. Oxford: Oxford University Press.

Walker, R. 2021. *Telling Stories About the Origins of the Covid-19 Pandemic*. Cambridge, MA: Harvard Shorenstein Center on Media, Politics and Policy, Working Paper. https://shorensteincenter.org/telling-stories-origins-covid-19-pandemic-investigation-biases-international-news-media/.

Walker, R. 2022. "The Ukraine crisis". *China Today*, 19–21 May.

Walker, R. & L. Yang 2021. "Stigma and shame in China during Covid-19". Scenes of Shame and Stigma in COVID-19 Project, University of Exeter, 3 June. www.youtube.com/watch?v=vo1135tXF0E

Walker, R. & L. Yang 2023. "The politics of poverty alleviation in China". In S. Pellissery, S. Biswas & C. Sambo (eds), *Politics of Welfare in the Global South*. New York: Oxford University Press.

Wang, Y. 2022. *Address at the High-Level Virtual Meeting of the Group of Friends of the Global Development Initiative*. New York: United Nations, 9 May.

World Bank 1990. *World Development Report 1990*. Washington, DC: World Bank.

World Bank 2015. *From Billions to Trillions*. Washington, DC: World Bank. https://thedocs.worldbank.org/en/doc/883731485963739623-0270022017/original/frombillionstoTrillionsMDBcontributionstofinancingfordevelopment.pdf.

World Bank 2017. *Monitoring Global Poverty*. Washington, DC: World Bank.

World Bank 2020. *World Development Report 2020*. Washington, DC: World Bank.

World Bank 2021. *A Roadmap for Countries Measuring Multidimensional Poverty*. Washington, DC: World Bank.

World Bank 2022a. *Development Policy Financing*. Washington, DC: World Bank. www.worldbank.org/en/what-we-do/products-and-services/financing-instruments/development-policy-financing.

World Bank 2022b. *Global Economic Prospects, June 2022*. Washington, DC: World Bank.

WEF 2019. *From Funding to Financing: Transforming SDG Finance for Country Success*. Davos: World Economic Forum.

WEF 2021. *Increasing Climate Ambition*. Geneva: World Economic Forum, Insight Report, November.

WFP 2020. *Minimum Expenditure Baskets*. Rome: World Food Programme, Research, Assessment and Monitoring Division.

Wietzke, F.-B. 2019. "Poverty reduction and democratization". *Democratization* 26(6): 935–58.

Wigley, S. & A. Akkoyunlu-Wigley 2017. "The impact of democracy and media freedom on under-5 mortality, 1961–2011". *Social Science and Medicine* 190: 237–46.

Wintour, P. 2021. "Can Biden's 'divisive' democracy summit deliver?" *The Guardian*, 9 December.

Wood, T. & C. Hoy 2022. "Helping us or helping them?" *Economic Development and Cultural Change* 70(2). https://doi.org/10.1086/713930.

Woodward, D. 2015. "Incrementum ad absurdum". *World Economic Review* 4: 43–62.

Wroughton, L., H. Schneider & D. Kyriakidou 2015. "How the IMF's misadventure in Greece is changing the fund". Reuters Investigates, 28 August. www.reuters.com/investigates/special-report/imf-greece/.

Xu, M., R. Walker & L. Yang 2022. "Poor and lazy: Understanding middle-class perceptions of poverty in China". *Journal of Contemporary China* 31(137): 756–75.

Xu, Z. *et al.* 2020. Impacts of international trade on global sustainable development. *Nature Sustainability* 3: 964–71.

Yang, L. *et al.* 2021a. "Determining dimensions of poverty applicable in China". *Journal of Social Service Research* 472: 181–98.

Yang, L., R. Walker & G. Zhang 2021b. "Children's dimensions of poverty". *Children and Society*, under review.

Yang, N. 2017. "East Asia in transition". *Journal of Asian Public Policy* 10(1): 104–20.

Ynet 2021. "Israel's poverty rate rises as standard of living crashes". *Ynet News*, 21 January. www.ynetnews.com/business/article/SyxaYXwJO.

Yonzan, N., C. Lakner & D. Mahler 2021. "Is Covid-19 increasing global inequality?" World Bank Data Blog, 7 October. https://blogs.worldbank.org/opendata/covid-19-increasing-global-inequality#_ftn1.

Zhou, J. & M. Latorre 2021. "FDI in China and global production networks". *Journal of Policy Modeling* 43: 1225–40.

Zimmerman, C. 1932. "Ernst Engel's law of expenditures for food". *Quarterly Journal of Economics* 471: 78–101.

INDEX